HE FOUND THE ANSWER

Lt. Larry Bleeker learned how to walk with God and bring glory to His name.

By

Betty Klamm Parkhurst

Bookman LLC
Publishing & Marketing
Providing Quality, Professional Author Services
www.bookmanmarketing.com

ISBN: 1-59453-562-0

TABLE OF CONTENTS

DEDICATION

To God;
To the entire Bleeker family; and
To the countless people who shared their experiences of knowing Larry.

ACKNOWLEDGMENTS

First of all, I want to express my deepest gratitude and love for the entire Bleeker family. They were such a vital part of Larry's story. They were willing to trust me, a complete stranger, with the immense task of helping to keep the memory of Larry's life alive and his purpose transferable to many more people down through the years. They shared with me so many wonderful events to help each of us better know this young man. Included here is also my thankfulness that Larry responded to God in such personal ways through his Bible study applications, his letters to God, and his prayers, that we in turn have the opportunity to look inside his life and better identify with the person he was.

I am indebted also to all of those who painfully and generously shared their thoughts, feelings and experiences with me through tapes, letters, phone calls, and e-mails. Without each of you, this story would lack the flesh and bone and energy to make it worth reading. I am thankful for all the encouragement I have received from my wonderful husband, Dale, who always stands behind me and beside me but especially when I take new steps of faith. I am grateful for Russ Johnston, who was the one in the beginning to encourage me to pursue this calling, and for the many friends who have prayed for me during these many years to see this come to completion. I thank my daughter-in-law, Dianne Parkhurst, and a dear friend, Harlean Mandell, for painstakingly correcting my punctuation and asking me to clarify my intent.

I am deeply thankful to Ron Bleeker who found the publisher who has made this dream come true.

Most of all, I am overwhelmed by God's love and faithfulness sticking with me, never letting me completely forget about this information, and challenging me to always believe that Larry's story needed to be shared with anyone desiring to know how to walk more closely with God. May He, above all, be well pleased, and may those who read find answers for their own unique and exciting walk with God.

NOTE: You will find the Navigator organization referred to often in this book since it played such a key role in Larry's spiritual growth and development. You may obtain any of the current materials for yourself by contacting the Navigators at website _www.navpress.com_ or writing to them at:

NavPress
% The Navigators
Box 6000
Colorado Springs, CO 80934

FOREWORD

It was the fall of 2001 and domestic travel in the U.S. was barely getting back up to speed following the September 11th terrorist attacks. I was in my office in Bedford, Texas on a Saturday afternoon putting the final touches on a cost management presentation I would be making at the Marine Corps Base in Beaufort, South Carolina the following Monday.

When I had finished my delivery preparations and before I left for the airport to catch my flight, I downloaded my e-mail as always to make certain that there was nothing pressing that couldn't wait until I checked into my hotel later that night. Of the 20 or so e-mails that had accumulated in my last hour in the office that afternoon, one noticeably caught my attention.

It was from a Rev. David Hatch in Green Bay, Wisconsin who was hoping to make contact with the family of a Marine Lieutenant named Larry Bleeker who was killed in Vietnam in 1967. The limited purpose of his exploratory e-mail was to merely ask if I were the brother of this Larry Bleeker.

Needless to say, his inquiry had piqued my interest. Who could this be looking for me a third of a century following my brother's death? But I barely had time to print off a hardcopy to put in my briefcase much less call him lest I miss my flight. So I just sent him a quick reply e-mail confirming that I was indeed Larry's brother and promised to call him when I got to my destination that evening.

When I arrived at the airport, I learned that given the public's still lingering post 9/11 fears, my flight had been delayed by several hours. This was fairly typical in the first weeks following the attacks, but nonetheless a situation normally dreaded by seasoned travelers. This time, however, I welcomed the delay and headed straight for the American Airlines Admirals Club to reconnect my laptop and try to make direct contact with this mystery pastor.

After making phone contact and the customary exchange of cordial hellos, he began by telling me the story of his father taking him as a young boy together with his older brother, who was a high school classmate of Larry's, to the funeral home during the visitation. Of the profound impact it had on his life, he would later write, "On that night, my eyes beheld the cost of freedom, of patriotic sacrifice and the symbolic significance of the American flag. I go there again and again in my memory. Looking back, I can see how hearing his tapes and seeing his body in that dress Marine uniform has shaped my thinking as a Christian and as an American. Through the years as a pastor, I've countless times told young people about Larry's witness."

He explained that he had listened to an album he found on the internet that had been produced by the Christian Business Men's Committee in my home town following my brother's death 34 years earlier.[a] Playing it again and again,

---

[a] The album that David Hatch had come across on the internet in the summer of 2001 had been posted there by a presumed non-believer almost as a mockery. He was a collector of rare "home-grown" albums and this one, entitled "I Found the Answer" had somehow made it into his hands...the same album that the C.B.M.C. of Ames, Iowa had funded the production and distribution of back in 1968. By his own words, the collector had described the album as "a little creepy".

Rev. Hatch had first attempted to negotiate the purchase of the album, but the collector refused, only agreeing to let David capture the audio for posting on his memorial website to Larry entitled "His Mission Lives On". In return David agreed to research and provide a little biographical information to post in

he providentially copied down the names of Larry's surviving family members enumerated during the memorial service captured on Side 2 of that album. Using those names and web search engines he had eventually located my e-mail address off of the consortium's website for which at that time I was Program Director.

Rev. Hatch further expressed how he had felt compelled to establish, of his own volition and expense, a memorial website at *www.wireservices.com/bleeker* where others would still have the opportunity to listen to those recordings on their own. Now he was looking for still more information to expand and enrich that website. Wow! I was utterly speechless....a condition Bleeker's are not normally accustomed to experiencing.

After regaining control of the high emotion attending a stunning moment for me personally, I told him of a lady up in the state of Washington whose life was similarly impacted by Larry and that had compiled a biographical manuscript of Larry's life. Unfortunately I had to also tell him that to the best of my knowledge my parents had lost contact with her over the years and that the book had never been published.

On the other hand, if he could track me down through the relentless employment of multiple search engines,

---

conjunction with the album. Hence the impetus to try to track my family down.

Little did the collector know that by putting that limited-production 30-year old album on the world-wide web he would unwittingly be the catalyst triggering a chain of events that would bring together the key players whose efforts have culminated in the preservation of Larry's testimony in the pages of this book and the accompanying audio CD.

Indeed, "the Lord works out everything for His own ends." Proverbs 16:4 (NIV) perhaps he could locate this lady as well and thereby a copy of her manuscript. Not surprisingly, her name had escaped me over the three plus decades, but I was confident that my then 86 year old mother would still be able to remember the author's name and provide her last known address. So I gave him the contact information on my mother and three siblings in the meantime and told him I'd follow-up when I returned home.

When I got back to Texas later the next week, my mother excitedly called to tell me of Rev. Hatch's follow-up call and the subsequent phone reunion he had helped arrange with the dear and patient author of this book, Betty Parkhurst. Ecclesiastes 3:11 speaks of God's timing, and while this is certainly not a time span tantamount to that of the dead sea scrolls burial and rediscovery, 34 years is still an astonishing amount of time for this document to lay dormant and still be resurrected. Yet as the Apostle Paul said in his letter to the Phillipians, "He who began a good work in you will carry it on to completion, until the day of Jesus Christ."

While all the elements were coming together to resurrect Betty's forgotten manuscript and finally get it to press, a Pastor Kevin Mungons, the then Minister of Youth & Music at my home church in Ames, Iowa was busy tracking down my little sister through the alumni records at Cedarville Bible College in Ohio. With the fading of the vinyl record industry in the 1970's, the old LP album "I Found the Answer" had eventually been transferred to and mass-produced on audio tape. But the tape in the church library had deteriorated considerably over the years with repeated playings and Pastor Mungons was hoping to get an original or at least a digitally cleaned up copy and the family's permission to reproduce it on the higher-tech CD medium of today.

When my sister told me of his work, I followed up with Kevin to assure him that the family enthusiastically supported his efforts to upgrade the recordings and do a limited non-profit distribution to church members. He was also genuinely interested in the progress on publishing Larry's biography. I found his passion to be sincere and it was he who first proposed the idea that we consider including the remastered audio recording on CD with the book distribution to further enrich its potential ministry.

We had all committed to keeping the book a non-profit endeavor and therefore as affordable as possible. To that end, the cost impact of commercially reproducing a CD for inclusion would have to be considered. He not only offered to help with that part of the project on a pro bono basis but also with the initial distribution of books and CD's to the many advance requests from folks that had learned of the pending biography's publication.[b]

Larry's witness did not die with him. Indeed the "work" begun in Larry many years ago is still being "carried on" through the faithfulness of people like Betty Parkhurst, David Hatch and Kevin Mungons. To these and the many other contributors that have sought to preserve the testimony of my brother's life, I express my and my family's deepest gratitude.

---

[b] Larry's mother had been contacting friends and family to get a feel for how many books to order with the inaugural printing. As Ms. Parkhurst was getting closer to completion in September of 2004, Ron inserted himself in the process of compiling his mom's list of advance commitments. He had a database of several hundred names, addresses and phone numbers, but prior to speaking with Pastor Mungons exactly how to logistically manage the distribution process, i.e. acquiring shipping/mailing envelopes, labeling, postage, collecting monies and the like had not yet become clear.

I'm grateful too to have grown up in a home where knowledge of the Savior was paramount, and a home where patriotism was not something scorned but applauded. I was indeed privileged to have had the example of a brother such as Larry and am thrilled to be able to share him with you through the pages of Betty's biography.

Having been involved in the publication of numerous books in recent years, my understanding of God's careful grooming and preparation has now become clear. For me to have had a small part of the production of Larry's biography and CD and see the Master's remarkable Hand in this endeavor is undeniably humbling. But we rejoice not in our own glory, nor even my brother's, but in the glory of the One who gave Larry both eternal life and the courage to live an earthly life of but 24 years that is still bearing fruit today.

Ron Bleeker
December, 2004

THE STORY BEHIND THE STORY

Many have asked me how I got started writing about Larry in the first place, and why it has taken me so long. So this is the story behind the story. As you will see, there have been many ups and downs over a period of 37 years. If I have learned anything from this, it is the absolute faithfulness of God to complete what He begins. He can and does use the most unlikely tools to accomplish His purposes. God wrote this story, and I thank Him for the wonderful privilege of getting to put it together to bring glory to God alone.

My husband, Dale, and I met a young college graduate named Larry Bleeker in 1967. We were at a Navigator conference at Warm Beach Conference Grounds north of Seattle, Washington, and Larry was the song leader. We were impressed that he was able to get everyone singing, even those who never sing, and everyone was having a great time! Next, one of the projects of that conference was to send each of us to Marysville, a small town nearby, to knock on doors to tell people about Jesus. For Dale and me, this was something at which we had never become proficient. It's called "cold turkey evangelism." BUT, Larry was the one who told us how to do it and, somehow, God used him to make each of us feel we could hardly wait to knock on the first door. As we looked back on that conference, we were deeply impressed with this young man whom we realized would soon be headed for Marine training at Quantico and eventually to Vietnam.

The very next information that we received about Larry was that he had been killed in Vietnam—only two weeks after his arrival. That news hardly registered with us. How could that be? But it was, in fact, true. At that time, I was taking a writing course. I had always enjoyed writing but had no formal education in it. One evening I made a comment to Dale that someone should write Larry's story. It would be so challenging. And then, the only time in my life for this to happen, I heard God say, "Why not you, Betty?" I checked. Dale didn't hear it. But it came through loud and clear to me. Again, it didn't make sense. I knew who he was, but I didn't really know him, at all. Besides, I wasn't a writer who could get his story out there for people to read. For two weeks, at least, I argued with God. Why me? It made no sense.

Then, in my quiet time one morning, a verse stood out as loud and clear as God's voice had. It was Proverbs 3:27 in the King James Version: *"Withhold not good from them to whom it is due, when it is in the power of thine hand to do it."* The only way it could be in the power of my hand to do it was if I wrote to his parents and asked them for permission to do this. They, in turn, would have to tell me all about their son. I was impressed that I needed to somehow make Larry real. What was evident in his life at the end was that he was the kind of a person we all would want to be, but would think was impossible. He hadn't always been like that. I was certain that I needed to help people grow with him and see what made him the young man he had become. So I asked what they could tell me about his life that would make him human and believable. I wanted the good and maybe not so good, so people could better identify with him.

Mom and Dad Bleeker called me from Ames, Iowa, and told me that they had been praying for someone to write about Larry's life, and then my letter had arrived. When Larry's body was shipped home, so were his belongings. Among them was his address book filled with names. The Bleekers had made copies of my letter, sent it to every name in the book, asking them to share anything that they could remember about Larry and to send that information to me. The Bleekers also said, "We're not thinking of an article; we're thinking of a book." Would I consider writing a book?

At that time, my writing assignments were 300 words long. Before I could say "No," Proverbs 3:27 came back loud and clear, and I heard myself saying: "Well I guess, if the Lord puts it in my hands to do it, I'll give it a try."

From that time on, I began to get letters and tapes from all over the world telling me about Larry. It was incredible. (I still have three huge boxes of notes, letters and tapes, and yes, I did get enough to put a book together.)

A little over a year after I began working on this book, a Billy Graham Writers' Conference was held in Minneapolis. They were accepting 200 writers from the United States and Canada to attend that conference. They gave a list of topics from which we could choose to write. One of those topics amazingly was, "A Marine Dying in Vietnam." So I wrote the end of Larry's story, sent it off, and it was accepted. The Bible study group we were leading really got behind me for this. They donated money so that not only could I fly to Minneapolis for the writing conference, I could also fly down to Ames, Iowa, where Larry's family lived to meet them in person. While at the conference, I talked with an author who wrote biographies, to see what help she could give me. Later in the conference, she sent someone from Harper and Row to talk to me because he had mentioned that he was looking for a Vietnam book. I assured him that Larry's story wasn't really a Vietnam book because he was only there for two weeks, but everything that he was looking for was true in Larry's life. So I made copies of my preliminary manuscript for him, and he gave me details about what I should do when I interviewed family and friends in Ames. Everyone in Ames was so helpful that I came home with reams of new information. I set about writing while I waited to hear back from Harper and Row.

The answer came about three months later saying "Sorry, but..." The editor said that since I was an unknown writer, and Larry was basically an unknown person, he had been unable to convince anyone at Harper and Row to take a chance on this. He did, however, suggest someone else to send my information to, which I did, and I kept writing. For five years I wrote. For probably about four of those years, I sent my information to nine different publishers who, each time, told me it was good, but they couldn't accept it for various reasons. Each of them told me a specific person to send it to at another publishing house and to mention their name so that my information would be read. I also mentioned to the Bleeker family that if they ever found someone well known who could get this published or use any of my research to put a book together, to go for it. And all the while I kept writing. I wanted to see if Larry's story could really remain interesting and challenging for the length of a book. Two hundred and thirty-two pages later, I was convinced that this was a story that could change lives.

My manuscript included some blank sections where I knew Larry had spent a summer, etc., but I had not found anyone to fill in details about that time. When I sent it to the Bleeker family, I asked the family in Ames to see if they could discover any of those details or give me the name of someone to contact. And again, if anyone was interested in taking this material and getting it in printable form, they had my permission.

Once that manuscript was sent, I waited 30 years for a response. I had concluded that my part in this drama was over, but I remained thankful for whatever purpose this had served.

Then came November 5, 2001. The phone rang, I said "Hello," and a woman on the other end said "Hello, Betty, this is Lillian Bleeker, Larry's mom!" You can imagine the excitement that flooded my heart and mind. I was sure that Mom and Dad Bleeker had long since gone to be with the Lord and their son, Larry. But here was this strong, happy voice that I remembered. Lillian was now 86 and in good health. In fact, she had just returned from a trip to Alaska when I spoke to her that night. Hiram Bleeker, her husband, died in 1973 down in Texas where they had moved for his health. She had sent me a letter after the manuscript arrived, but it came back saying we had moved and there was no forwarding address. (She had written to an old address we had when I first started writing about Larry) So, for 30 years, we both thought that Larry's story had come to an end. She had tried to read it but, at that time, it was still too fresh and she was too emotional so she had passed it on to her children. Where that copy is now, no one is sure.

Lillian explained to me that she had just received a call from the Reverend David Hatch, who had been a boy of 12 when Larry went to be with the Lord. This pastor remembered the tapes Larry had made. Over the years he had done Internet searches on Larry and had recently found a page featuring the "I Found the Answer" record album made after his death. Through some negotiation, he obtained a copy of the sound track. On that sound track was Larry's obituary, read at the funeral by his pastor. Mr. Hatch quickly jotted down all the names of the family and began Internet searches on all of them. With the initial contact of Larry's brother Ron, he now had the contact information on Larry's other two brothers, sister and mother and would one by one connect with them as well. Ron also told him about a lady who had started writing a book about Larry, so Reverend Hatch called Lillian Bleeker to find out more about the book.

Lillian only had my name but, with that, they were able to find all they needed to get in touch with me. Thus, she called me on November 5 to tell me about all that had happened through the years, and now, Pastor Hatch would like to talk to me about the story.

True to his word, Rev. Hatch called me the next night, November 6. He had an older brother who was one of Larry's high school friends. When Larry's memorial service was held in Ames, David Hatch, then 12 years old, along with his brother and dad, had gone to the funeral home to see Larry. He had never forgotten the impact that visit made on his young life. There was Larry in his dress uniform, white gloves and a bandage on his head. This young boy of 12 realized for the first time the tremendous cost that was paid for his freedom, and Larry's life continued to speak to him through the following years. As a pastor, he has shared Larry's life as a wonderful example of a person who wanted wholeheartedly to follow his Lord and to get His message out to the world. His question to me was, "How would I feel about putting my manuscript on his web page (*www.wireservices.com/bleeker*) so others could read about Larry?" The fact that it was over 200 pages didn't bother him. He said he could do that. WOW!

As I had prayed about this, Proverbs 3:27 was as vivid and vital to me as it had been 34 years earlier. I knew I must go back and finish the story so others could read it. If one person's life could be changed, it would make it all worthwhile. Because I wanted Lillian to see the end result, I felt I must get those pages into the computer and send them to her once again. Lillian has now read the manuscript, and it is at long last going to publication.

I am more convinced than ever that if we are waiting for a prayer to be answered and it has taken so long that we're tempted to give up…we must not! God's timing is perfect and HE always finishes what HE has started! (Phil. 1:6)

Betty Klamm Parkhurst

INTRODUCTION

Larry found The Answer. He learned how to walk with God and bring glory to His name. Larry's life still holds the answers to many of our hopes and dreams of living a life well-pleasing to the Lord. Larry's life was a manual of "How to" walk with a personal, loving Father-God.

Larry invites you to walk with him through the pages of his life. Find ways to stretch your faith when he stretches his; let God pick you up and encourage you onward, as He did many times with Larry. When Larry applies new principles of Bible study, Quiet Times, prayer, etc. ask God to give you a similar hunger to spend time with Him and to obey Him with all of your heart.

Like Matthew 5:7, when Larry asked, it was given him; when he sought, it was found; when he knocked, the door was opened unto him. The principles Larry learned and applied to his life can be just as vital and powerful for you as they were for him.

God isn't looking for another Larry Bleeker. He already has one living with Him right now. What God is looking for however, is YOU-to step in the gap in your world and let Him walk with you and work in your life to produce the willingness, obedience and wholehearted devotion to be used by God to reach your world for Christ.

Larry found the answer. He learned to walk with God. He invites you to come along on the journey of his life and learn right along with him what an exciting life God has waiting for you. In Larry's case, the Navigators happened to be the organization that most ministered to his life. For you, it is important to find a Christian group like the Navigators, Young Life, Youth for Christ, Campus Crusade, YWAM, etc. or an active church youth group, where your faith will be challenged to grow and you will be held accountable for your choices.

Ask God to open your eyes and your heart to listen to what God wants to say to you personally. Then get ready to begin at the very beginning and, please enjoy!

CHAPTER 1 - FAMILY ROOTS

A tall, lanky, young man walked down Main Street in Ames, Iowa, with bold strides, whistling as he went. Now and then he'd exchange friendly "howdy's" with passers-by because Larry Bleeker was naturally attracted to people and they to him. He dressed like any other collegiate; he looked perhaps a little more handsome than most, but there was something about this young man that seemed so alive, so ready and able to meet any challenge cheerfully and wholeheartedly. People found his smile genuine and his enthusiasm contagious.

Unlike the population of many larger cities, the people of Ames crossed the street almost any time the other side looked more interesting. So it was not unusual on this particular lazy afternoon for Larry to step off the curb in the middle of the block. What was unusual took only the next few seconds to transpire. Suddenly he was aware of a little red Fiat on Duff Avenue that was hidden by the truck that just passed. Larry was right in the way of the oncoming car. It was now only a few yards away! With all the life, enthusiasm and wholeheartedness he could muster, he leaped into the air to let the little fellow pass, but instead, gravity deposited him on his back on the windshield.

"Way to go, Bleek," he told himself as he slid off the hood. It was Larry who stood apologizing and checking on the physical condition of the driver, who was still not sure what hit him. It took a week or two for both Larry and the little Fiat to feel as good as new. But Bleek wasn't one to complain. He'd had a few close calls before and was thankful to still be around to praise God for His undeserved love and protection.

* * * * *

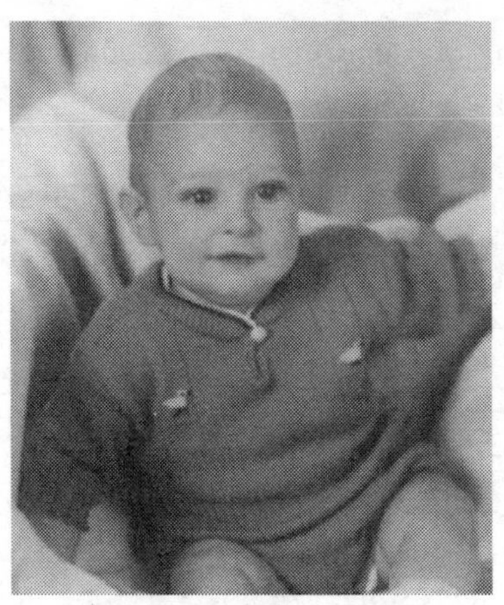

Larry

There hadn't been a dull moment in the Bleeker household since that sunny morning of June 21, 1943, when Larry Dean Bleeker first put in his appearance only a few moments after his mother arrived at the Mary Greely Hospital in Ames. He was the second, tow-headed son of Hiram and Lillian Bleeker and, from the outset, he and his 16-month-old brother, Gary, became the best of buddies.

Those were happy days for the Bleeker family. Each morning Hi, a big hulk of a man of German extraction, would kiss his family goodbye and then begin jogging his physically fit 225 pounds along an old cow path, crossing vacant lots and railroad tracks, and finally arriving at the Bennett McDaniel Furniture Co. store on Main Street. Each day Lillian, a young woman with determination, zeal, and an English ancestry, kept busy with her two lads who were growing ever healthier and more inquisitive.

Then, one morning in November, as the cold winds whistled down South Maple Avenue, the mailman brought an unexpected letter from Uncle Sam saying, "Hiram William Bleeker, we need you in the Army." Plans were quickly made to keep and store two overstuffed chairs, dishes, pots and pans, the washing machine, and the bed with some friends in nearby Perry. They sold the rest, including their car. After only two weeks, Lillian and the boys headed for her Grandfather Gillman's farm in Blackstone, Illinois, to stay during Hi's two years in the European conflict of World War II. Lillian's father had died at age 29 and her mother, Mary, had to pursue a career as a practical nurse for 17 years. When Grandmother Gillman took ill, Mary quit her job and moved back to the farm to help care for her parents and have more time with her own children, who had been raised there on the farm. Mary and her children continued living there with her father after her mother died. Mary was delighted to have her daughter Lillian and Lillian's two little boys come to stay while their daddy was away in the war.

* * * * *

Those days on the farm were ideal for two, mischievous, fun-loving, little boys as they managed to keep Gramp Gillman, their great-grandfather, their Grandma and Mom ever busy with their adventurous spirits.

One day Lillian was summoned by their frantic cries and found two frightened little boys as bumble bees orbited around and around them. As was often the case, Gary got the worst of it, getting quite sick from the stings, while Larry exclaimed over and over, "The bees was bizzin, Mommy!"

* * * * *

Larry and Gary on Great Grandfather Gillman's farm

Gary and Larry became quite the farmers at a very young age. They loved shelling corn for the chickens and watching baby chicks. And they were eager company while the big folks milked the cows or fed the pigs. One day they decided they were big enough to help count eggs from the egg bucket to the egg case in Gram's pantry. Normally, slips with eggs didn't matter; they just enjoyed scrambled eggs or sponge cake. But the slips that day were significant, when it was discovered that many "humpty dumpties" had been deposited in the wooden sugar bucket in the corner.

There was a great variety of things to play with on the farm, like the cistern pump on the water tank when mom wasn't on guard. The boys loved to pump the water until there was a nice pool where they could get soaked from head to toe. There was also the coal shed and the mountains of coal to be climbed—and later picked up—which wasn't nearly as much fun.

* * * * *

A really grand place for two inquisitive little boys was Gramp's shop. Even with its high latch, they'd somehow manage to work it loose and, if it wasn't screws and bolts, then sacks of new nails would find themselves in interesting patterns in the ground where busy hammers had done their work. When they tired of their building blocks, Gary and Larry found Grandma's balls of colorful carpet rags a great substitute and created some rather psychedelic pieces of art. All they lacked to make their world complete was Daddy, so they prayed daily for him, "God, please keep Daddy from the Germanies." And God answered their prayers. The war ended in May but Hi was kept longer because of his ability to speak and interpret German. He was, however, discharged in early November and back with his family by Thanksgiving.

With Hi's discharge, he returned to Ames in November 1945 with a wife, two sons, no home, no civilian clothes, no car, and very little money. But what they lacked in worldly possessions, they made up for in their faith in God, Whom they knew loved them and would provide for their every need. One night around midnight, they made arrangements for a home on Wilson Avenue and then got an old cotton mattress from the Bennett & McDaniel Furniture store where he was again working, this time as manager. They slept on the floor that first night, filled with thanksgiving for God's goodness to them.

From their home on Wilson Avenue, Hi would bicycle to work and Lillian would grocery shop at a store five blocks away. She carried the groceries home in the stroller while neighbors watched the boys. Friends always picked up their family for church on Sundays until the Bleekers could buy a car, two years later.

Gary and Larry immediately began adjusting to city life, and there were a few anxious moments. One day the phone rang and a neighbor reported that the boys had nearly been run over. They had been sitting in the cinders behind a grocery truck. The driver had not seen them and, except for a quick move by their guardian angels, the boys would have been hit. Not too long after that, both boys disappeared. Mother called, looked in the garage, yard, all over the neighborhood, a nearby fish pond, and then called the police. The boys were finally located in their own garage behind a big box, playing with their cars.

* * * * *

During the spring before Larry's fourth birthday, the boys were told the good news that they would soon have a new little brother or sister, and Mom and Dad Bleeker were careful to answer their many questions. One morning after Gary and Larry had piled in bed with Mommy, Gary asked how she knew the baby was in there. Mother replied that he could hear its heart beat if he put his ear on her tummy and listened.

As usual, Larry was talking. His brother impatiently told him to be quiet while he listened. Then Gary's eyes got big and sparkling as he announced to his brother that, "He's in there all right, cause I can hear him playing with a rattle."

In June, Ronald Ray was born. Larry really missed his big brother when Gary started school, but he loved having Ronnie to entertain and help him develop new skills.

* * * * *

Just before Larry started first grade, the Bleekers moved to Fort Dodge, about 65 miles to the north. Their home on

South Nineteenth Street was an old two-story house, and now there were three young boys to fill it with constant adventures. One of their favorite sports was sliding down the stairs. They kept a large piece of cardboard hidden beneath one of the boys' beds. When their folks were out in the garden, the boys would shut the door at the bottom of the stairs, scamper back up and climb on the piece of cardboard, let go of the railing and zzzzzzzmmmm to the bottom. They would hit the door and it would fly open, much to their delight! It wasn't until they had outgrown that sport that Mom and Dad were told why that door would never latch right and why the carpet got worn through so quickly.

* * * * *

Three growing boys needed milk, although this was not their favorite food. So Dad played a game to develop milk drinkers, and it worked. The boys were delighted to find that when their glasses were empty, their ears would whistle. If their glasses were not empty, their ears would just growl. Dad had a magical way of holding their ears, twitching them and getting the appropriate sound effects—and results.

It was about this time that the fourth son, LeRay Eugene, was born to the Bleeker family. Hi was a great dad for four boys, and he enjoyed playing ball, wrestling and boxing with them. From the time they were all small, Hi enjoyed boxing each of his sons on the chin and calling them his little Tunney, after his favorite boxer, Gene Tunney. By the time LeRay was old enough for boxing, his three big brothers listened to dad calling him Tunney. And it was his brothers who decided to alter his name slightly and LeRay became Tony from that time on, to all but his relatives. In fact, LeRay told his Sunday School teacher and his school teacher his name was Tony Bleeker. When Lillian came to speak to

LeRay's teacher, the teacher said she didn't have a LeRay in her class. Mom said, "Well, that's him." The teacher was as surprised as Lillian. LeRay had really changed his name. He was Tony—and is to this day!

* * * * *

The Bleeker family was more than religious in name only. The life of the church was their life, and they always supported it with their time, their money and their talents. So when an evangelist named Reverend Stukey came for revival meetings, Mom, Dad and all four sons were present. That first night, quite a number of young people came to the inquiry room following the meeting to find out more about the Christian life. One of these young people was eight-year-old Larry. That night he talked to Jesus in prayer and admitted he had done some wrong things and needed His forgiveness. He wanted to be like his Mom and Dad, pleasing God with his life. But this didn't come natural for a stubborn, adventurous boy like Larry.

* * * * *

When he and Gary were nine and ten, they would walk along the street and pick up the longest cigarette butts they could find, take them out to the garage, take off the paper and try to roll the tobacco in newspaper. They were all thumbs, and it just didn't work. So they decided they'd have to get some real cigarettes. Down on the corner was a store, so they wrote a note saying that their grandpa had sent them for cigarettes and handed the note to the girls behind the counter. The girls just laughed and sent them back home.

The boys were determined, however, and finally one day after pestering just too long, they were sent around back, given a package of Pall Malls and some matches, and told to get out and stop bothering them anymore. The boys were delighted. They dashed up the alley to their garage and thus began their experience with cigarettes. Before long, Larry was blowing smoke rings and getting quite professional at it, while poor Gary was only succeeding at choking. They finally agreed they'd had enough for that day, so Gary stuck the remainder of the cigarettes in his pocket and they headed for the house. They quickly started upstairs, but Mom became suspicious when she smelled smoke. She asked them if they had been smoking.

They hemmed and hawed and said they hadn't.

So Mom asked the next question, "Had they started a fire and burned some papers?" At first they said "no," but then they decided to accept her explanation. Pleased with that way out, they hurried on to their room.

It wasn't long before Dad came home. As Hi walked across the yard, he found a fresh cigarette and wondered if the boys were about the age to be experimenting. Just a few words with Mom and he was sure that they were. It was time to call the boys down for dinner, but Hi decided this would be a good time to show them how to smoke.

The boys knew they'd been caught when they saw their dad holding a cigarette. Hi asked them to get their cigarettes and join him outside. They were going to learn how to really smoke.

He would show them. The boys were surprised, because they had never seen their father smoke. Gary skeptically brought out the cigarettes and they went out on the front porch.

Hi then told them how to be a real cigarette smoker. He said they should take a drag and breathe it way down. Larry was tough and stubborn, so he did just as he was told. He took a big drag, breathed it way in, turned white, but didn't say a word. Gary did the same, and coughed. Dad encouraged them to take another deep drag. After only a few more drags, all three became sick and couldn't eat any supper.

Later, when they were feeling a little better, Dad encouraged them to go out and have another cigarette. In unison, they declined his generous offer. Then Hi asked them where they had gotten the cigarettes and together they went back to the store. Hi gave strict orders not to give his boys any more cigarettes. Then the next day he again called the boys together and offered to buy them each a package of cigarettes. Again they declined the offer. Then he told them that if ever they decided to smoke, to let him know and he would buy the first package. After that, they would be on their own. He told them it was a dirty habit and expensive, but if that's what they wanted to do, to let him know.

They both deeply respected him for giving his counsel but leaving the decision up to them. Their curiosity over cigarettes was satisfied.

* * * * *

Larry's care-free, farm-boy nature was still being nurtured during those days on South Nineteenth, because the family made many trips to the farm in Cornell, Illinois. Here the boys would tramp over the countryside, cutting across fields that their cousin Dick knew so well, and fishing in the creek, sometimes with bobby pins. One very hot day, the boys couldn't resist a swim in the deep part of the creek and, since they knew it was forbidden to get their clothes wet, they carefully left their clothes on the bank. But somehow, Uncle Harold and Mom found them splashing around in the buff and the three little boys got paddled soundly.

* * * * *

When Larry was 10, Dad opened a beautiful, new furniture store just east of Fort Dodge on Highway 20—the Mikos and Bleeker Furniture Co., and the family moved from South Nineteenth Street to a large farmhouse with an acre and a half on Tenth Avenue North. All the boys loved it. There was a cornfield stretching out to the north, and behind and across from them was another field. Down about three blocks was where the railroad tracks angled across Tenth Avenue North. By this time, Gary had developed a new friendship with a boy his age named Bud Beamer and, for the first time, Larry didn't always feel welcome with his brother. One day, though, he decided to tag along. They were walking along the ditch by the railroad tracks and catching tadpoles in pockets of water. Then they decided to build a cave in the mounds of dirt beside the track. It was full of cinders so, as they'd dig, it would cave in. They found only Larry was brave enough to go in and start digging again. Finally, it was junked as a bad idea when the whole thing caved in when they were only half done.

There were always forts to make and to man. The old hog houses sitting clear back in the fields were ideal. And so was the storage shed.

To the side of the house was a large garage, 25 feet by 50 feet, in which the previous owners had stored an airplane and well-drilling equipment. Dad had built a wooden floor in one half and walled it up. He stored furniture in it from the store and shut the one side door and locked it. The only way to get in was to have a key or go up in the shed side, climb the rafters and drop down. The boys, of course, chose the latter. Nothing was more fun for young boys than to lay one mattress flat and prop the others up so they could run down the rafters, grab hold of a V-bar, swing, let go, and slide down the mattresses!

On Saturdays, their friends would join them to play gangsters with their cap guns. They'd shut the doors, climb the rafters, slide down the mattresses, jump out of windows, and all the time popping their caps until the shed was blue with smoke.

* * * * *

Not all the activities there were that wild, however. It was here that Larry became aware of some abilities that God had given him. His marionette and puppet friends could bring smiles and laughter to the whole neighborhood. He had a little stage and, after personally depositing invitations in the neighbors' mailboxes, he'd sell popcorn and Kool-Aid to his audience as they arrived, toting little chairs, benches and sacks to sit on, to watch his puppet and magic shows. Before long, even the parents came, and they seemed to enjoy the show as much as their youngsters.

* * * * *

When Hi would go to the furniture market in Chicago each June, he'd return with something special for each child. Larry's magic acts began with a coin trick Dad brought him one year. He'd put the coin in a special container, push and pull it while uttering his magic words, Akarba-arbad (abraka-dabra backwards) and suddenly the coin would disappear. The magic was simple in the beginning but, through the years he developed it into a complicated and fascinating show and was asked to perform at school programs and church events clear through college. Larry had an ingenious way of always working the gospel into his shows.

From those early shed performances, his guillotine act created the most audience response. While the children watched, Larry would insert a carrot on the chopping block under the tiny sharp knife. Then with a mighty "whomp," he'd cut the carrot in two pieces. Then he would look at his audience and select an eager child from the front row. He'd ask him to stick his finger on the block. No one was ever willing to do that.

Larry would then bravely stick his finger on the chopping block, whomp it real hard, and pull his finger out without a scratch. This was followed by "Ooohh's" and "Aaahh's" and "How did you do that?" But being a good magician and a good talker, he'd already be accomplishing another act of magic before their eyes.

Larry and magic act 1961

* * * * *

Although there was a lot of time for play, there were chores to be done on an acre and a half. There was a large lawn to mow, chickens to be fed and watered, and raspberries to weed. Larry liked the latter least of all. So when Dad told them to weed the raspberries, Gary and Larry would get "busy" climbing trees or building forts. Those berries were sticky, and it was hot and tiring, so they could think of all kinds of excuses to put it off. When Dad came home one evening, the boys were downstairs and Dad asked again if they had weeded the raspberries yet. When they said they still had not gotten around to it, Hi decided they needed some motivation. He reached over to pick Gary up by the hair. Gary quickly agreed to head for the berry patch. When Hi reached for Larry, Larry flatly said, "No."

Hi was not a father who would take "no" from his son. He could have pulled out all of Larry's hair, and Larry probably would have still remained firm. Larry never did <u>say</u> he would, but his dad made sure he did go out and weed the raspberries.

* * * * *

Gary and Ron enjoyed Larry's stubborn streak, sometimes. And they took advantage of it with the garden tractor, which had all the potential of being a cultivator, a plow or a lawn mower. They had such fun roping a tree and pulling on the rope while the huge claw-like tires dug holes in the ground. When the tractor wouldn't start, they'd pull on the starter cord and touch the metal to see if it was getting a spark. Gary would touch it and jump because he said it was getting sparked. Then Ronnie would do the same.

Finally Larry would touch it and always say he didn't feel anything. So whenever they couldn't get it started, they'd ask Larry to put his finger on the metal because they knew he was getting shocked, though he never let on.

Gary and Larry had a pump BB gun. Larry had unloaded it, but Gary had reloaded it. One evening Larry was messing around with it and faking like he was pumping it out the window. Gary told him not to mess with it because it was loaded. Larry disagreed because he had unloaded it, and he didn't believe that Gary had reloaded it since then. Finally, to stop the argument, Larry told his brother to shoot him right in the chest.

So Gary, who had had enough, took the gun, pointed it about six inches from Larry's tummy and pulled the trigger. Larry let out a howl; there was a little BB stuck right in his stomach which later left a swollen red spot.

* * * * *

Larry didn't always ask for his close calls. He was sleepwalking one night and woke everyone up. Mom saw him coming out of his bedroom upstairs and told him to go back to bed. Gary and Ron were awake so they decided to help. Larry was headed for the stairs and the kitchen for something to eat. When he walked toward Mom, she again told him to go back to bed. Then he turned and walked toward Gary, who also told him to go back to bed. He turned again. He went to step over the railing that ran around the top of the stairwell and fell 10 feet to the bottom. Landing on his feet, he walked to the kitchen, came back, walked upstairs and climbed into bed while the others still stood there. Next morning he had no recollection of the incident at all, but a banana peel and an empty glass of milk were still on the table where he had left them.

* * * * *

Larry loved kids and was perhaps the proudest in the family when his new baby sister, Marlene Kay, with strawberry blonde hair, was born when he was 12. After four boys, she was all girl, and her feminine charm found its way into what for Larry had been a boy's world. They were all deeply concerned when Marlene developed a severe asthmatic condition. Larry would spend special time with her, which made them close, even though years did not. It would be safe to say that Larry enjoyed all ages and either sex. He just liked people, and during his high school days at Fort Dodge, he was out for a good time.

Bleeker family, Christmas 1956
Marlene, Lillian, Gary, Ron, Larry, Tony, Hiram

* * * * *

Larry liked music, but not piano lessons which only lasted one year. But he was good on the cornet, much to Gary's amazement. All Gary ever saw for weeks was Larry blowing on the mouthpiece. He'd find Larry lying on the sofa holding his breath and blowing it out slowly, or lying on the floor counting and making his lips in a funny shape, but all he blew was the mouthpiece. Gary kept asking him when he was going to get the rest of the horn. Larry would patiently explain that he needed to get his lips ready first. And off he'd go around the house with this little mouthpiece, blowing and blowing. Then came the day Larry got the horn and he did surprisingly well. He played in the junior high band. When he was a junior in high school, he organized an orchestra of young people in their church in Fort Dodge. In college, he was chosen to play in an all-men band of 50. He loved music.

* * * * *

When Larry was 16, his grandfather died. Larry and Ron were moving some of his farm equipment in a tractor and wagon on an old country road. Neither one knew what they were doing for sure, but a car was coming along in the rear, so Larry pulled over to the shoulder to let the car pass. Then, as he pulled back onto the road, the tractor jerked the wheel and broke the pin that held the steering wheel in place. Ron flew out. The tractor and Larry continued on across the road, down into a ditch and up the steep bank on the other side before the motor died. About this time, Dad appeared in his car and was certain the tractor would turn over and crush his boys. Thankfully, it had come to a complete stop and all was well.

* * * * *

Not many months later, Dad bought the furniture store on Main Street in Ames. He and Gary and sometimes Larry would work and commute or, as was often the case, just sleep there all night, while Mom, Ron, Tony and Marlene were still in Fort Dodge. Mom had her eye on a place in Ames, so when someone came to the house on Tenth North, she sold it and the furniture and, with the help of church friends, loaded a truck and went on down to Ames, arriving there about 9:00 p.m.

Hiram in front of the Bleeker Store in Ames, Iowa

She went into the store and announced to the surprised men in her family that she had sold the house. When they asked where they were going to live, she mentioned the home she wanted; they called the realtor, got the key, and moved in that night!

Dad thought she'd lost her mind when he discovered she'd sold the piano and the sofas, but had kept *The National Geographic* magazines. There were, however, still things left in the shed in Fort Dodge. So that next Saturday, Gary and Larry piled in the store's big red Ford van, with rollback doors on the sides like a bread truck, and drove back to Fort Dodge to get the things from the shed while Dad followed in the car.

They loaded everything and started back to Ames. On the way, Gary remembered he had made a sale and had left the delivery ticket in the pocket of his dirty shirt in the back end of the truck. He gave Larry the wheel while he climbed into the back to retrieve the ticket. They got about as far as Highview, where the road bends, goes over to the big grain elevator, the drug store, a gas station and one house, then turns back. It was here at Highview, while Larry was driving and Gary was in the back end, that Larry's long legs presented a problem. While Larry was trying to get better situated behind the wheel, Gary began to notice out the tiny opening on the side, that the side of the road was getting closer. He hollered up to Larry that they were headed for the ditch. But there was no answer. As the truck began to slide into the ditch, Gary hollered again. Larry just said, "I know it" and, now on the soft shoulder of the highway, he whipped the wheel to the left. They came up out of the ditch and headed across the road right in front of an oncoming semi-truck. Larry tried to turn the truck back the other way, but being top heavy, they spun around, missed the semi, flopped over and slid backwards down the ditch, upside down. A compartment door inside the truck flew open, and a large jack sailed past Gary's head as he was now in the midst of falling tools and motor bikes. The truck finally came to a stop, but the motor was still running and oil was pouring out. Larry sat there, saying over and over, "I wrecked Pop's truck, I wrecked Pop's truck." He knew his dad had just finalized its purchase earlier that morning!

Gary came scrambling up on the roof of the cab to see if Larry was okay. As Larry reached up to turn off the ignition, all he could think of was that he had wrecked Pop's truck. Once again, Dad came on the scene of the disaster and was amazed to find both boys only shaken up. The semi driver had notified the highway patrol and Larry got an accident reported on his record.

With a wrecker, they righted the truck. It was so bent out of shape, it looked like a parallelogram, but Dad pulled it back to Fort Dodge. With a torch they cut away everything from the frame, with the exception of the windshield part (without glass), the steering wheel and the front seat. The truck ran smoothly as they drove back to Ames, their load from the shed tied on the back end, and the wind blowing in their faces.

The truck was such a sight that Dad refused to use it to deliver furniture, although the boys thought it would be great fun. Instead, Hi bought a cab with a chassis and had a body built for it. That truck was a monstrous 7-ton behemoth that got pitiful gas mileage. The tailgate alone was 175 pounds of quarter-inch steel.

* * * * *

As they settled down in their new home on Furman Drive, Larry, though still out for a carefree good time, began to think more seriously about life itself and that Someone up there must love him to have protected him so well. He realized, perhaps for the first time, that his life could be taken in a split second. What was he going to do with his life while he still had it to live?

The answer lay farther down the road.

CHAPTER 2 - REASSURANCE

It was a sunny day in early fall, the beginning of Larry's senior year at Ames High School. As usual, this Saturday found him working in his father's furniture store arranging displays and waiting on customers. Larry was busy with Dan Furman, working on the second floor where he, Gary and Dad had slept during the interim before they moved to Ames. It now accommodated furniture not on display. Outside a young man stopped in front of the store, hesitated for a moment, and then came in.

Hi Bleeker looked up from his office in the back of the store when he heard the door chimes and smiled a welcome. The young man smiled back and began to look around. As Hi walked cheerfully toward his customer to offer his assistance, the young man seemed to recognize Hi as someone he had met before.

After introducing himself, Hi asked him if he could be of any help.

The young man introduced himself as Don McDonald. Then he asked if he had met Hi in Fort Dodge about seven or eight months before, at a singspiration in his home. It had been a wonderful evening of singing and sharing testimonies of what God was doing in the lives of the young people.

Hi studied Don for just a moment and realized that was where they had met the first time. Hi was happy to see him again. Hi explained that his family had just moved from Fort Dodge and asked if Don lived in Ames.

Laura & Don Mac Donald. Don helped Larry find assurance of his salvation

Don said that he did and was now setting up an apartment near the campus of Iowa State University. He was looking for a used sofa and wondered if Hi's store carried used furniture.

Hi said they only carried new merchandise, but he encouraged Don to look around. While Don was looking, Hi asked him if he would be working with the students at ISU that fall. Don said that he would be and that he was excited about the good nucleus of men returning to campus that year. He asked if Hi had a son about college age.

Hi told Don that his first son, Gary, was out of high school and working in the store during the week. His next son, Larry, was a senior in high school and was working in the store on Saturdays. Larry had led the songs at the singspiration in Fort Dodge.

When Don said he remembered Larry, Hi assured him that Larry would like to see him again so he went over and called up the stairway for him. Soon Larry's lean figure came bounding down the stairs and over to them with the same strong, friendly strides of his father.

Hi introduced Don as the Navigator who came to their singspiration for Gary's birthday.

Larry was glad to see him again and they shook hands vigorously. Then Larry asked Don how things were going for him.

Don again explained that he and a couple of other guys were moving into an apartment there in Ames and that he was out looking for a used sofa.

Just then the doorbell chimed again, and Hi excused himself with an invitation for them to continue their talk. He'd take care of the business.

Don expressed his appreciation of Larry's dad, telling Larry he had never met a more positive man and how refreshing it was to talk with him. Larry agreed with Don's evaluation of his father. Although Pop was not one to physically show his love much, Larry and the whole family knew that his love was strong for all of them. No matter what their family might have to face, Larry was confident that his Pop would always hang in there, strong and sure in his faith in God. Larry's mom, always busy doing for others, was very vibrant, lively and energetic. She had a tremendous heart for the lost and shared her deep faith easily. Although Hi and Lillian were opposites in some ways, still their desire to put God first in their marriage made them a rare couple, strong in love and faith. As Larry watched his dad greet the new customer, however, he wondered if his dad ever felt unsure of himself or puzzled by life like Larry now felt. Did he try not to show it, like Larry did? Larry looked back at Don, only a few years older than himself, but excited about his work for the Lord. Perhaps Don held some answers to Larry's questions about God's will for his life.

Larry invited Don to sit on the sofa beside them, so they could turn it into a "used" one, and Don laughed good-naturedly. Larry told him he planned to go to ISU the following year and would like to hear what Don did on the college campuses and more about the organization he represented, the Navigators.

For the next few moments, Don filled Larry in on a little of the Navigator background. Don told him it's an international, interdenominational, Christian organization begun by a man named Dawson Trotman. During the early stages of WWII, Daws began to build into the life of a young serviceman some of the basic things a new Christian needs to know to grow in his Christian life. These two men met together, one-on-one, in Bible study, prayer, evangelism and fellowship until the young serviceman was ready to share what he knew with another. Then those two reached out to two more, those four to eight more, and before he knew it, Daws was receiving mail from servicemen around the world, asking for some of his materials for Bible study, Scripture memory, etc. Men were sharing Christ on more than 1,000 ships and military bases during World War II. So much mail came to Daws's home in Los Angeles from military installations the world over, that the FBI held an investigation and finally came to Daws with more details of how big this thing had gotten than Daws himself knew. Because of the magnitude of the work and it's miraculous success, the FBI encouraged Dawson's group to become a non-profit organization. Since Daws had been navigating young men through their Christian lives, the name "Navigators" was adopted and thus the official organization was born.

Don told Larry that, after the war, many of the servicemen returned to the states and entered college, and so the ministry spread to college campuses and had been going strong ever since. It was still a "man-to-man" or "ma'am-to-ma'am" ministry—one person meeting with another. On the campus of ISU they were seeking to help young men and women come to "a sure knowledge of their salvation" and then helping them become more effective in their Christian lives.

Don had mentioned a "sure knowledge of their salvation." This was something Larry had been searching for—sometimes consciously, sometimes subconsciously—ever since his close calls with death in the tractor and truck that summer. Larry decided it was time to ask just how a person could be sure. What was it that they would tell a person who asked that question?

Don sat back and began to tell Larry what he would say to help a person be sure that his or her sins had been forgiven and that they would go to be with the Lord when they died. He said he would sit down with them and pull out his New Testament, which he always carried in his jacket pocket. He said the Bible is very clear on this matter of how we can know if we're a Christian or not and that he liked to turn to I John 5:11-12 for that assurance.

He showed Larry the verses while he quoted them to him. Larry had never realized there were verses like these in the Bible.

Don went on to explain what God had said in those verses. First of all, since God doesn't want anyone to die without knowing Him, God has offered us the gift of eternal life, which can be received when we believe in His Son. Don said it is important to know that to "believe" does not mean simply agreeing with our head that Jesus died for our sins, but to place our lives in His care. The Apostle John had continued to write that *"God hath given to us eternal life, and this life is in His Son. He that hath the Son of God hath life; and he that hath not the Son of God hath not life."* John had written this *"unto those that believe on the name of the Son of God so that they would know that they had eternal life..."* That "sure knowledge" came because God doesn't want anyone to "wonder" about their salvation. God had made it very clear and had it written down in black and white that we may know that we have eternal life if we believe in His Son.

Then Don asked Larry a question no one had ever asked him before: "If you were to die this very day, do you know for sure that you will go to be with God?" Larry wondered how Don had zeroed in on his problem so quickly. Larry found himself recalling as an eight-year-old his need to have Christ forgive his sins, but had that experience really made him a Christian? Why, through the years, hadn't he always felt that he belonged to Christ? He thought of the camps and retreats and church services he had attended faithfully, but somehow he still hadn't found any assurance in his own heart that he had eternal life.

Now Don had really put his finger on the problem. What if he did die right now? Was he sure he'd be with God? For the first time, Larry heard himself admitting, "No, Don, I'm not sure."

Then Don shared with him how only a few years before a young man named Jim Williams, who could only move his head and one hand, had led him to a relationship with Jesus Christ. Don had not only invited Christ to be his Savior, but also to take over and rule his life for him. Don had known ever since that he would go to be with God when he died.

He told Larry he had that assurance because of I John 5:11-12 that he had just quoted. He said the assurance came in knowing that Christ was in his heart. Then Don turned to

John 5:24, where Jesus says, *"Verily, verily, I say unto you, He that heareth My word, and believeth on Him that sent Me, hath everlasting life, and shall not come into condemnation, but is (right now) passed from death to life."*

To the age-old question, "Isn't 'just believing' too easy?" Don explained that God wanted salvation to be so simple for us, that anyone—young, old, weak, strong, disabled, or highly gifted, could come to Him. If we had to do anything, it would automatically leave some people out. God doesn't want to leave anyone out. Consequently, He did everything necessary. All He asks of us is that we believe in Him. He meant everything He said. By simply praying and asking Christ to come into our lives, we can know He will come in and with Him comes eternal life. The Bible says so!

Larry determined then and there to make this the prayer of his heart. Right there in the store Larry told God that he realized that he had messed up his life by trying to run it himself. He knew he had sin in his life that he needed to have Jesus take away. He realized that he was not sure of heaven, but that he wanted to be. So, he asked Jesus Christ to come into his heart right then and to become Lord of his life. Then he asked God to please let him know for sure that he would go to heaven when he died.

Although no one else in the store was aware of any great miracle taking place, Larry felt a strange new satisfaction and peace down inside such as he'd never experienced before. At last, on the basis of God's Word, he knew he had eternal life. That was all the assurance that he'd ever need.

When Don left the store that morning, he had already begun to apply the Navigator principle of man-to-man with Larry. They had an appointment to meet together on Sunday afternoon a week later to share some of the basic things about the Christian life. In the meantime, Larry was to memorize I John 5:11-12.

Larry lost no time in getting his dad's Bible off his desk, looking up I John, and copying the eleventh and twelfth verses of chapter five on a receipt from the wastebasket. He had it committed to memory before he left the store that day. He also found, as the day went on, that he now felt genuine when he walked up to a customer to greet him or her. He really did want to help them find what they were looking for. He really was interested in them. The customers also seemed to sense it.

Larry could tell that God had done something in his life as that next week wore on. He seemed to have developed a whole new viewpoint on things around him. Much of it was glorious, but some of it was discouraging, too. He had never before realized how much he did out of wrong motives. Larry had always liked people and enjoyed making them happy. The question was, "Why?" Wasn't it often so that they would like him and that it would make him happy? Why was it that he so enjoyed being the party clown, or being good in sports? Still, he knew it was not wrong to be good at what one was doing. He could remember his parents teaching them the Biblical principle of doing everything they did "heartily as to the Lord." No one could have had a finer example set for them than he and his brothers and sister had in their parents.

A new understanding came to him. Everything was to be done wholeheartedly and well, to please God and not for the praise of others. Through Christ, he must seek to do everything out of the proper motives and to the best of his abilities.

One of the first battles Larry now faced was with pride. God had richly endowed Larry and he knew it. Larry now discovered that he had far more pride than he had ever imagined. For some reason, it frequently reared its ugly head during the weeks to come. There was, however, one area in which Larry could take no pride. That was his study habits. He was not a student at heart and studying came hard. That first Sunday afternoon when he and Don got together, Larry expressed his uneasiness about ever being able to get involved in Bible study.

Don immediately thought of the illustration Dawson Trotman had developed to show how important the basic steps of spiritual growth were for believers. On a piece of paper, Don drew for Larry what the Navigators called "The Wheel Illustration." This illustration showed how a believer could live a balanced Christian life. To do this, certain areas of his or her life needed to be strong, just like the spokes of a wheel. He had Larry label the four spokes on the wheel now before him. The bottom spoke was the Word, the top spoke was Prayer, and the two horizontal spokes were Witnessing and Fellowship. Then Don shared a little about each of those spokes.

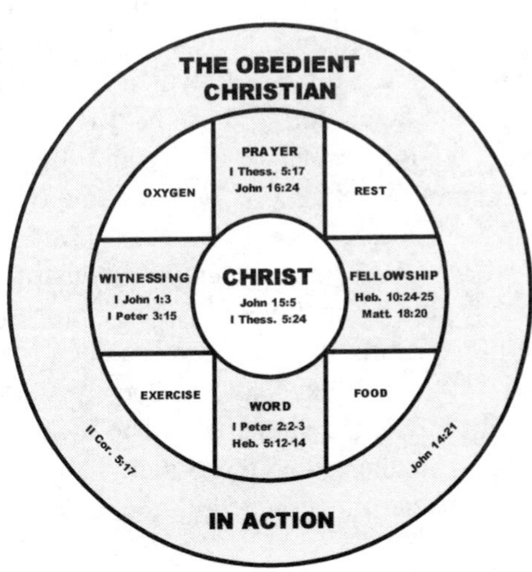

He showed Larry that those same four areas that were important to spiritual growth also represented the basics of physical growth. He challenged Larry to think of the Word, not as a thing to study, but as his necessary Food; Prayer as his Oxygen; Witnessing as his Exercise; and Fellowship as his Rest.

For the first time, Larry began to realize the correlation between people's physical and spiritual lives. Just as in their physical lives they need food, oxygen, exercise and rest to grow to maturity, so the same things are important if they are to grow spiritually. They have to feed upon God's Word or they will starve themselves spiritually. They have to keep the door to prayer open continually, just as they have to continually breathe oxygen to survive. They need to tell others about what Christ has done for them and is still doing for them. They need to be daily doing those things which God wants them to do. This will give them their spiritual exercise. Finally, they need to fellowship with other believers so they can enjoy their much-needed encouragement and challenge to rest in God's ability and power to equip them for any task to which He may call them.

Don was encouraged during those next few weeks to see Larry grasping the importance of getting into the Bible daily and of memorizing Scripture. As winter came on, they both became busier and busier. Don became a pastor of a local church and worked 50 hours a week on a construction job a half hour away, plus he continued his Navigator ministry on the ISU campus, gearing in with three key men there. Since Larry was not yet in college and was busy with his own senior activities of Ames High School and his church, as well as working at the store, the Sunday afternoons were soon lost in the maze of busy schedules.

With his new love for the Scriptures and new realization of the difference the Bible could make in his life, Larry wanted his family to attend a church that was strong in the teachings of the Bible. He and Ron began to look around. One evening found them in the Campus Baptist Church in Ames, across the street from the campus of ISU.

An attractive, friendly looking woman came in the door at the foot of the stairs and smiled up at the two brothers. As she neared the top of the stairs, Larry asked her if she could tell them where the high school group met.

She not only said she could, but she gladly led them down the hall to the room they wanted. She said she was Mrs. Switzer and that she had just dropped off her daughter while she had parked their car. The Switzers lived on a little farm just north of town, and she brought her daughter, Carla, in early because she played the piano for the youth group. Mrs. Switzer invited them to introduce themselves to Carla, and they said that they would.

When they arrived at the room, they found a large group of friendly young people who greeted them at the door and made them feel very much at home.

The evening service also impressed Larry, as the minister, Milton Dowden, explained the Bible clearly and with enthusiasm. After that evening, both Ron and Larry highly recommended the church to the rest of the family. Before long, all the Bleekers were active members of Campus Baptist Church.

As Larry became more and more involved with the young people's group, he became the song leader and he and the pretty, little brunette who played the piano got to know each other better. Therefore, when Mrs. Switzer again saw him and invited him out to their farm, he eagerly accepted the invitation. He was still a farm boy by nature. He loved horses, the smell of hay and the outdoors. The Switzer farm soon became his home away from home. He was welcome anytime, as the whole family "took a likin'" to him and he to them; especially to the eldest of the farmer's daughters. A great deal of the rest of Larry's busy senior year was shared with this young lady named Carla.

In the early spring of that year, Don McDonald stopped by to see Larry with an interesting proposal for his summer. He told Larry about a place in Nebraska called Maranatha, where the Navigators held a training program for about five weeks of the summer. He went on to explain what was involved in such a training program, which was like a Christian "boot camp." There would be manual labor to do as well as concentrated time daily in the Scriptures and prayer, learning to grow in their Christian lives and how to share Christ with others. These were all the ingredients of "The Wheel Illustration" Don had shared with him back in the fall.

Larry thought it sounded really challenging, but when Don said it would take five weeks of his summer, he was sure that just before entering college he would have to spend the entire summer working. Dad was counting on him working at the store.

He expressed his concern about his job but his mother, who was also present, said she thought they could probably work something out at the store. So Larry agreed to pray about it.

Another thing uppermost in his mind was what did God want him to do following his graduation in May. Gradually, things fell into place and he was accepted at ISU as an Industrial Administration major for the fall of 1961. This would keep the cost down as he could live at home. Maranatha, therefore, was becoming more and more of a possibility.

About that same time, in the early spring of '61, Larry met a young man from a farm near Glidden, Iowa. His name was Duane Bundt and they hit it off immediately. Although he, too, came from a Christian home, Duane felt that Christianity was only for women and children. He came to ISU in 1960 to major in Farm Operations. Then, as the year progressed, he felt he was living two lives. His life at home and his life at school were opposites. He figured he had to go one way or the other. At first, he decided he might as well eat, drink and be merry because he could not seem to live the way a Christian should. After he met some men who really were living the Christian life and were engineers or agriculture students like himself, he decided to give it another try. Duane got involved with Christian men on campus and at church where he met Larry. He was sure they could help him grow spiritually. He told the Lord that if there weren't men walking with God as a result of his own life in college, he would consider his college education a waste.

Larry and Duane began to meet together for Bible study in the spring of 1961, and Duane asked Larry to go with him to the ISU campus for evangelism. They would knock on doors in the dorm and talk to men about Christ. This was Larry's introduction to ISU, dorm life, and sharing his faith with young men who would invite them in. After only a few times of being asked questions for which he had no answers, Larry became more and more convinced that he needed to know more.

Just before Larry's high school graduation on May 26, Don McDonald again stopped by with the suggestion that Larry take five weeks out of his summer to attend Maranatha. This time it was an answer to prayer for both Larry and Duane, and they started to make their plans to attend.

Graduation went well. Larry had a group of his friends from Campus Baptist Church over to his home to help him celebrate and, of course, Carla was an important part of that group.

Then, in July, Larry and Duane headed west with what they felt was great anticipation. They had no idea that God was, even then, preparing to give them *"...exceeding abundantly above all that they could ask or think" (Ephesians 3:20).*

CHAPTER 3 - MARANATHA

On the morning of July 19, 1961, Duane's little 1950 maroon Ford pulled away from the Bundt farmhouse in Glidden, Iowa, 65 miles from Ames, at about 8:30. Larry and Duane were filled with a hearty breakfast and lots of loving advice for the 300-mile trip ahead of them. It was a beautiful day with clear skies and just enough wind to make it comfortable.

It was decided that Duane would drive the first shift. As they pulled away from the Bundt farm, Larry settled back to enjoy the rich farm lands and the wide open spaces.

Duane was impressed with how much Larry knew about farming. Larry had held quite a conversation with his dad the night before, and Duane wondered how he knew all that. Larry assured him he didn't know much, but what he had learned had come from listening to farmers tell about their land, their livestock or their crops. Larry felt you could get to know a person pretty well by listening to what was on his or her heart, and he had found most farmers thought of their land as an extension of themselves.

Duane agreed that farming and the Lord really turned his own dad on. Duane had been guilty of taking all that for granted. Ever since high school, he'd been totally involved in farming with his dad. And yet, Duane didn't think of himself as a gentle person by nature, like his father. There was something inside of Duane that really responded to danger and the rougher the activity, the better he liked it. He enjoyed nothing more than breaking horses or teasing and dogging dairy bulls. For the next 70 miles to the Nebraska border, Larry relived Duane's bronco-bustin', bull-teasin' days until both of them were ready to ditch the Ford and rustle themselves a couple of fine stallions.

Now, as Larry took his turn driving, he was becoming more aware of the Nebraska landscape. It looked impressionably flat, flat, flat. For the next 100 miles, they saw nothing but corn and soybean farms across the horizons and US-30 plowing straight down between the boundaries. It wasn't until shortly before noon that they entered the Platte Valley. Corn fields and acres and acres of alfalfa lay in every direction.

As they drove past a weighing station, Larry began to chuckle and it was just loud enough to awaken Duane. He sat up to see what he was missing.

Larry hadn't realized Duane was almost asleep, but he explained that they had just driven past a weighing station which brought back to Larry's mind a really dumb thing he had done not so many months before. He'd had his dad's furniture truck and it was overloaded. He saw a weighing station up ahead and realized that his load was too large, so he turned around to go back to unload some of it when a patrolman stopped him. Larry shook his head as he told Duane how he had proceeded to explain to the officer that he was overloaded and the weighing station would never let him get by. He guessed he thought the patrolman was going to help him out or something. Instead, the officer told him to drive back to the station. Sure enough, the truck was overloaded, and Larry was fined. His brothers had never let him live that one down. How naive could he be!

Duane had a good chuckle over that one, too.

A few more miles down the road they passed an alfalfa plant and Duane frowned at Larry. They were both thinking, "What happened to our fresh country air?" All it took was an alfalfa dehydrating plant to change not only the freshness of the air, but their attitudes as well.

When they got to Grand Island, Nebraska, Larry pulled into a gas station on what must have been gas fumes, because the attendant put 21 gallons in the car and Duane thought it only held 20. They thanked the Lord for still being in the business of multiplying things to meet their needs. Then they grabbed a couple of hamburgers each and Duane opted to drive on into camp.

The rest of the trip ran parallel to the North Platte River which was still very wide but extremely shallow this time of year. Instead of the fertile land they had expected along the river, it was gray and dry and nothing at all like their good old Iowa.

As the remaining 100 miles or so swept past them, Larry mentally reviewed the letter from Reverend Olson, the founder of the Maranatha Camp Grounds. Phrases like 5:30 reveille, morning calisthenics, four hours of daily manual labor, concentrated spiritual growth, no fellowship between guys and gals, and strict discipline, sounded like a real challenge—especially the last three.

The final 50 miles went the slowest of all but, finally around 3:00 p.m., they arrived at Maxwell, Nebraska and knew their destination lay one mile south and two miles west, which was just east of the forks of the North and South Platte Rivers.

Finally Larry, with his head poked out the window, announced that he could see the buildings of the campground just ahead and Duane got the message.

As they came to a stop, they had to wait for the gray dust to settle before they could make out their new home. Duane's maroon Ford now looked like a gray tank. As they surveyed the setting, they knew that, although not at all elaborate, this place would suit them just fine. Then they saw a friendly-looking young man, who looked to be in his late 20's, coming toward them.

Larry, eager to get out and stretch his six-foot-two frame and start his camping experience, jumped out to shake the man's hand. The man introduced himself as Walt Henrichsen. Duane walked around the car to greet him as well. With introductions over, Walt recognized them as part of Don McDonald's gang and offered to show them where to get settled. Together they walked a few yards down a cedar-strewn pathway, and then Walt pointed to a long building off through the trees.

Walt told them that was where they would be living. It was called Marsh Chapel and would be housing all the male trainees. He explained that there were two rooms up there. One was a little room in the back for the counselors, Don McDonald and Frank Meyers. The other was a big room which was to house about 30 guys. They were to take their pick of whatever bunks were left. He suggested that they drive up and unload and then park their car under the trees where it was cooler. While the three of them walked over to registration, Walt told them that dinner would be at 5:00 so they had time to look around and meet some of the gang, which they were both eager to do.

In the registration building, they met the first trainees. Soon about six of them were on their way up to Marsh Chapel as another three or four came out the door. To the "Oh, no's" of those leaving, Larry greeted them with a friendly "Howdy!" and asked if it was getting crowded inside.

One of those exiting the premises said it was, but he was certain there was still plenty of room. Larry sat by him at dinner that night and found out his name was Keith from Caldwell, Idaho. This was one of the thrilling things about this camp. In their bunkhouse that night, they discovered their bunk-mates were from California, Colorado, Idaho, Illinois, Kansas, Minnesota, Nebraska, North and South

Dakota, Pennsylvania, and even another Iowan named Dennis.

After dinner, the 65 new trainees gathered at Yeutter Hall for the evening meeting. It began with real spirit as they joined voices in singing songs, some old and some new. Interspersed with the singing, Walt Henrichsen introduced the rest of the staff and Reverend Olson, the camp's founder and pastor.

Walt outlined the schedule for the coming days. When he said they would be getting up at 5:30 every morning and lights out would be at 9:30 every evening, he got the loudest groans! However, somehow, Larry felt it was going to be good. Then Walt introduced Jim White as the speaker for that first evening. The majority in that room, like Larry, had their hearts tuned in for a challenge, and they got what they were looking for.

The strong, deliberate way Jim approached the speaker's stand in the center of the platform spoke to Larry of a man's man. After a joke or two, of which Larry took mental note, Jim asked them to turn to II Timothy 2:3-4. As they looked at the verses, Jim quoted to them the King James Version word for word. *"Thou, therefore endure hardness, as a good soldier of Jesus Christ. No man that warreth entangleth himself with the affairs of this life, that he may please Him Who hath chosen him to be a soldier."*

Jim went on to tell them that this was not to be a summer camp with a Bible emphasis. They were there for training and they had only five weeks in which to receive it. This was going to be the closest thing they'd find to a Christianized Marine Boot Camp and both the guys and gals would be given opportunities to "endure hardness as good soldiers of Jesus Christ."

He shared Luke 14:33, where Jesus said: *"So likewise, whosoever he be of you that forsaketh not all that he hath, he cannot be my disciple."*

There were two qualities that were essential to character building and that was what they would talk about that night.

The first was to be able *"to endure hardness."*

The second was *"to give everything."*

Jim wanted them all to look at their next four-and-a-half weeks as training in at least those two areas. The bulk of their instruction would be, first, from messages given—so they should begin that night to take notes. The second part of their instruction would come from personal time spent with those on the staff that they had met that night.

Then he began to outline for them some things that the staff would be expecting from each of the trainees. Those disciplines were expected to help them carry out their training objectives.

The first two they had pretty much already taken care of:

1) *They felt God wanted them there.*
2) *They had really wanted to come.*

Larry looked at Duane and grinned. They'd talked about this on their way down. Jim continued:

3) *They should be willing to let 168 hours of their week be governed, and that was all of them!*
4) *They should be willing to be open to instruction and reproof.*

Jim shared some thoughts from verses from Proverbs 9:8-9, about the wise man loving reproof.

I Peter 2:20, what their attitude toward reproof should be, especially when they didn't feel they had it coming and, finally, Hebrews. 12:11, the benefits that yield the peaceable fruit of righteousness.

Jim went on to say that they trusted that if or when rebuke was necessary—one word would do it. Then he continued:

5) *They would be expected to do their work thoroughly and correctly.*
6) *They expected there to be no complaining or murmuring.*

Jim had them look at Aaron and Miriam in Numbers 12:1-11 and Paul's advice in Philippians 2:14-16.

7) *They expected them to be gentlemen around the ladies.*
8) *There would be absolutely no dating or fraternizing. I Corinthians 1:7. If they were busy thinking about the opposite sex, they would not be thinking of discipleship and the Person of Christ.*
9) *They needed to be considerate and think of the other person—watch their volume, etc.*
10) *They must develop good table manners.*
11) *They were expected to get along harmoniously with others.*
12) *They should maintain good personal hygiene.*
13) *They would be expected to be at all the meetings.*
14) *They must be on time.*
15) *They would be expected to take notes.*
16) *They expected them to complete assignments.*
17) *They must maintain a strong devotional life.*
18) *They were expected to maintain absolute integrity.*

19) They expected them to check with their leaders before leaving the grounds, and
20) They needed to maintain the spirit of a servant. II Corinthians 4:5

As Larry listened to this list of expectations, he began to realize that these weeks ahead of him were going to be very different. He had come to enjoy the freedom he had in Christ during this last year and now he felt somewhat boxed in. Every hour of his week would be "governed," every moment "planned" by someone else. Many similar opinions from his roommates were vented into the chapel air that night after lights out. As Larry drifted off to sleep, he realized he was not the only one for whom this would be a whole new way of life.

CHAPTER 4 - MORE MARANATHA

The sharp bugle notes of reveille sliced through the early morning Nebraska air and, with somewhat more difficulty, penetrated the minds of most of the new trainees. The others were only awakened after four or five of their roommates bodily hauled them out of their bunks.

"You've got to be kidding" some of them were still mumbling, as they staggered out to the open field where once again Walt's big smile greeted them. With all the efficiency of a drill sergeant, he spread them out and soon a very energetic <u>looking</u> group of young men were running in place, jumping up and down, bicycling their feet in the air, doing pushups and a number of other exercises using muscles seldom, if ever, used before. Even some of the simplest were tests of "endurance" as Larry and Duane held their arms straight out like big birds until they thought their arms would fall off. And there was Walt, who kept his arms out just as long, but without even a sag! Walt did everything he asked them to do.

Thirty minutes of this and thirty now very wide-awake young men rushed back to the chapel to clean up their bunks and themselves. At 6:45 they met with the girls over at Yeutter Hall for group prayer. Following this, the fellows and girls split up for instructions on "The Quiet Time," which from then on would follow the group prayer each morning until breakfast at 7:30. Frank Meyers, Larry and Duane's Bible study leader, spent the next 15 minutes sharing "Quiet Time" principles. What exactly does one do when getting together with God in a quiet place? Frank turned to Exodus 34 and again Larry took detailed notes, although Don McDonald had shared some of this with him back in Ames.

From Exodus 34, Frank explained that a Quiet Time is *"cultivating a relationship with God through a definite time spent with God in the Word and Prayer."* He explained that the Scriptures give some clear instructions about this time spent with God.

In Exodus 34:2 God told Moses, *"And be ready in the morning and come up in the morning unto Mount Sinai, and present thyself there to Me in the top of the mount."* This verse said God wanted Moses to present himself to Him *"in the morning."*

In Mark 1:35 it said that Jesus, *"... in the morning, rising up a great while before day, went out, and departed into a solitary place, and there prayed."*

I Corinthians 1:9 said we are "*called unto the fellowship with His Son, Jesus Christ our Lord.*" And David said in Psalm 5:3, *"My voice shalt thou hear in the morning, O Lord; in the morning will I direct my prayer unto Thee, and will look up."*

Frank went on to share several reasons why the morning was the key time to spend with God.

1) *The mind would be fresh and the thoughts He gave could stay with them throughout the day.*
2) *It prepared them for what lay ahead. God alone knew what they were going to need for each new day.*
3) *They would receive their orders for the day during this time spent with Him.*
4) *There would be fewer interruptions. Once the whole world came to life, it would be almost impossible to get alone with God.*

Another truth that Frank shared from Exodus 34:2, was that Moses had a definite place—the top of Mount Sinai. In Mark he showed that Jesus also had a definite place—a solitary place. He assured them that this would be easier there at camp than it would be once they were back home. He asked them to find a place somewhere on the grounds where they could be alone with God, a place that would have as few distractions as possible.

Larry read Exodus 34:3 and thought to himself that God told Moses not to let any man come with him nor even to be seen throughout all the mount nor were even the flocks and herds to feed there. This reminded Larry of the New Testament concept of entering their closet and shutting the door on every kind of distraction.

Frank continued in Exodus 34:4, to share that God commanded Moses to take two tablets of stone on which He would write a message from Himself. So the trainees were encouraged to take a notebook with them so they could record all that God would say to them.

In verses 5-7, Frank showed them that God had revealed Himself to Moses there on the mount. He descended in the cloud and passed by before him and shared with Moses some new truths about Himself. Then Frank asked them how it was that God revealed Himself to them now.

They all agreed that God reveals Himself through His written Word, the Bible.

Frank nodded his approval. He explained that it is through His word that they can get a good look at Him and learn new concepts and principles for daily walking with Him. He reminded them again to always have their Bible and a notebook when they approach God in their devotional time.

Then Frank took this a step further. From verse 8, he showed them that *"Moses made haste and bowed his head toward the earth and worshipped."* Frank spelled out the fact that God would speak to them through His Word and they could speak to God through prayer, as they responded in worship and praise. Together, he said, the Word and prayer would cultivate a deep relationship with God in their hearts.

Proverbs and James had been selected by the camp for the trainees to read, so they would get into both the Old and New Testaments. Since they still had another 15 minutes left, Frank sent them off to find their own spot alone and to at least read one chapter. In the future, they would shoot for one to three chapters daily. This day they were all to meet back in the dining hall for breakfast at 7:30.

Larry headed for a picnic table not far from the dining hall. It seemed like he'd been up for hours without any food. He turned to Proverbs thinking those chapters would be shorter than those in James. Again the words of Proverbs 1:5 were impressed upon him from Jim's talk the night before. *"A wise man will hear and will increase learning..."* and verse 7—*"...but fools despise wisdom and instruction."*

Verses 24-33 spoke to him of those who refused to listen to God's reproof and counsel and who, as a result, would *"eat of the fruit of their own way and be filled with their own devices."*

As the breakfast bell rang, Larry prayed, *"O God, I believe You want to show me some things about Yourself and about myself while I'm here. Please God, give me a willing heart to receive instruction and reproof."*

After a quick but hearty breakfast, Larry reported for his work detail on the maintenance crew and Duane headed for the paint crew. They had one hour and that was sufficient to get them acquainted with the grounds and lay the foundation for the jobs ahead and the ways in which they could most efficiently be realized. Then it was time for personal Bible study and, since Larry was in a group with some Navigator experience behind it, the assignment was to do an ABC Bible Study on the first chapter of Philippians.

Each person was given two small pieces of paper. One was "How to do the ABC Study" and the other, the ABC study plan on which to fill in the proper information about the chapter to be studied. *The "A" was for "A Title." The "B" was for "The Best or Basic passage." The "C" was for "Challenge," the "D" for "Difficulties," and "E" for the "Essence or summary/outline."* Then they were sent off by themselves to study.

This was one aspect of the training that Larry expected to be his hardest. He was not a student. Studying had never come easy. It seemed to Larry to take too much valuable time from living. He liked being with people, not with books, and doing things, not sitting still. So it was with great misgivings that he slowly headed for a table as far away as possible while he prayed to God to give him the desire to study. He finally took a table way down by the Platte River. It took that distance for Larry to find himself willing to talk to God about his attitude and, even then, it seemed like a long hour with very little recorded on his study sheet.

Bible study at Maranatha
Bk. Row-Larry, Duane Bundt, Jim Baxter, Terry Bell, Leader-Frank Meyers
Frt. Row-Ed Murphy, Mike Potter

On the "C" for Challenge, however, he wrote Philippians. 1:6, and asked God, Who had already made him His child, to continue to work in him and even to make studying a joy. That was not a request that God granted right there on the spot so, with no apparent answer yet, Larry headed once again to Yeutter Hall for Reverend Olsen's "Pastor's Hour."

As Rev. Olsen began his series on "Major Doctrines of the Bible," Larry found him to be a man who could stir up excitement about passages of Scripture that Larry thought he already knew. A keen interest began to grow in Larry to internalize the Scriptures, like "spiritual food" into which he could sink his teeth. Following this, six of them headed out under the trees with Frank Meyers for what was called Bible Study Discussion. This was the time to share what they had discovered in their personal study that morning and how they could best apply it to their lives. Only a couple of the six trainees had really known what to do, so Frank went over each point carefully with them, answered questions, and encouraged them to be obedient to the Word of God.

This was the beginning of what led to some of the most meaningful times of the training program as each young man learned to share what God was speaking to him about, as spiritual questions were answered, and as applications were making changes in their lives.

God had purposely brought together these six young men: Jim Baxter from Notus, Idaho; Terry Bell from Senora, California; Ed Murphy from Artesia, California; Mike Potter from Oklahoma City; and Larry and Duane from Ames and Glidden, to hold one another accountable, *"as iron sharpens iron."*

After lunch, it was off to the work crew. It was during these hours of manual labor each day that they began to learn the valuable lessons of working for the Lord Himself. Thoroughness, wholeheartedness, and following instructions were basic principles put into action as the trainees freely gave their time to maintain the camp grounds for the campers of all ages who came for a week at a time.

They received on-the-job training on how to work well and efficiently. The principles of completing the job, flexibility under pressure, training in leadership, and following instructions were vital parts of these hours of "hard labor."

It wasn't until 2:30 p.m. that anyone had time to wonder what to do, and it was cherished when it came. Each afternoon from 2:30-5:00 was free time to do a number of things. They were: horseback riding, swimming and boating, shuffle board, trampoline, ping pong, handcrafts, hiking, tennis and just about every kind of ball game. There were also some necessary activities such as: washing, ironing and letter writing.

After the evening meal, there was one more work detail from 5:30-6:30 for any job needing more attention and, for the rest, a time for what the Navigators call "Man to Man" or "Ma'am to Ma'am." Two young men or two young women would pair off to discuss what God was teaching them, to help each other learn or review memory verses, to share any problems they were having, and to pray for one another. Several had never heard another person pray for their concerns specifically. This time became more and more meaningful and productive as the days went by and they got to know one another better.

Then came an hour for personal study, where they could work more on Bible study or go over notes from messages. They were actually tested on some of the talks given, to make sure they were paying attention and understanding the principles that were being shared.

The evening meeting wound up the day with vigorous singing, skits or quartets, and then one of the staff would share a message basic to leading an effective Christian life filled with joy and anticipation. Such topics as Obedience, Witnessing, Follow-up, World Vision and Prayer were shared at this time. A half hour later, it was lights out.

So went the days. That first week they began to experience the reality of *"enduring hardness as a good soldier of Jesus Christ."* It was a struggle to keep on top of everything. The schedule was packed and the conditions were new. They were learning a variety of valuable lessons like how to *"redeem the time,"* how to keep their bunk and clothes neat, how to be wholehearted in their work and how to work fast, yet efficiently. Had there been a mountain in Nebraska from which to observe the activity, it would have looked like a disturbed ant hill. There seemed to be a hustle and bustle from 5:30 a.m. until lights out, and it was mighty tired young people who hit the rack at 9:30 in the evening during those first couple of weeks.

By the end of the second week they seemed to reach a plateau—they were all used to the schedule and used to each other. The newness had worn off. Problems arose not so much in what the trainees were learning, but in their heart attitudes toward others and toward God. They were gaining head knowledge, but they weren't relating or applying it much to each other yet. There were bad attitudes of "not my fault" and "sour grapes."

One hot night when they couldn't sleep, Duane and Larry quietly reviewed the whole program.

Duane complained about how they picked on such little things, like how straight his bed was or where he put his shoes. He said it made him feel like he was about ten years old. Larry let Duane talk, but couldn't help thinking, if only his own problems were a messy room instead of incomplete studies and dry Quiet Times.

Once Duane got wound up, he shared what had really been on his mind. He was tired of Larry always trying to be in the spotlight or the center of things. He thought, as a friend, he ought to call that to Larry's attention.

Larry hesitantly thanked him for sharing that and said he would pray about it. Larry, however, wasn't at all convinced that he agreed with Duane's evaluation, but the next morning in his Quiet Time, Larry did talk to God about it.

His journal from that morning read, *"God, I know I'm more outgoing than a lot of these guys, but You made me like this. Yet I've offended a good friend. Show me what to do."*

During the third week, Frank asked each of his men to begin praying that he, their discussion leader, would have insight and wisdom concerning areas of their lives that needed help. Then, one by one, Frank spent personal time with them. For one, it was a matter of wholeheartedness in his work; for another, his ability to redeem his free time; for another, not getting specific applications in a personal Bible study.

For Larry, he zeroed in on something he had told them all. If he wanted to be effectively used by the Lord back home, he must begin right there to be a "giver" in all areas of life. He should give himself to studying the Scriptures, to sharing the gospel with others, and to being concerned about his brothers and sisters in Christ. He must make it his goal to give himself wholeheartedly to God and others there at camp and to continue applying those principles once he was back home with family and friends and in his ministry on the ISU campus. Frank assured him that God had given him a lot of potential. He must give it all back to God and then the attention would be drawn to Christ and not to himself.

Here it was again. He'd been drawing attention to himself. But here was also an answer. Give it all to God.

During those last weeks, there was a marked change in attitude among all the trainees. They were more wholehearted in their work, more concerned for one another, and had more team spirit and concern. Consequently, the days ran much more smoothly and quickly.

The individual time spent for "man-to-man" began to really come alive as the trainees had been encouraged to pray for an individual about some specific need with which they could be used by God to help. Strengths were shared and weaknesses were overcome by strength in the Lord and in their united prayers during those last two weeks. The Lord gave wisdom and insight, hearts were receptive, and a good rapport was established as they became really eager to learn.

One afternoon during their free time, Larry and Duane just walked around the grounds and talked.

Bundt shared with Larry that he felt he was finally beginning to understand the principle behind some of the little things that were being stressed at the camp. They weren't using discipline simply for discipline's sake—they wanted to build in them some lasting habits that make a Christian sharp. God had used cleanliness and good manners, and doing all his work to please God to deepen Duane's desire to be a real disciple of Christ.

Larry had noticed some good changes in Duane, and he heartily agreed with the principle of being faithful in little things.

Duane said he had always looked at what other people had looked at—the outward things. Now he saw that these little things speak of heart attitudes, of how God sees us.

Bleeker was amazed, too, at how miraculously God could work in so many of them simultaneously. He thanked

Duane for letting God use him to point out his own pride and ego.

Duane tried to apologize for that, but Larry assured him that what he had said was true and he needed to be told. In fact, he related how all the guys—Walt, Jim, Frank and Reverend Olsen—seemed to be preaching to him on that point. God had really been using it in his life. Larry shared that that very morning during his Quiet Time, God had seemed more real and personal to him than He had ever been before. God had reminded Larry that as long as he had his eyes on God, old Bleeker wouldn't be so important. He confessed to Duane that he knew this wouldn't happen to him overnight and that he would no doubt need a reminder now and then to get his eyes back on Jesus.

Duane agreed that was true for everyone. Their great theological discussion was then abruptly interrupted by an invitation to join the others in a soccer game in the Platte River. In a matter of moments, the Platte became an enthusiastic battleground and a wonderful way to let all their energies explode and their tensions evaporate.

Playing soccer in the Platte River at Maranatha

Larry didn't have everything worked out yet. A couple of times he and Duane got so involved in praying together over the Iowa State campus that they were late to meetings and were assigned extra pushups as a result. His study-time attitude had improved considerably but it still was not easy.

The Sunday afternoons spent in the towns of North Platte and Valentine, witnessing from house to house, or in the bus stations or at Cody Park were becoming easier, and Larry had gained much more confidence in his ability to share what he knew about Christ. So with real eagerness, he looked forward to making a difference in the dorms of ISU that fall.

Graduation was held Sunday afternoon, August 20. Then 65 young people left for their 14 different states, with the basic principles of the Christian life beginning to bud in their lives. It was a joy to see their hearts eager to trust Christ in the everyday situations that lay ahead of them. Some had even decided that they were willing to obey God at any cost.

CHAPTER 5 - AN ISU FRESHMAN

The Bleeker family had gathered around the breakfast table heaped with bacon, eggs and toast. Everyone was there except Larry. Gary could hardly believe that Larry wasn't coming down to eat. Not him. Mom asked why Larry wasn't there. Gary frowned when he said that it was because he was "studying."

That comment got dad to his feet. He had never known Larry to skip a meal for studies. Hi walked over to the short flight of stairs that led to the upper level and told Larry they were all waiting for him. Their breakfast was on the table.

Larry apologized and explained that he had overslept. Then he said something that caused them all to believe that the time at Maranatha had indeed changed him. He told them that if he didn't have time to feed his soul, he didn't have time to feed his body.

Larry was as surprised at his new attitude toward his morning Quiet Time as the rest of the family. Dad understood and was obviously very pleased as they went on with breakfast that morning. They had all been up late the night before listening to Larry's thrilling accounts of Maranatha and of the trip he and Duane had made from Maranatha to Colorado Springs for a men's conference at Glen Eyrie. A gang from Iowa State had been there, too, and Larry was now eager for school to begin. That, too, was another strange phenomenon in his life. Dad had given Larry the rest of the week off from the store, so after a good time with the Lord and a few odds and ends around the house, Larry headed off for the Switzer farm. (There were no rules about fraternizing now!)

As Larry drove the seven miles out to the Switzer farm, he rejoiced in the Lord's provision even for a guy's desires. He didn't have to have a farm to retreat to, nor the smell of hay, nor country rolls nor even the beautiful and talented young lady whose dark eyes conveyed her interest and whose dimples were as sweet and coy as she was. He certainly was very grateful for all these extras.

He had been so busy for the past six weeks and so much had happened, that girls had not been seriously considered for perhaps the longest time in his maturing life. Larry had enjoyed the feminine wiles of the opposite sex ever since they entered his life at the age of 12 when his baby sister, Marlene, was born.

Now he found himself wondering if Carla would be as excited and thrilled as he was over his new-found joy in the Lord. Since she was only 15, it would be awhile before she could experience anything like Maranatha but, in the meantime, hearing about it would be good.

Larry was out of the car almost before it stopped, ran up to the door of the farmhouse and pressed his nose against the screen, calling out an exuberant, "Hi—anybody home?"

Mrs. Switzer, who couldn't help hearing him come, welcomed him with a motherly hug. She told him that the girls weren't home from school yet and her husband, Sam, was out in the lower 40. She knew they would all be home shortly, so she invited him to come in and tell her all about his vacation.

Larry laughed good-naturedly at the term "vacation." He enjoyed telling her that it was a far cry from a vacation. It was more like a boot camp where they learned to "endure as good soldiers of Jesus Christ."

Mom Switzer had pulled her rocker over closer, as she anticipated hearing about his time in Nebraska.

Larry reassured her that it was a "good deal." They had no rest or relaxation because they had really gotten involved in the spiritual battle.

Mom Switzer, sensing his enthusiasm for the program, then asked just what they did at a training program like Maranatha. This sent Larry off and running through a typical day, beginning with the 5:30 morning calisthenics. That hour didn't sound all that bad to a farmer's wife, but she knew that was something very different for Larry.

For the next hour, he shared with Mrs. Switzer some of the highlights of his summer at the training program until they heard feminine voices outside.

As Carla and her younger sister, Nancy, entered the room, they saw Larry. Carla stopped in mid sentence, a huge smile spreading across her face as she put her books down and stood for a moment grinning at him in the way he remembered, her dimples in full bloom. Then she asked him how long he'd been there.

Larry told her he had forgotten she would be back in classes already, so he had arrived about an hour early and had talked her mom's ear off. Then he asked what he had really come to find out, how she was and what was new with her.

Carla told him there was nothing much new around there but that she, too, was eager to hear all about his trip. She suggested they go out and grab a couple of horses and go for a ride, while he shared his adventures. Mom nodded her approval and they were off.

Once out of earshot from the house, Larry told her he had a new name for her. In answer to her questioning eyes, he said that he thought "Dimples" better suited her. Carla's quick reply of "Okay, Bleek," though said without a great deal of thought, stuck just the same. Many people would come to know Larry as "Bleek" in the coming days.

They laughed and joked as they walked over to their two favorite riding horses: then as they trotted off, Larry began to recount his past six weeks.

Carla groaned about the Maranatha schedule in all the same places the trainees had groaned that first night, but Larry sounded convinced that five weeks of that had really been good for him.

He told her that the best advice he had gotten was to spend his first moments in the morning with God, before the whole world woke up to compete for his time. He explained that he had overslept that morning and found many more temptations to put it off than when he had the time with God early. But God was so faithful. Larry had met with Him even though he was a little late, and they'd had a wonderful time together.

Carla's eyes danced. Larry was notorious for being "a little late"!

Then he told her about Reverend Olsen and how impressed he had been with him. Reverend Olsen's burning desire had seemed to be to reach the world before Jesus returned. Just listening to him had made Larry begin looking for Christ to come at any moment. Larry told her that, as a result of five weeks of the "Pastor's Hour" and a week of Dr. Jack Mitchell at the Glen, he had decided to set up a prayer map.

By this time, Carla's mind was swirling with all these new concepts. She felt that she must have missed the meaning of all he'd been so carefully explaining to her. Somehow, he seemed so much older now. She wasn't sure she liked it, but she did ask him to explain a prayer map to her.

Larry shared that that morning he had gotten out a world map and that he intended to pray for different areas of the world. He planned to spend two weeks on each area. First, he would pray for the people there, and second, for the work going on there. He explained that this was what Dawson Trotman, the founder of the Navigators, had done in the beginning. He and some other guys had gone up on a hilltop overlooking Los Angeles and had begun to pray for the city, then for Los Angeles County, and then for California, the West Coast, for all the states, and, finally, for the whole world. By the end of World War II, there had been Navigator contacts on a thousand ships and bases all over the world. Now there were Navigator ministries on college campuses all over the United States and Canada.

Carla could only respond with a "Wow!" Then a thought struck her, and she asked Larry if he thought God might someday send him to a mission field some place.

Larry could tell that that would worry her, so he tried to reassure her that probably not. They both knew that God could make them missionaries at home as well. In fact, if they weren't missionaries at home, crossing an ocean wouldn't turn them into missionaries. That pretty much ended his part of catching her up on the summer, and he felt she had a good understanding of all he had said.

Then Carla caught him up on the youth group at church and how, recently, it hadn't had much life. Before they got back to the house, they stopped for their customary time to pray and really commit Campus Baptist Church and the youth group to the Lord.

Shortly after this, God began to show Larry a basic principle in the way He worked. If God put a concern on an individual's heart, He was usually going to ask that individual to, in some way, become a part of the answer. God began using Larry that very next Sunday.

If the youth group lacked life, its heart began to beat again as he shared the challenges he had received during the six weeks he had been gone. He had a kind of contagious enthusiasm that challenged those who had become somewhat bored with a Christianity they felt was for kids or older people. Several youth began looking for opportunities to talk with him further about his joy in knowing Christ. One such person was Jim Brygger, who had come to Ames to attend ISU and study architecture. His dad was a minister in Sioux City. Jim sought Larry out after Sunday school, and they immediately felt a strong bond in Christ. The more they talked, the more clear it became that God had a real purpose in bringing them together on the campus, in the church, and later as they both worked in the Bleeker furniture store.

Those first weeks at ISU were an adjustment for them both. It wasn't like high school where Larry never cracked a book. He had decided on an Industrial Administration major, but this first quarter he took a full load. He took: General Botany, Plant Kingdom, English 101, General Psychology, Air Science I, Algebra and Trigonometry, plus some things like P.E., Men's Glee Club and the Iowa State Singers to spark it up and keep him really hopping.

Although Larry got together with Duane and some of the guys on the Navigator team, he also got involved with Jim in Intervarsity Christian Fellowship on campus. Larry was eager to find God's place for him, and he investigated everything he saw as a possibility. During Christmas vacation that winter of 1961, Intervarsity held their big missions conference at Urbana, Illinois. Larry went to the conference and, again, God used it in a very definite and needful way in his life. After he returned home, he wrote this letter to a friend.

> *Did you make it to Urbana? If not, let me spend a few, brief, simple words and tell what it has meant to me. Even in the first meeting of the conference, I*

felt sure that God had directed me to Urbana and had something in store for me there.

The theme of the conference was COMMISSION-CONFLICT-COMMITMENT, and the Lord had an abundance of words to say to me through the speakers. In the meetings, both large and small, we carefully considered the commission that Jesus Christ our Lord and Savior had given to us. There were speakers, including nationals from different countries, who brought us face to face with many of the conflicts that confront us as we undertake Christ's commission. Finally, the Lord has showed me that if we are determined to undertake the commission and meet the conflicts, whatever they might be, the only formula is commitment, total commitment to Jesus Christ, and this isn't the Tuesday, Thursday, Saturday routine. Nor is it the Monday, Wednesday, Friday routine, but this is the complete surrender and commitment of ourselves to Jesus Christ.

This conference has challenged me in many ways, and may I take this opportunity to challenge you to consider the cost that Jesus paid, in dying for you. How much? What is the cost of your commitment to Jesus Christ?

Larry Bleeker

Because of the interest and ideas that Larry and Jim had poured into their college youth group, it was not surprising that in February they elected Larry as president and Jim as his vice-president. Together they took the total responsibility of setting up all the college activities and programs. Their desire to know Christ better, plus their keen love for fun and action, began attracting many new collegiates. Larry and Jim met more and more frequently in Jim's small off-campus room, kneeling beside his bed, praying and sharing, and then planning the youth programs. These times were invaluable in the lives of both the church and the guys themselves.

The youth in the church took on a new zeal, and Larry found his interest not only in his college group but in the high school group as well. He wanted to see them get into the Word and begin to grow spiritually. He set about organizing a Bible study group in the high school department and faithfully met with them to challenge and instruct them. Carla liked this because, as she had feared, she had been seeing less and less of her "knight in shining armor."

The times of sharing with Jim showed both Larry and Jim that young guys all faced the same temptations and that, by talking their problems over with God and each other, they stood a much better chance of experiencing total victory in their lives as they pulled together in the same yoke.

As responsibilities began to snowball, it was not surprising that many of these times together were closed with a prayer for physical and mental alertness to study late into the night, which they often found necessary just before a test.

One afternoon, just after an exam, Larry was walking across the snow-covered campus. He was really worn out mentally and physically. He hadn't done well on that test, and he knew it was because God had only had about half a man to inspire that day. He felt totally washed out. Just then an ice ball whizzed past his ear, and he looked up to see Vic Zetta coming toward him.

Vic said he had been trying to track him down for some time. He invited Larry to go out to the Navigator headquarters at Glen Eyrie with some of the guys during spring break, for a work week. Expecting to have to talk

Larry into this, he said it would be a good opportunity to get away. Before he could say another word, Larry said it sounded great, he would pray about it, and could he bring a friend? Vic laughingly said yes, as long as it wasn't a girl. Larry assured him that Jim Brygger was no girl, but he was sure Jim would enjoy the experience also.

Vic found himself looking forward to the time at the Glen even more after talking to Larry. He told Larry that they would be getting all the interested guys together in the little room just off the cafeteria at noon on the coming Friday. If possible, it would be great if he and Jim could join them.

After thanking Vic for the information, Larry began to wonder if Pop could let them both off for spring break. He headed over to the English office building where he was to meet Jim before going down to the store. Larry chided himself for doubting that God could work everything out for everyone's good. He knew that if God wanted them both there, He would take good care of Pop and the store.

Jim had several questions about Glen Eyrie when Larry told him about it on their way downtown. He knew it was the Navigator headquarters in Colorado Springs, but he wasn't clear if just anyone could go or did one have to be a Navigator first?

Larry was able to reassure Jim that he would be more than welcomed. He told him they had all kinds of conferences for high school, college, adults, pastors, and churches. The grounds were great. They could hike clear up to Eagle Lake. A person could almost forget that there was a world outside that peaceful valley that needed Christ. However, one visit to these headquarters made it abundantly clear that it existed for the purpose of reaching the world and it was doing it!

Jim said he had been planning to go home, since he hadn't made it for Christmas, but that this sounded like a trip he didn't want to miss. Larry was happy with his response and suggested they pray about it and watch to see how God would open or close the doors. They decided to go to the Friday meeting, and then Larry would see what his dad thought and what could be worked out at the store.

Five weeks later, Jim and Bleek were part of the Iowa gang that pulled through the gate at Glen Eyrie and drove down the pink road past acres of green lawn to the 67-room castle where dinner was in progress. They were soon totally involved and, after only a few short days, also totally impressed by its impact on their lives.

Jim commented to Bleek on the way back home that they had seen Christianity in action in very practical ways there. It had been thrilling to be a part of helping to make it easier for people to know Christ and to make Him known. Jim shared that he wanted that to be his primary aim from then on. He added that he wanted to apply these new principles to his life. He said he knew Larry had always had a knack for Scripture memory, but now he could better understand why it was so important. After all, the Word was their sword and their only offensive weapon against the enemy. He felt he couldn't afford to have it back in his room anymore. It had to be in his heart and ready to be used at any moment.

Larry was excited. Jim was starting to sound like a Navigator! His new goal in life corresponded so well to Larry's. They eagerly anticipated the coming spring quarter on the ISU campus.

That change of pace at the Glen and the spiritual challenge they received by "taking in" after "giving out" for so long was just what they both needed. That spring, no one could hold either of them back as they began putting their knowledge into practice. Actually, no one really wanted to hold them back. They found Christianity more exciting than they had ever imagined possible.

With June came the plans for Gary and Millie's wedding. With Larry not so busy now, he spent as much time as he could with Gary and in prayer with and for him. This was a "big step." It seemed strange to have one leave their family circle. They had always expanded it quite easily to include anyone and everyone, but for one to move out and begin a life of his own, well, it was as it should be but different.

The beautiful ceremony was held on June 20, 1962. As Larry watched and listened to Gary and Millie recite their wedding vows and then fairly dance back down the aisle as husband and wife, Larry was genuinely happy for them. The prayer of his heart was, *"Father God, make theirs a good marriage, grounded upon You and Your Word. And make it a glory to Your name! Amen!"*

CHAPTER 6 - MAKING LABORERS

In the fall of 1962, Campus Baptist Church had a freshman reception and Larry and Jim Brygger put together quite an act for entertainment. They dressed up in overalls, old shirts and farm hats and sang some humorous duets. Then Jim, the intelligent one, turned to Larry, the not-so-intelligent one, and asked him to pick up the bandana from on top of the piano. Jim wasn't looking when Larry walked over to the piano and picked up a banana instead. Larry told him that he had it but now what was he supposed to do with it.

Still not looking, Jim asked him to tie the two opposite corners together. Larry scratched his head and stared at the banana while the group began to laugh in anticipation. Then, at just the right moment, he began to try to tie the banana in a knot. He had everyone in stitches except Jim, who, still not looking, was getting impatient with how long it was taking him to do such a simple thing.

Finally Larry asked, "Now what?"

Jim told him to walk over and stand behind him. Larry agreed and slowly shuffled his way over to stand right behind Jim, with the banana skin all split and banana oozing out. Jim told Larry that as soon as he uttered a couple of his magic words, Larry was to take what he had just tied in a knot and shake it over Jim's head, assuring him that the knot would come undone if he shook it hard enough. So Jim asked him if he was ready. Larry smiled and said he was, and then asked if Jim was ready. Jim furrowed his eyebrows at that question and then went on to utter his magic words. Well, Jim had been absolutely correct, and his magic worked. When Larry shook the banana over Jim's head, it came completely undone. It ran down Jim's face and dripped off his nose as he appropriately looked surprised. Larry made sure the blackened peeling was draped over one ear.

Instead of stopping there, they asked, "Do you have faith? Do you understand your faith? Do you know what it is? Strange and surprising things can happen if we don't know the meaning of a word—like bandana, like faith." Then they asked their audience, "Where does your faith lie? Are you confused?"

That set the background for the evening message and, once again, God had used the talents of these two young men to loosen up the group, break down resistances, and help them relax and enjoy themselves. They were now open to seriously consider the One Who could dispel their confusion and put lasting joy in their lives.

Many new students came to the Sunday Suppers and meetings during Larry's sophomore year. He and Jim continued to meet twice a week to pray and plan for it. But Larry and Jim were puzzled that the ministry on the campus did not seem to be as fruitful as they had anticipated. Most of the Navigator team from the year before had graduated, and there was no Navigator staff leader for the campus. Yet, God was faithful to build in the lives of those who did respond. In fact, that fall God had called out five young men with personalities as unique and different from each other as the first 12 disciples. Their hearts were united in wanting to see God really open up the campus to respond to Jesus Christ and to live for Him. They began to meet and pray toward that end. These five guys were Dick Ikenberry, Vic Zetta, Duane Bundt, Larry, and Jim Williams.

Dick was from nearby Des Moines, and Don McDonald had introduced him to Jesus during Dick's senior year. Now he was working on his Ph.D. in plant pathology. Dick was sharp intellectually, extremely neat, and a great asset in helping with details. His keen sense of humor and big smile naturally attracted others to him.

Vic came to ISU to get his Master's in Agricultural Engineering. He had already received his B.S. from Virginia Poly-technical Institute. He had a deep Virginia accent and was slow and deliberate, unlike the others, but his warm hospitality and deep walk with Christ made him a refreshing asset.

Duane was now a junior in Farm Operations. He hadn't lost his love for danger and excitement, so he was always on the lookout for new and exciting things to do and was finding that serving Christ held all the excitement he could comprehend and more.

Larry was the life of the party and the life of the team. His enthusiasm and optimistic attitude were contagious, and his leadership qualities came to the fore when any kind of challenge was presented. Whether it involved how long he could stay standing on a racing toboggan or how many bananas he could eat at one time, he was always ready to jump in and give it all he had. Consequently, others followed him with similar enthusiasm. Now that he realized more fully what a great challenge it was to follow Christ completely, he got involved with his total being.

Every Wednesday evening, these four would go to the nursing home in Ames to meet with their fifth member, Jim Williams. Jim had had polio, which left him only able to move his head and one hand. However, what he lacked in physical strength, God had generously endowed him with tremendous strength in his soul and spirit. Although he was only in his 20's, he was actually a spiritual grandfather to Larry and Dick since he had led their spiritual father, Don McDonald, to Christ several years before.

God richly blessed their times together in the Word and prayer. During one such get-together, toward the end of fall quarter, God challenged them all to claim some verses from Matthew, chapter 9, for that year. Verses 37 and 38 said, *"Then saith Jesus unto His disciples, 'The harvest truly is plenteous, but the laborers are few; pray ye therefore the Lord of the harvest, that He will send forth laborers into His harvest.'"*

With renewed fervor, they began to ask God to use them as laborers to find and make more laborers. That was a prayer God would answer! The way God would do it, however, was as unique and exciting as each individual involved in it.

Each young man began to pray that God would give him another man to which he could minister, who would consequently pray for another guy to which he could minister. The Apostle Paul knew that was good advice for young Timothy in II Timothy 2:2. *"And the things that thou hast heard of me among many witnesses, the same commit thou to faithful men, who shall be able to teach others also."*

What Paul had shared with Timothy, Timothy was to share with other faithful men who, in turn, would be able to share it with still others. This concept of "man-to-man-to-man" was the foundation of the Navigator ministry. This was the principle the four on campus applied as they went back to their dorms to share their faith. In the meantime, Jim, confined as he was, could still soar to the heavens as he prayed for them and praised God for what he knew He was able to do.

A couple of Sundays later, Duane stopped by Steve Krumen's room. Steve had a personal relationship with Christ, but he knew he should be telling others about God. He realized, however, that he didn't know how. So Duane took Steve with him that afternoon to share with him what he knew about evangelism. They picked a room at random, knocked on the door, and Duane shared what Jesus meant to him.

After they left the young man inside seriously considering Who Christ claimed to be, Steve turned to Duane and asked him, in amazement, if he knew who that man was. Before Duane could say that he didn't, Steve told him that it was the man he had been out drinking with the night before. Whether that young man made a decision or not, Steve knew he himself had just made one. If he was going to witness for Christ, his life had better start backing it up. Steve determined that he was going to start filling his life with God's Word, instead of man's liquor—and he did. He got involved in Bible study and Quiet Times. He began to meet with the men in prayer. It wasn't long before he, too, was sharing his faith with other men.

Then Rick Uhl joined the team. He had become a Christian the year before but, like Steve, had been out of fellowship, was now seeking God's will again, and was excited about sharing Christ.

In January, their evangelism efforts brought them to Dean Senning's door. Dean had just asked Christ into his life two weeks before and, as a new Christian, was praying that God would send someone to help him. God did!

And so their laborers grew in numbers. To them were added Jim Brygger and Chuck Swanson from Campus Baptist Church, whom Larry was teaching to do personal evangelism. Larry also met regularly with a freshman named Marlin Bricker. Every Thursday evening, they'd pray together and then visit the dorm. At first Larry did most of the talking, bringing the conversation quickly to the One he knew to be the most exciting Person in the world to know. He would tell them about the claims of Christ. Then he began to include Marlin more in the picture by asking him to share his own testimony—about what Christ meant to him. Larry had spent personal time with him on this beforehand, so when the time came he was ready, eager, and, of course, a little nervous. As they left each room, whether a definite decision for Christ had been made or not, a definite impression had been left that there must be something to Jesus if He could get men like these so excited about life. Even when they obviously didn't agree with Larry's point of view, a bond of friendship and respect was laid to build on at another time.

One day Larry came bounding into Marlin's room full of the enthusiasm he always showed when he had talked to someone about Christ. Marlin asked him what had happened because he was sure Larry had a good story to tell. But Marlin didn't know how good.

Larry said he had just given a young man a lift to the dorms and talked to him about becoming a Christian. He seemed wide open so he asked Marlin to pray for the man. He told him the man's name was Floyd Constant. When he said that, Marlin dropped his book right in the middle of the floor. He told Larry that Floyd was a man he had gone to school with and when he had gone home to Des Moines the weekend before, Marlin had shared his testimony with Floyd about how Christ had changed his life. Marlin said he seemed a little interested then, but that he was active in gymnastics and that had occupied most of their conversation. Marlin was ecstatic. They both prayed for Floyd right then and there, that he would make that most important decision!

A couple of weeks later, Floyd asked Jesus to come into his life, and his gymnastic buddies began to hear more and more about a Person named Jesus, Who could give real meaning to life.

It was during winter quarter that Duane got a new roommate. His name was Stan Nolte. Stan had two goals.

One was to get a 4.0 grade point average and the other was to meet as many girls as possible. As the quarter progressed, he witnessed several guys giving their hearts and lives to the Lord in his room as they talked with Duane. Finally, Stan changed his two goals to one—serving Christ with his whole heart.

During this time, Larry was learning another of God's principles. When you ask God for something, you'd better be prepared for His answers. Larry was busy. He couldn't say "No" to anyone. The college department at church could have taken his full time, aside from classes and work. But God had really laid people on his heart, both in the church and on the campus. Larry was committed to three guys from church: Marlin, another freshman named Ron Bennett, and a graduate student named Ben. Larry decided to work these young men into his campus ministry, get that needed time with them, and have it be productive as well. Still, it seemed that every moment was spent with people or thinking and praying about people.

One of the people he didn't have time for, but thought about often, was Carla. He longed to be with her, but lately it seemed every time he could she already had a date.

He and Jim Brygger spent time praying about the gals in their lives, but it was difficult. One afternoon, as Larry and Jim were unboxing furniture in the store, Jim said he couldn't understand why God had created women in the first place. They sure were complicating his life.

Larry jokingly responded that he guessed they were just one of those necessary evils. He knew they both enjoyed them, but they certainly were complicating his life as well. He knew his feelings for Carla were stronger than he wanted to admit, because seeing her with other guys really hurt. And yet, he couldn't blame her. She was a beautiful, talented girl who enjoyed life and doing things. With her just a sophomore in high school, their activities didn't coincide. When Larry said, "Naturally, she is going to be dating other guys," he was thinking out loud about Carla, but Jim assumed he was talking about his girl. He responded as you would expect until he was assured by Larry that he had been speaking of Carla only. Larry decided that it would be a good idea for him to date other girls as well. Jim agreed that Larry should probably broaden his horizon. Jim knew, in fact, of several girls in the youth group that would like to date Larry.

Larry laughed it off but didn't forget it. During those last weeks of winter quarter and on into spring, with the buds on the trees and crocuses on the ground, Larry's mind, like other young men's, turned to girls. In Larry's case, however, it was still one girl in particular. This was usually during his idle moments, so he began to wonder where his own emotions fit in and where God's will fit in.

It was during one of those confusing moments for Larry, when God's will seemed unknowable and the fear of blowing the whole thing loomed largest, that Ben Buskohl came to the house and asked to see Larry.

Mom cheerfully told Ben Larry was up in his room and went to call him down while Ben took a seat in the living room. Just then the phone rang and Marlene answered it. When she told Larry it was for him, he checked to see if Ben had a moment. Ben assured him he did, and told him to take his time. No one minded waiting for Larry too much because they enjoyed visiting with his mom or dad. Mom Bleeker commented that they hadn't seen much of Ben for some time, except for glimpses at church now and then. She asked him what he had been doing. Ben said he hadn't been doing much, especially not like her son Bleek. Larry seemed to always be doing something for someone else.

Mom had to agree with Ben. In fact, she said he had always been that way. He loved people and really enjoyed helping them in any way he could. When Larry returned from the phone, he told his mom he had a meeting on campus the next day at noon and wouldn't be home for lunch. Then he greeted Ben with a firm slap on the shoulder and asked him how he was doing. When Ben responded "Fine," Larry looked him in the eyes and sensed that he really had more he would like to say. Larry said he needed a good rap session with him and led him up the short flight of stairs and down the hall. As they walked to Larry's room, he figured Ben was possibly frustrated with his walk with Christ, but Larry didn't know why.

Once in the room with the door shut, Ben began at the beginning. He told Larry that it had started back in the fall. His first recollection of Larry was when he had been trying to tie that stupid banana into a knot at the freshman reception. He hadn't known Larry at all, but he could tell he wasn't dumb and that he wasn't confused about his faith in Christ. It was Larry's faith that showed in so many ways that gave Ben a real hunger to have that same kind of a walk.

Larry was feeling uneasy because he didn't want anyone looking at him, but at his Lord. But Ben went on to say that he was probably four years older than Larry, physically, but that Larry had a kind of spiritual maturity that he wanted to pattern his life after.

Larry wanted to stop him, but for a quiet young man Ben was really opening up and sharing his feelings, justified or not. So Larry decided he better let him say all he'd come to say.

Ben shared that he had tried to do the same things he saw Larry doing and he was really frustrated because he just couldn't measure up. Ben continued to say that God had impressed him that He didn't intend for him to be another

Larry Bleeker, but he didn't know what God did want him to be. Why was it that God couldn't use him, too? Wasn't it okay for guys like Bleek to be a challenge to guys like himself? In desperation, Ben again said he had tried to pattern his life after Larry but…

Larry could sit there no longer. His heart went out to Ben as he asked him to look at what he had been doing. Ben was making himself a bigger stumbling block to Larry than Ben was even to himself. Ben looked shocked, but Larry went on to tell him that if he continued to look up to Larry as his example, then the Devil would go after Larry all the more. If the Devil could trip Larry up, it would mean that Satan could get two-for-one, because Ben was sure to fall as well.

It was obvious that Ben had never thought of it that way before. Larry continued that no one should pattern his or her life after any other Christian. Christ was to be the ONLY example, and God wanted us to be like Him in our own unique and important ways. Larry said he was very glad that God didn't want more than one Larry Bleeker. His life was not as great as Ben might think and that Ben, being the best Ben he could be for the Lord, would be awesome.

When Ben left the house he had a new appreciation for himself and his potential. Even Marlene noticed the difference as he flipped her pigtail on his way out the door.

During the spring break, Larry and Ron Bennett took off for Glen Eyrie and came home with new vigor and vision. One day soon after their return, while reading his Bible, Larry felt a strong desire to respond to God and, later, he used this as a paper for one of his classes. He called it:

A LETTER TO GOD

Dear Lord,

While I was reading Your letter to me, the Bible, last night, I thought that it would be interesting to write one to You. Of course, You already know everything that's going on down here, and this will be old news to You, but I'd just like to give You my point of view on some things.

First, I want to thank You again for all the wonderful things you've given me. I have a loving Christian family, although I don't appreciate them half as much as I should; I have good friends; I have a good church to go to and worship You, with so many wonderful friends there. Thank You for a beautiful world to live in; everything in it—trees, flowers, animals, the moon, stars, and sun—remind me of Your power and glory.

Thank You for always supplying my needs: basic needs like food, clothes, shelter; and other needs, like helping me with my problems and decisions; or supplying something that is needed right away; and helping me with tests and schoolwork. I really need help there! But most of all, Lord, I thank You for Your wonderful gift of salvation, for the sacrifice You made for me. When I think of You leaving all of the glory of heaven to come and live on earth and then die on the cross, I am amazed and ashamed, amazed that Your love for a sinner like me could be so great that You would be willing to go through that shame and suffering, and ashamed that I'm so stubborn and selfish about giving things to You and living completely for You.

The world itself has changed so much since You left it. Now people travel hundreds of miles an hour, go to work in huge skyscrapers, use electronic brains to compute problems (that's what I need, remember my last algebra test?), watch color TV, and talk about atomic war. But the people haven't changed. We're still selfish, self-centered, and egotistic. People are too anxious to shut You out of their lives completely, to prove that they don't need God, that they can do everything by themselves. They try to prove that You don't exist when evidence of Your existence is all around them—even in life itself. But, they say, "We can produce life." And they'll keep trying, even though You've said, "All things were made by Him (God) and without Him was not anything made that was made" John 1:3. They say all life evolved from a single cell (but can't seem to decide where that cell came from), when just reading Genesis 1 through once should remove all doubt and show that You created everything. But human nature won't accept this. Man won't be dependent on anyone; he's too convinced of his own worth and importance. Everyone is too wrapped up in his own life and affairs and pleasures and has no time for You. It's like it was at Bethlehem when You came to earth; there's no room. And I think that even if You were to come to earth again, people would still be as blind as they were 2000 years ago. They wouldn't see You as the King, but only as a man who was trying to take some of their power. And again, people would shun and ridicule and try to get rid of You. They would harden their hearts as

Judas did and not acclaim You as their Savior, or they would turn away as the young ruler, because the price was too great and they couldn't make the sacrifice.

But there are some, Lord, who have room for You in their hearts. There are countless missionaries who leave their families and encounter danger and hardships to spread Your Word throughout the world: ministers, teachers, and Christian workers who have been called into Your work and just ordinary people who, though we aren't in a special area of Your work, are living their lives for You and trusting You day by day. There are so many times when I doubt You, Lord, but I know that You forgive and that You'll give me stronger faith in the days ahead.

Now I have to go, because the bell is going to ring in just a minute, and I can't be late for class. Thank You again for Your love and grace.

All my love,
Larry

Back on campus that spring, God was still raising up laborers and reaping harvests. He used Duane to reach Dennis Munch and Larry to reach Dick Dexter and the hearts of the team remained encouraged. By now, Larry was getting to campus by 6:30 a.m. to spend personal time with some new Christians for their morning Quiet Time. They'd meet in a room or out under a tree, read the Scriptures together and discuss what that meant to each of them at ISU in 1963, and then they'd pray. It was one thing to be told how to have a Quiet Time, and quite another thing to have someone show them how with the enthusiasm Larry had.

One morning, as he met with a couple of guys in their room, he noticed some girls' pictures on the bulletin boards. He thought back to some of his own struggles when he had shared his room at home with Gary. So he prayerfully mentioned that he didn't know about them, but he had found it so easy to get sidetracked during his Quiet Times. It didn't take much to get the old mind on something besides God. It was a constant struggle to get quality time with God. He told them that at home he used to get up before anyone else and go down to the basement and sit on the washer or dryer. He had decided that if he sat at the desk in his and his brother's room, the picture of Gary's girlfriend would distract him, and Gary didn't appreciate it too much when Larry covered the picture with a t-shirt.

The young men laughed, but they also identified with the problem because the girls' pictures soon came off their bulletin boards.

The evenings were warm now, and on Sunday nights after church, Larry would walk out on central campus and meet Dick Ikenberry under a spreading Larch which they called their "Prayer Tree." Many battles were fought and won there, as they shared their hearts with their problems, confessions, encouraging times and recent blessings from the Word. They'd read together a portion of Scripture and pray, and the quietness of the campus plus the quietness that would come to their own hearts, made it a time of spiritual refreshment and encouragement to which they both looked forward.

One of the battles that Larry frequently fought there was his date life. Dick asked him one night who the blonde was that he saw hanging on Larry's arm a few days before and questioned him on what had happened to Carla.

He told Dick the blonde's name but had to admit he had wished she were Carla. Carla couldn't be involved in all he was doing, still being in high school, so they hadn't spent much time together lately. He said he got out to the farm when he could and they were still friends, but he wished things were different. Larry was surprised that he could put this into words so easily, but he'd been doing a lot of thinking and praying about this.

Then Dick asked him if he had ever asked himself just why he dated. Larry quickly answered that it was because he was a red-blooded American boy.

Dick agreed he was, too, but because of that, he had to constantly ask himself whether dating really fit into God's plan for his life right then. Did it add to his effectiveness or did it detract?

This gave Larry much to think about that night as he walked the three miles home. He always enjoyed that time to formulate his thoughts and plans for the coming week. But some things were not settled in a night.

Dick's questions continued to eat away at Larry. Then one night in June, God worked in his life in such a way that Larry realized he could now share his victory with others. To make his testimony clear in his own mind and to be a reminder of how God had brought him to this conclusion, he typed up the following details.

JUNE 1963

WHY DID I BEGIN DATING ______________?

1) *As Carla became more interested in others, I wondered about my deep interest in her and whether God was clearly showing me His objection.*
2) *As _______ was interested in developing a closer relationship and since I was greatly attracted to her spiritual maturity, we*

experienced an enjoyable time. I feel as if God has taught us both new things.

WHAT DOES CARLA MEAN TO ME NOW?

1) *Carla means as much to me now as she ever has—I hope she always will.*
2) *My desire to see her spiritually grow and mature means more to me now than my actual going out with her. As only God can produce this interest and desire with her, I must only be confident in Him.*

WHY AM I NOT DATING CARLA OR ANYONE NOW?

1) *I was studying 2 Timothy 3 and God began to speak to my heart. Just before spring quarter finished, it came to my attention that there was some question in my example before younger Christians in this matter of dating. Then this came:*
   Verse 2 "For men shall be lovers of themselves..."
   Verse 4 "...lovers of pleasures more than lovers of God..."
2) *In question was my motive for dating. As I presently feel that God would have me finish college before I seek to get married and, also, that He would have me go into the service to specifically work with single men, my only real motive for dating right now is to participate in these relationships which I do enjoy and take real spiritual pleasure in. I feel no emotional guilt about dating, and I don't expressly feel as if my motive is entirely wrong, however, because I enjoy these relationships (in light of things which I know God wants me to do) am I going to let this desire of mine exceed my desire for God*

and His will? Or will I give God even my time in potential date life, to let God have the pre-eminence? Am I going to live entirely or only partially according to Matthew 6:33, "But seek ye first the kingdom of God and His righteousness, and all these things shall be added unto thee?"

3) *I have chosen to let God have control in these and all matters of this area and desire only to do His will and give Him the pre-eminence in all things (Colossians 1:18). I will give myself entirely to Him and be available to him until I finish school and my service.*

Larry had no idea how important this page of notes would be to his life and to others.

CHAPTER 7 - HARVESTING

The summer of 1963 was one of the few summers in which Larry basically stayed in Ames. Being there meant seeing Carla and with that came the old questions.

"God, is she the one for me?" Of one thing Larry was certain, if she were the right one, God would give her a heart for the things He had made dear to Larry. But then, he would reason, how can she know what's on my heart if I don't tell her? I'm really just concerned about her walk with Christ.

Many a sunny summer day or evening found Larry driving the old '48 Dodge out to the farm. Mom Switzer was always interested in Larry's feelings about things. He spent many a conversation with her about his concern for knowing and following God's will for his life. One afternoon he arrived later than he had expected. Carla had had to run an errand and was not there when he arrived. He and Mom Switzer had just had such a conversation while he waited for Carla's return. He knew God wanted him at ISU for this phase of his education. What he didn't know was for what God was preparing him after college.

Mom Switzer had naturally expected him to go into business with his dad. After all, he was such a good salesman. But Larry was pretty sure that was not the direction God was leading. Larry felt very strongly that he had to give himself to something really big. He just didn't know what that was yet.

Mrs. Switzer thought for a moment; her own daughters would be facing that same question before very long. What an important question for young people to ask! How important it was to find the right answer from God! She reassured Larry that she was confident God had a marvelous plan for his life and that he would find it when the time was right.

Larry responded with just as much faith, that he was certain God would let him know and that was what kept him going toward whatever that goal was. But he said he still had trouble being patient. That was when Carla entered the room. Larry stood to his feet and grinned. He apologized for being late, and called her Charley.

Carla looked around as if he were talking to someone else. Realizing she had no way of knowing that in his circle, everyone was Charley, he took time to explain and then asked her how she was. She responded by calling him Charley and saying that she was tired and hot.

There was a bit of tension in the air so Mom offered to go get them something cool to drink. Larry told Carla her Mom was really great. Carla agreed, but got back to the source of the problem between them by asking him what his excuse was for being late this time.

Larry told her he had stopped to see Jim Williams on his way over and he didn't get away as soon as he had expected. Larry again marveled at how Jim, who could only move his head and one hand, could rejoice in that fact! Larry would go to cheer Jim up and always be the one to come away blessed. He was just the person to talk to if he was ever feeling down.

The tension was gone. Carla also admired Jim and said she was sure the nurses must really appreciate such a positive patient. Carla decided it was time she, went to see Jim again. Larry agreed and said Jim would really like that.

Larry felt like the summer sped by. His life was now the farm, the nursing home, the furniture store and Campus Baptist Church. He was still busy, but it was a different pace and a different routine from the school term. It was definitely a welcome and much-needed break from a constant responsibility to so many people.

Although Larry was still not a student at heart, he was eager for ISU to begin in the fall, which it did with a bang!

In the fall of 1963, they again had a Navigator representative at ISU to help coordinate the ministry on campus, so with real enthusiasm and expectation the key guys from the year before met with their new representative, Darrell Thompson. The fall quarter began with a nucleus of ten men who were believing God for big things. Larry, Dick Ikenberry and Duane got together and prayed that they and the other seven guys would be fruitful. Within two weeks, each of them had led at least two other guys to Christ. Before he knew it, Larry was once again vitally involved in personal, individual time with guys sharing Christ and helping them grow in their new-found faith.

The basic approach that year was to be actively involved in personal evangelism in the dorms each week. Every Christian they met, they would try to get into the Word and get them out witnessing. Every non-Christian they met, they would seek to introduce to Jesus Christ.

Soon, Monday, Wednesday and Friday noontimes were spent in Duane's room praying. This really knit together the hearts of the young men. It became such a vital time that they soon outgrew the room. One of them suggested that they try to get the conference room near the cafeteria. They could meet from 12:00-12:30 and still have time to eat lunch. They chuckled at this comment. Food, after all, was the second most important thing in their lives. It sounded like a good plan, so they prayed about it and then sent a delegation to ask about it.

The secretary seemed understanding but said she was sorry to deny the request because they were not allowed to let religious groups use the facilities. They had already turned down two other groups that week with the same request.

The delegation said they understood, but would she please try one more time because they really felt God wanted them to be able to use that room. She looked surprised but impressed. She said that it wouldn't hurt to ask, but that they shouldn't count on it because it was a policy they just had to follow. She did promise to check again, and the men left knowing God would be the One to open or close that room. As they met together back in Duane's room that evening, they unanimously felt that as they gave this to God, He would change the policy. It was as good as done!

Larry still included Jim Williams in on any of the special prayer requests regarding the team. Jim enjoyed being a vital and necessary part of those out doing the leg work. Larry planned to stop by and have Jim pray about this one, but there was not a free moment until about midnight which was obviously too late. Larry decided the first chance he got the next morning he would share it with Jim. Then Larry drifted off to sleep.

The next morning Jim was still on Larry's mind as he came down to breakfast. Once downstairs, Mom asked Larry to come into the kitchen for a moment. One look at her told Larry something was wrong. She said she had just gotten a call from Jim's nursing home. Jim had contracted pneumonia and died during the night.

Larry just stood looking at her for a moment or two. No wonder Jim had been so much on his mind yesterday. Then Larry praised the Lord, because he knew Jim was now walking and running all over heaven.

It was only a couple of days later that word arrived that the conference room was theirs for Mondays, Wednesdays, and Fridays from 12:00-12:30. It was a wonderful confirmation from God that nothing was too hard for Him.

God blessed. Twenty-five men were soon gathered for the noon prayer meetings and about twenty of those would then go out to share Christ in the dorms. Every interested guy they met and talked with would then be met with individually by an older Christian who could help him do Bible study, memorize Scriptures, and encourage him in his Christian walk.

One of the men Larry spent time with was Bob VanZante. One day Bob told Larry about a time the February before, when Larry had invited him along with some of the Navigator men to go over to his home. Bob remembered that Larry and his dad had asked him that night if he was a Christian, and he had answered yes. Bob also remembered the empty, sick feeling in his heart. All those months since then, as he had observed the guys demonstrate the abundant and victorious Christian life, he decided he was missing something vital in his own life. That something was Someone—Jesus Christ. He then asked Christ to come into his life.

Right in the middle of the hall, Larry let out a yahoo and slapped Bob on the back. Larry was so pleased that he thanked and praised the Lord as they stood together in the dorm hall. Those words and their beaming faces were observed by several guys walking by, but Bob and Bleek were unaware of their reactions as they continued to Bob's room.

Bob asked Larry what he should do next. Larry explained that what he had done was just the beginning of a whole new life for him and that, like his physical birth, Bob needed to grow spiritually. That was just what Bob wanted. Discovering that they were both free for the rest of the afternoon, Larry took Bob over to the Thompson home, explaining to Bob that Darrell was the new Navigator representative. Larry needed to stop by and pick up more

Bible study blanks and materials so he could get Bob moving ahead. On the way over to Darrell's, Larry asked Bob lots of questions to see if he was reading the Word, what studies he'd been in, what his knowledge of the Scriptures was as far as the number of years he had attended church, and so on. Then he shared the exciting fact that, according to Song of Solomon 2:14, God, His Father, wanted to fellowship with him. God longed to see Bob's face and hear his voice. He told him that meant that when Bob had fellowship with God, he would be making God's day special just as God would be making Bob's day special.

Larry always liked to see a new Christian get established early on in his Quiet Time. Bob confessed that he had never been very good at or consistent at that. Larry shared his own battles in the early days of not wanting to study or have a consistent Quiet Time, but that God had since brought him to the place where he actually liked doing it and never wanted to miss it. Larry stated that he was confident that God could and would do the same for Bob.

Darrell wasn't home but his wife, Wendy, was. She was happy to supply Larry with more materials. Early the next morning, Bob found himself still only half awake sitting next to Larry out under a tree opening the Word together. Bleek told him that during his Quiet Time he enjoyed just reading through the Bible to find out all he could about God the Father, Son, and Holy Spirit. Larry introduced him to always reading his Bible with a pencil and a notebook handy. He said that when he asked God to speak to him God would, and Bob wouldn't want to forget a single word God said!

Bob took hold of these new principles quickly. God began to speak to him, and he began to respond with an obedient and willing heart. Bible studies and memorizing from one to three verses a week began to fill in those times that used to be filled with things not nearly so pleasant. Soon, Bob was a regular part of those who were sharing Christ with other guys in the dorms and on the campus.

Larry also felt a real responsibility to his own brothers, Ron and Tony. Whenever he could, he was thrilled to have a Quiet Time with them to see how God was working in their lives. It was during those times that God put Ron's and Tony's friends on Larry's heart as well, even though they were from four to eight years younger than Larry.

Campus Baptist was another area on Larry's heart. Chuck Swanson had been elected the new president for the college age, and Larry gave him his full and complete support. Larry also spent personal time with Chuck and with Ray Vogel, who got involved in campus evangelism and follow-up. Reverend Dowden was thrilled on Sunday mornings as a number of pews were filled with college men with vibrant testimonies of what God was doing in their lives and on the campus of ISU.

Just before the students broke for Christmas vacation, Darrell invited Russ Johnston, the Navigator representative in Lincoln, to bring his gang to join them in campus evangelism. A rally was held on Saturday evening. Russ was a stocky, fun-loving guy with a warm smile and a delightful way of saying things. He made taking notes fun.

On rally night, Larry led the singing and, in addition to Russ speaking, Larry was responsible for a short message on which he had spent some exciting hours of preparation. Larry had been seeking God's will on whether he should consider joining the Navigator staff when he got out of college. The topic for the evening was "God's Need" and Larry felt that, at least for then, God had other work for him to do. Larry used Ezekiel 22:30 and this is how God spoke to and through Larry that night.

GOD'S NEED-Ezekiel 22:30

I would like to pose to you a question. What is God's greatest need today? May I, along with this question, also suggest an answer? I believe the need that God has today is for disciples, that is men. *Ezekiel 22:30 very adequately portrays this situation where it says, "...I sought for a man among them...but found none." God wanted men then; He needs men today.*

We don't fully realize the meaning and significance of the word "men." One might well define "man" as those individuals which are of the highest type of animal, differing from other animals by their extraordinary mental development. Okay, but God's man has an evident sort of manliness.

God's man is an ardent carrier of God's concern, which is that "...all men be saved and come unto the knowledge of the truth" (I Timothy 2:4). If people are going to hear what Jesus Christ can mean in their lives personally, someone is going to have to tell them.

God's man is wholehearted in the things that he does. Colossians 3:23 says, "And whatsoever ye do, do it heartily..." A football player doesn't play half-heartedly and neither does God's man.

A real man of God is faithful in his service. Luke 16:10 talks about "being faithful in things both small and great." Faithfulness is of qualitative importance, not quantitative.

The man God needs today must be a laborer, that is, willing to roll up his sleeves and sweat—to be a real workman. Notice that Christ says to his men (disciples), "the harvest truly is plenteous but the laborers are few; pray ye therefore the Lord of the harvest, that He will send forth laborers into His harvest." *Christ didn't say, pray for church buildings; He wanted men. Rockefeller once said, "You can take away all my businesses; you can take away all my banks; you can take away all my possessions; but leave me my* <u>*men*</u> *and I'll build it all over again."*

Paul tells us, as Christians, that we ought to "Watch...stand...be like men...be strong" (I Corinthians 16:13). Paul saw a need for men. A noted person of our day once said, "There are only two types of people today that are actually accomplishing anything. This is the committed Communist and the committed Christian." With our population pushing well over 2.8 billion, there is a mighty need for men, God's men, today.

I found the true and personal reality of Jesus Christ as a senior in high school. A friend of mine shared with me how I might be sure of eternal life and know that I had a personal Savior. I needed Jesus Christ, so I just asked Him to be my Savior and give me the assurance of eternal life. Now that I know I am in God's family, my desire is that I might grow to be usable as God's man. But you see, God needs <u>*men*</u>*. That's plural. What about you? Are you a man—God's man?*

E.M. Bounds said this, "Men are God's method. The church is looking for better methods; God is looking for better men...What the church needs today is not more machinery or better, not new organizations or more and better methods, but men whom the Holy Ghost can us—men of prayer, men mighty in prayer. The Holy Ghost does not come on

> *machinery, but on men. He does not anoint plans, but men—men of prayer."*

Although Larry directed his talk to the men, it was evident that it applied to the ladies as well.

Winter quarter was cold, as it always was in Iowa. The next rally they had with an out-of-town gang was concluded with such a severe snowstorm that no one was able to leave the city. The phones began to ring. "Do you have room for one or two young people in your home, until the roads are passable?" Several were taken in, but it was getting late and Larry suggested all those without a place to stay come to his home. They piled into a few cars and the "dead rabbit," as Larry's old '48 Dodge was now fondly called. With added weight in the cars, they all got safely home to Furman Drive. The family was already in bed, so Larry helped the girls find room in the living room to sleep and the guys, including Larry, took to the basement after raiding the refrigerator at Larry's invitation.

On Sunday morning, Mom came down to fix breakfast and was greeted by one of the three girls sacked out on the living room carpet. The girl explained that they were from out of town, but the highway patrol had said no one could leave the city because of the road conditions, so Larry had graciously offered his home. They hoped it would be all right.

Mom, every bit as generous as Larry, assured them that they were very welcome and only wished she had been up to help them get more comfortable.

Another girl spoke up and said they had slept real well, and she would be happy to help with breakfast since the three of them weren't the only ones who had spent the night. When Lillian discovered there were guys in the basement as well, she called down to Larry to see for how many she should prepare breakfast. When the tally was taken, Mom more than rose to the occasion and set a lovely breakfast before her family and the 11 guests for the morning. Then they all piled into their cars and got to Sunday school only a few minutes late. Once inside, Mr. Boyland in the college class and Reverend Dowden in the sanctuary continued to feed them all morning from the Word of God.

Larry was really proud of his family, for not only their ability but their desire to be available whenever needed. Grandma often thought her daughter should have advance notice, because Larry was always waiting until the night of to mention everyone was coming. He was careful only to do this when he was sure his family had no plans of their own.

Larry explained to his grandmother that if he told his mom ahead of time, she would just go to a lot of fuss and bother getting ready and there was no need to do that. He knew she was great at coming up with just what he needed when he needed it. Besides, Larry was convinced that she liked it best that way. Mom and Gram weren't as sure about that as Larry, but the fact was that it always did work out well.

Another habit of Larry's was never to tell his family when he had done something really well. He felt that would be boasting, and he was trying hard not to call attention to himself. Consequently, unless someone else said something or they read it in the paper, Mom and Dad were usually the last to know.

One afternoon, therefore, Lillian was amazed when Larry came home from the University and commented that he wanted her to know that his name would probably be in the newspaper that evening. Mom was surprised but said nothing more than "Oh?" Larry continued to explain that he was flying low that morning as he went to the college, or at least a policeman saw it that way. He had been given a ticket. The speed limit on 13th Street had been lowered and he hadn't noticed. He warned the rest of the family to be careful.

During the middle of winter quarter, Darrell got some of the key guys in the dorm together with the team to listen to Bob Boardman, home on furlough from Japan. Larry had never heard "Bordy," just heard about him and knew they were in for a special treat.

Bob Boardman had been a Marine in Okinawa, and when the Japanese hit and destroyed the tank he had been driving, Bob and the others tried to escape back to their lines. In that process, a Japanese sniper's bullet penetrated Bob's voice box. As a result, he could only speak with a whisper. Then, to the amazement of many, God called Bob to go back to Japan with the message of hope, peace, and forgiveness found in Jesus Christ. God was using his whisper to win Japanese people to the Lord!

They had a good turnout that evening. Everyone who had been invited came and Darrell, with his strong deep voice, enthusiastically introduced their speaker. Bob responded with a raspy, "Thank you, Darrell."

Those in the back strained to hear him. Bob went on to explain that he had what was called "Japanese laryngitis." As Bob continued to speak, he captured their rapt attention, as well as their hearts. Before many more words his voice seemed as big as he was; that was 6'2" and a firm 210 pounds.

Bob sensed their hearts were especially open that night. At the close of his talk, God led him to give an invitation for those there, to consider going themselves into all the world with the Gospel. Larry had seriously considered this possibility for his own life before this night, and now, as he listened to Bob's presentation, he was one of those who responded with, "God, I'm yours to send anywhere, to do anything, as long as it's for You."

A couple of nights later, Bleek was even more thankful that God had brought him to that commitment, because he found himself in a situation he was sure God had put him in, but one for which he would not have asked.

Friley-Hughes Hall at I.S.U. One of the world's largest dorms, housing 1400 men

The men had met for prayer and then gone out to share the Gospel in "The Towers," a new men's dorm. As they stepped on the floor to which God had led them, they were met by a reception committee, self-appointed to throw the Navigators out if they came up there. A crowd had formed to watch the expected route of the Navigators. The air was filled with electricity. Then, to the surprise of all, Bleek's gang viewed them as men who were there to hear the Gospel; they proceeded to share their testimonies and the crowd listened. They listened so well, in fact, that one young man invited Christ to come into his heart, and all the rest quietly and thoughtfully returned to their rooms. The team learned once again that it really paid to be committed to Christ, Who could do all things well.

On May Day, 1964, the ISU gang took off for Tarkio, Missouri, for the Navigator spring conference. It was there that Larry gave a workshop on prayer, which followed a message that Darrell had given to everyone.

Duane greeted those in the workshop and then introduced Larry, who would be sharing some of the practical aspects of prayer with them.

Larry began by appealing to those who maybe weren't well-organized in their prayer life but wanted to be. He had them review Darrell's message on "Conditions for Answered Prayer." They recalled things like being in God's will, obeying God's will, praying in faith, having a pure heart, praying specifically, praying in Jesus' name, persevering in prayer, and remembering that prayer was a two-way communication so that they must take time to listen and not do all the talking. Larry was pleased with the list and added just one more item to it, praying in sincerity with all their hearts.

He shared that to pray well, they would need to have a plan. Larry realized that some of what he would be saying was going to be repetitious, but he figured if they could listen to commercials over and over about things like Cheerios and Spearmint gum, they could stand to hear practical truths about prayer over and over as well. He knew his product was of much more value.

Larry began with some of the things Don McDonald had shared with him that had helped him have meaningful Quiet Times over the past few years. They were things like having a "time" to pray. That was one of the basics. The way the world competed for their attention, they would have to work to set aside time to talk to the Lord. He knew they could find time in their busy schedules to do a lot of things that they felt were important, but they probably had found it very difficult to set aside a time to pray. Then he challenged them to look at the lives of people who were dynamic and effective for God, and they would find that those people took time to pray. Some of them got up in the wee hours of the morning, at 2:00, 3:00 or 4:00, to pray. We know Jesus got up a great while before day to talk to His Father (Mark 1:35). Jesus was, in fact, man. He was hungry at times. He got tired. He was confronted with the same things as they were, yet Jesus found it important to get up a great while before day to spend time with God. In Psalm 5:3 it says: *"My voice shalt thou hear in the morning, O Lord; In the morning will I direct my prayer unto Thee, and will look up."*

Larry shared an illustration that had impressed him about a pastor. Early in the morning the pastor's wife had awakened to find her husband out of bed and on his knees. When she asked what he was doing, he replied, "How can I sleep when I have the souls of three hundred of my congregation on my heart?" He had to pray for them when he had the chance, in the wee hours of the morning.

He also shared about a man from England, who really believed in prayer. One day this man asked his servant to please call him after 30 minutes, because he was going to spend some time in prayer. A half hour later, the servant came but found his master in such a spirit of communion that he thought it would be a shame to disturb him. He let him go another half hour, and another half hour, and another. After two-and-a-half hours, the servant thought maybe he'd better call him or the man would have his whole day's schedule fouled up. His master's comment when he finally interrupted him was that "a half hour sure goes fast when we've spent it with the Lord!" That man really enjoyed his "time" in prayer.

Secondly, Larry shared that they needed to have a "place" to pray. He told them that sometimes he liked to pick a place on the spur of the moment. Walking across campus sometimes he would go over to a nearby tree and plunk down to pray, only to be interrupted by a lawn mower. His suggestion was to choose a place where they could meet with God on a regular basis and not be interrupted by the world. He suggested a closet or attic where they could make it their chapel and spend time communing with God.

Then Larry stressed the importance of making their place free from distractions. Things as simple as a picture, or a bright book, or a radio that could be heard, were all things that could often turn their minds to other things. Since prayer was so important, he warned them that once they had found a time and a place, Satan would try his best to keep them from accomplishing anything. He would be right there to give them the hardest time he could. Just knowing who the enemy was, he reminded them, could help them be *"more than conquerors"* (Romans 8:37) of the moment.

Larry quoted George Muller as saying, "The thing that brings me the greatest joy in my life, I find, is the hardest to do." If Satan can't get us by fouling up our time or fouling up our place, then he'll foul up our "desire." This, he said, was the third area of importance to prayer. They needed to get their hearts set on Christ. They needed to be convinced that God wanted them to pray. They needed to remember they were meeting with God Himself, and when it seemed hardest to pray was the time when they needed to pray the hardest!

Next, Larry went into some of the practical questions of, "How do we pray?" He called their attention to the words of Psalm 66:18: *"If I regard iniquity in my heart, the Lord will not hear me."* He explained that this meant that if they were going to pray, they needed to have the attitude of prayer. They needed to get their hearts prepared. They must get sin out of the camp, out of their lives. Then he shared Psalm 139:23-24: *"Search me, O God, and know my heart: try me, and know my thoughts: and see if there be any wicked way in me, and lead me in the way everlasting."* They all needed to come to God with a clean heart.

Next, Larry challenged them to be specific and definite in their prayers. He asked them to turn to Ephesians 3:14-21. From those verses, he showed them that Paul prayed specifically for this and this and this. Here, he said, was where prayer lists came into the picture. This was one thing that God had really laid on Larry's heart that year. He told about a time during winter quarter when he and a friend of his had spent some time on Sunday mornings praying, and they had decided that they would specifically write down the things that they felt God would want to have happen. Then they waited in expectation. Larry said they found that they could hardly keep up with the answers that came. Having a written record of what they had prayed and how God had answered was a terrific way to encourage them to bring everything to their heavenly Father.

Larry showed them two prayer pages published by the Navigators. One was a yellow page on which they could write their specific requests on one side and record the answers on the other side. The second page was blue and to be used as a permanent list of prayer concerns.

Another important factor was "to wait in expectation." They needed to believe that God would answer their requests. They should write down their requests believing that God would answer in the best possible way. They were not to write just to be writing. Larry shared how amazed he had been at how faithful God always was in answering. He had prayed for a person's heart concerning Bible study. He asked that God would give him an interest so that he would ask about a Bible study. Only a few days later, that young man had come up to Larry and said that he thought it would be good if he could get a Bible study group going. As Larry had encouraged him to do that, his heart rejoiced at God's faithfulness and the answered prayer.

Another suggestion Larry made was that they look into "prayer guides." He explained that these were another Navigator tool. They were set up by the month, and Larry found them helpful to expand his understanding of what was going on in other areas of the world. This gave him other things about which to pray. Another advantage was that it reminded him daily of the need for prayer. People everywhere were depending on the prayers of others to enable them to serve God more successfully.

The last suggestion Larry left with them was to get a prayer map. He told them how he used the world map and began praying for people he knew in foreign lands, or even just in another city or state. If they didn't know anyone in a certain place they could pray anyway, that the good news of Jesus Christ would reach their hearts and that laborers would come to share the Gospel and show them how to grow. They might even pray for those in leadership in the country and for God's will to be done through those leaders. They could spend a week or two on each area and watch the newspapers, etc. for clues about what to pray. By doing this, they could pray around the world.

Larry shared an incident from his own life. When he came to Egypt on his map, he hadn't known what to pray. The very next day, God put an article in front of him from a World Missions magazine concerning what was going on in Egypt. He knew that if they were willing to pray, God would tell them what to pray.

Going back to his question of "How to Pray," he likened it to learning to play football. They could enroll in a class; they could go see the coach; or they could get by somebody that knew how to play football and play football with them. They would learn to play football as they faithfully practiced daily. The same was true of prayer.

Larry suggested that they pray out loud, another reason for going to a solitary place. He explained that this would help them concentrate on what they were praying. It would make them think and speak and hear. That would involve three of their senses. They also should pray with thanksgiving. He asked them to look up Philippians 4:6 which says: *"Be careful for* (be anxious about) *nothing, but in everything by prayer and supplication with thanksgiving, let your requests be made known unto God..."* He challenged them to remember to thank God for the answers He brought. They could use the answer side of their prayer list to fuel their thanksgiving to God in prayer.

Then Larry shared a point that he found difficult to maintain in his own life. It was to be consistent in prayer, to persevere. He told them of a man who prayed so much that his knees were leathery from praying. When someone looked in his room they found grooves worn in the hardwood floors by his bed where he had consistently prayed. That man had spent hours and hours in prayer. If they were to pray, they should pray and continue to pray. I Thessalonians 5:17 says: *"Pray without ceasing."* That meant that when they prayed, they should continue to talk to the Lord about the things on their hearts all through the day, wherever they were, just as they continued to breathe all through the day and not just for five minutes in the morning.

Larry had still one more thing to share about prayer, and that was the help they could derive from reading about prayer and about people who prayed. He suggested the following books:

Hudson Taylor's Spiritual Secret. It was a biography and told about how he believed God in prayer. It was a good book to challenge any person to pray, to step out in faith, to trust God in different areas of their lives.

Master Secrets to Prayer. He showed them Duane's dog-eared copy. He said it was loaded with information on prayer and that they wouldn't be able to read it and not find helpful suggestions and examples for their prayer lives. It talked about the school of prayer, the approach of prayer, how to intercede, hindrances to prayer, and practical hints on how to pray.

E.M. Bounds, Power Through Prayer. This was another little book packed with helpful information and filled with challenges for a healthy prayer life.

Next, Larry reiterated what Darrell had shared earlier in the morning. They should remember that "they might understand all the mysteries concerning prayer; they might know of all the things that are written about prayer; and they might have the whole scoop on prayer; BUT, unless they prayed, they'd never learn to pray." Larry left them with the challenge to pray and to trust God.

Meanwhile, back in Ames, the Thompsons were preparing to go to the mission field. Chuck Hunt would replace them in the fall. God had richly blessed Darrell's time there, and the rest of that spring quarter was no exception. Almost before Larry knew it, summer had arrived and his summer plans to spend the next three months at Glen Eyrie for training had materialized. Only one thing dampened his excitement just a bit. He was not looking forward to saying goodbye to Carla for an entire summer!

CHAPTER 8 - GLEN EYRIE

Glen Eyrie-castle and grounds

As a group from the Ames area left for Glen Eyrie, there was laughing, singing, and talking about the Lord and their expectations for the summer. When they pulled up to the gate that evening, a surge of excitement rushed through their veins. Indeed, God had called them to this place for a purpose.

On each of Larry's previous visits to the Glen, he had wanted to stay longer than the week's conference. Here was his chance. Three months on an 1100-acre estate of rugged mountain beauty! As Larry moved through that summer, he could see God's hand still mightily at work in this quiet Valley of the Eagles.

The Glen Eyrie story began back in 1867. William Jackson Palmer, born in Delaware and raised in Pennsylvania in a Quaker home, had always loved railroads.

At age 17, he went to work for the Hempfield Railroad and, at 19, he began to study railroading and coal mining in England. In 1856, he returned to the states to become the private secretary to J. Edgar Thomson, president of the Pennsylvania Railroad. In 1861, he formed the Anderson Troop and joined the Union forces in the Civil War. At age 29, he became the second youngest brigadier general commissioned in the Civil War. Throughout the rest of his life, he was known as General Palmer.

In 1867, he came West in a survey party with the Union Pacific Railway Eastern Division. They were investigating the best route to California from Kansas City. During the days that followed, trying to get the railroad located, Palmer came across a beautiful valley approximately four miles north of Colorado City and just north of the Garden of the Gods. He had decided then and there that this was the place he wanted to one day build his estate.

One of Palmer's business associates had a beautiful daughter named Mary Lincoln Mellen. Mary's grandmother gave her the nickname of "Queen." General Palmer married Queen in 1870. He promised to build his Queen the grandest of homes. Palmer purchased 10,000 acres for $1.25 per acre and established what became Colorado Springs. He also purchased 2,225 acres in the valley he had been drawn to for his estate and built a 22-room frame house. They originally planned to call it "Bijou," but it was also referred to as "Little Garden of the Gods" since it was a continuation of the Garden and had its own magnificent rock formations. However, when a landscape architect, John Blair, came from Scotland to help General Palmer plan his bigger venture on the property, he looked up and saw an eagle's nest high up in the rocks. In his Scottish brogue he exclaimed, "Ah, Glen Eyrie, valley of the eagle's nest." The General and Queen immediately decided that was what they would call their estate.

General Palmer and Queen had three daughters, but Mrs. Palmer had a heart attack in 1880 and had to move with her daughters to a lower altitude. They went first to the East coast and then to England where she died in 1894. She was only 44 years old. General Palmer brought his daughters back to Colorado Springs, along with his wife's remains.

General Palmer, remembering his promise to his wife, began remodeling their home in Glen Eyrie into an English Tudor castle for his Queen. Construction began in 1904 and was completed in 1906. He had the outside made from stones brought in from the Bear Creek area that had the appearance of being very old, just as he requested. During the construction, he and his daughters took trips to Europe seeking fireplaces, artifacts, and heirlooms to fill the completed castle.

Engraved on the entrance door was General Palmer's creed, "We should a guest love while he loves to stay, and when he likes not, give him loving way." Guests were always welcome at the estate, and General Palmer enjoyed showing them around the grounds and the Garden of the Gods. One day in 1906, mounted on a horse he seldom rode, General Palmer took some guests to the Garden of the Gods. His horse suddenly stumbled, throwing him to the ground and breaking General Palmer's neck. He remained paralyzed from the neck down until his death on March 13, 1909, at the age of 72. At the time of his death, the estate was valued at $3,000,000.

The estate was sold in 1916 to a group of Oklahoma businessmen who paid $150,000 to turn it into a private resort and country club boasting an 18-hole golf course. The castle would be used as a clubhouse and the Glen divided into 150 home sites. That dream never came to pass however, because of World War One. Finally, in 1922, the Hillbright Corporation bought the estate for $450,000 along with five ranches to the north. In 1925, the Pink House was built and the castle was closed.

Several attempts to sell occurred during the next ten years. In 1938, it was finally purchased by George W. Strake, an independent oil producer from Houston, Texas. He used the property for a summer home and cattle ranch until 1950 when it was again placed on the market for $500,000.

In 1953, a Colorado Springs real estate broker contacted the Reverend Billy Graham, who was considering a headquarters for his ministry. When the owner, Mr. Strake, heard it was Billy Graham considering the purchase, he lowered the price to $300,000 plus $40,000 for furnishings. Mr. Graham contacted Dawson Trotman, who was then responsible for counselor training and follow-up of the Billy Graham Crusades. He asked Daws to take a look and see what he thought of the place for a Billy Graham Academy and Retreat Center.

In the early 50's, Dawson Trotman and the Navigators were enjoying phenomenal growth. Daws' headquarters in California was having trouble keeping up with the growth as military men now entered colleges and universities all over the States. Daws began searching for headquarters for the Navigators that would be more centrally located and he envisioned a dude ranch, maybe in Colorado. Daws was considering a ranch called Pine Valley when Billy's request came to take a look at the Glen. For Daws, it was love at first sight. He was eager to call Billy and tell him about the 700-acre valley of spectacular beauty with 21 buildings, the largest being a massive 67-room castle.

Billy liked it and signed a purchase option readily underwritten by 30 businessmen. Mr. Graham and Daws talked together of Billy using the grounds for prayer and Bible study retreats for international students, sports personalities and government leaders. Billy also thought the Glen would be ideal as an international home and year-round training facility for the Navigators. Together, the Graham Association and the Navigators could share the facilities. They excitedly met to work out the details.

It was a great disappointment to both men when it was decided that the Graham Association felt it was too far-a-field from evangelism, and Billy had to abandon his dream. At first, Daws felt his dreams had also been shattered. There was no way the Navigators could afford such a place. Or was there? Didn't God lay this place on his heart for a reason? In a couple of hours, Daws had his answer from God, and he called Billy to say he felt, most definitely, that the Navigators must attempt purchase of Glen Eyrie. Billy agreed and turned over the option solely to them.

With that decision, Daws was then looking at six weeks in which to raise $100,000! From the ridge high above the grounds of Glen Eyrie, Daws talked to God and said, "Lord, if You entrust this all to us, I want to dedicate it now to You as David did, to be used for Your glory, to make known Your holy Name in all the world." Phenomenal things happened during those next six weeks. People sold their cars and mortgaged their homes; two small boys gave a jar of 902 pennies; and servicemen in Japan rallied together to give more than $10,000. The newspapers, Western Union, the Post Office, everyone got involved in the countdown which went right down to the wire. In the end, they received more than they thought they would need, but with fire insurance and closing costs they had needed $108,000, and that is what they had! A week or so before the deadline, Daws had written, *"On the lips of thousands will be praise to the God Who has shown He can do the impossible. The world will see what can be done by a band of Christians whose hearts are united, who know how to trust their God and how to roll up their sleeves and work. Many will get their first glimpse of this kind of faith in action."* Larry knew that was exactly what had happened back in 1953, and it was still happening as he stood there surveying the grounds in 1964.

Larry and the others were soon settled in and then Warren Meyers, in charge of the summer training, oriented them to the summer schedule, goals and objectives, and made their specific work assignments. Larry's lot fell for the kitchen crew, as it did for about 16 others. This was perhaps one of the hardest jobs at the Glen, because of the busy summer schedule of conferees besides trainees. There were three deadlines to meet every day. You couldn't serve a meal tomorrow.

Jim Wilson was in charge of the kitchen gang. One of the Navigator principles was to do anything you did the very best way possible. Jim felt the meals in the castle had to be next to perfect, and they were.

At the outset of the summer, they had a formal banquet for the staff in the Great Hall. A couple of the guys dressed in suits of armor, and the girls who served wore long dresses and pointed hats with ribbon streamers down the back. The guys who served were dressed for the occasion, too. Flaming torches lit the room, and the food was absolutely superb.

Each of the summer conferences started on Saturdays, so Saturday evenings were buffet suppers. The tables donned their white linen clothes. The plates were piled high with huge slices of succulent roast beef, baked potatoes with sour cream and garnishes, fruit salads that could have been the main course, and vegetables with special things added to make them not only delicious but beautiful. Literally hours went into the preparations, but it really did welcome the conferees in fine style.

Larry and a German fellow named Eb Roell were the breakfast cooks, which meant rising a great while before the rest of the camp. This had its advantages, though, as the air stayed somewhat cool in the kitchen until time to eat breakfast.

The pressure of deadlines coupled with heat and long hours, ten to twelve a day, was a real test of Christian attitudes and cheerfulness, and they each found it hard.

One morning after an especially difficult time in the kitchen, Larry climbed Razorback Ridge, where the air was cool and clean, and his mind could get a new perspective. He found a spot in what Moses might have called "a cleft in a rock." The 1100 acres of spreading green lawns and towering evergreens laced with pink ribbon roads lay below him. Buildings were nestled here and there beside tall, pink, rock formations like those in the Garden of the Gods just over the ridge.

Then an eagle soaring into the heavens called Larry's attention upward. It seemed suspended above him, resting on the One Who had so marvelously created him. Larry thought of the verse in Isaiah 40:31 that says: *"But they that wait upon the Lord shall renew their strength; they shall mount up with wings as eagles; they shall run and not be weary; and they shall walk, and not faint."* Out loud, Larry prayed, *"Father God, thank You for this object lesson. Teach me to look to You and wait on You, that I would not live under the circumstances, but mount up with wings as eagles."*

Those few moments on the mountain were God's way of preparing Larry's heart, because that morning their assignment was to spend some time thinking through the things they wanted God to accomplish in their lives that summer while they were there. Some of those desires God had given him in the cleft of the rock. This was what Larry wrote down for that assignment:

Things I want God to Do this summer, and How

I. A. To give me a love for Jesus Christ superseding any other love and to make me to long and hunger for time alone with Him.

B. I plan to make a schedule of my time and spend one hour per day alone with the Lord.

II. A. That God would take the Word through my time in Bible study and prepare my heart to be receptive and to know the Spirit's teaching, eliminating my own wisdom and knowing that the Spirit is showing me new truths.

B. I am going to develop a reading program to stimulate an acquaintance with the Word and ask God specifically to teach me as I study.

III. A. I want to know how to meditate on the Word, to take a passage and ponder it and think through it with God Himself.

B. I am going to check with some of the personnel here at the Glen and get some ideas as to how to meditate. Then I want to enact some type of system of meditating and recording new thoughts.

IV. A. I want God to give me a willingness to die completely to myself in every area and to give me a hatred for lust and sin.

B. I am going to use mediation and just surrender to remove self and substitute the Word for lust and evil thoughts.

V. A. I desire that God would give me specific direction through counsel, the Word, and prayer, as to His will concerning my military service and how I should enter, as enlisted or as an officer.

B. I am going to talk with Jim Downing and other servicemen to find the overall picture and then to spend some time with God deciding what His will is.

VI. A. I want God to reveal His will and direction concerning the insurance business—whether to proceed, retreat, or wait.

B. I am going to take the information that I have and consider the potential pluses and minuses of this position, as to the profession and timing. I am going to spend at least one day really praying about this alone with God.

One by one, God worked away at those six points during the rest of the days Larry spent at the Glen that summer.

In their Navigator Basics class, Warren Myers had them spend an hour in prayer with God alone and then comment on their time spent. After that one hour, Larry came to these conclusions.

An Hour In Prayer Alone With God

To begin with, I was somewhat scrambled in my thoughts as to how I was going to spend this hour. I

> *finally began to pray and soon I was deep in intercession and petition.*
>
> *One thing that I became aware of is that I was thinking about my comfort, and this was sprinkling itself into my mind frequently. I prayed on my knees for awhile and also in a sitting position.*
>
> *I didn't have a prayer list with me, it being some time since I made one. I began to pray for others. As I was praying, God seemed to bring these others to mind that I should remember to Him. Then after I closed praying for others, God brought to mind several more that I should remember to pray for.*
>
> *I found that, unaccustomed as I am to just sitting and being quiet, it was hard to keep my mind free while waiting before God. My mind would plan, dream or wander vaguely. Another thing that I was conscious of was the time. In deciding to spend one hour in prayer, I found myself checking the time as if this was a rigid appropriation of time.*
>
> *In all, I think that I was poorly equipped in familiarity of extended time spent alone with God. There have been times in my life when hours would go by and I was entirely unaware of the time. I think that I have ceased to learn what is meant by "pour out your heart before Him" (Psalm 62:8). This comes with the intimacy of knowing God and, boy, this intimacy is something that I really don't know.*

God, therefore, had more work to do with Larry that summer. Besides Larry's spot on the mountain, the Lord showed Larry a closet in the depths of the castle where he could shut the door and be alone with his Maker. According to the time Larry spent in these places, so went his days.

But, there still was a problem with "give me a love for Jesus Christ superseding any other love." Carla had left for Winona Lake, Indiana, a few days before Larry left for Colorado. He had picked some roses from home, packed them in plastic bags with water, sealed them up tight, packed them in a box and sent them to her. He hadn't really expected to hear from her before he left, but now, several weeks had gone by and even his letters had been unanswered. During this time of anxiety and soul searching, Larry found a man he could talk to who was not only understanding, but helpful and encouraging. Larry could pour his heart out to him.

To make matters harder for Larry, there was a trainee who went through the meal lines who had Carla's brown eyes, Carla's brown hair, Carla's fair complexion, and even Carla's dimples. Larry couldn't look at her anymore. He knew she couldn't help it, but he really had a battle. He asked the Lord to give him a willingness to die completely to himself in every area and to give him a hatred for lust and sin, but he really hadn't found victory in his desire for Carla.

Larry's friend could remember similar problems in his younger days, so he encouraged Larry from the Word, to substitute Christ and the Scriptures, if he could not literally flee. This did help him to see the need to discipline his mind, but he was surprised at the amount of time he spent thinking about Carla compared to the time he spent thinking about God. He knew he had not yet come to the place where his love for Jesus Christ superseded any other love, and this broke his heart.

God used the Navigator Basic's class also for the area of getting into God's Word. The Navigators had what they called the "Word Hand." This was an illustration that vividly showed how a person could take the Word into his or her life. The illustration used a drawing of an open hand with the fingers spread apart. They represented five ways in which they could get the Word into their lives. Beginning with the little finger, those five ways were: hearing, reading, studying, memorizing, and meditating.

Warren Meyers explained that an illustration was meant to increase and broaden their vision. The eye gate, as well as the ear gate, are "windows" to the soul. Ezra 7:10 says: *"For Ezra had prepared his heart to seek the Law of the Lord, and to do it, and to teach in Israel statutes and judgments."* Warren explained that the Word Hand illustration would help them better understand how they could go about seeking the Law of the Lord and searching the Scriptures.

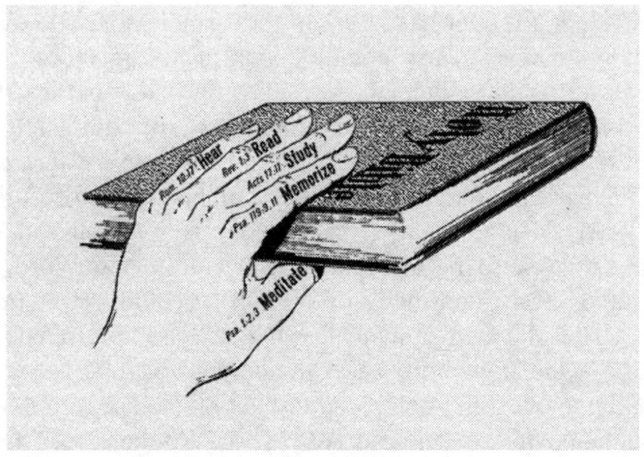

First of all, he explained that through the preached Word, they could HEAR it. Romans 10:17 says: "*So then faith cometh by hearing and hearing by the Word of God.*" HEARING was represented by the little finger of the hand. There were few people in the world who had not at least heard the Word preached. And by HEARING, they could get some grasp of the Word. Then Warren took hold of his Bible with his little finger and the palm of his hand. It was very easy to pull the Word out of that grasp. He said that only about five percent of what was HEARD would be retained.

Next, he explained that, through the printed page, they could READ the Word. Revelation 1:3 says: *"Blessed is he that READETH, and they that hear the words of this prophecy, and keep those things which are written therein: for the time is at hand."* Warren went on to explain that many people HEAR the Word, but fewer READ it for themselves. By READING, they could increase their grasp of the Word.

Then Warren used his last two fingers to grasp his Bible, but again, it was not held securely. Only 15 percent of what they READ would be retained.

The middle finger represented STUDY, and he stated that even fewer people STUDY the Bible. But II Timothy 2:15 says: *"Study to show thyself approved unto God, a workman that needeth not to be ashamed, rightly dividing the Word of truth."*

Warren showed them that through question-and-answer Bible studies, they could actually STUDY the Word, *"comparing Scripture with Scripture."* This would enable them to have a greater grasp of God's Word, and they could retain about 35 percent of what they STUDIED.

The index finger represented MEMORIZATION. Through MEMORIZATION, they were able to "write God's Word upon the table of their hearts." Deuteronomy 11:18 says: *"Therefore shall ye lay up these My words in your heart and in your soul, and bind them for a sign upon your hand, that they may be as frontlets between your eyes."*

MEMORIZATION was not easy, and still fewer people would do it, but how much better a grasp of the Word it would give them. It could result in 100 percent retention of God's Word.

Warren reiterated what he had said. They could seek the law of the Lord by HEARING it, READING it, STUDYING it, and MEMORIZING it. But, he called attention to the fact that a hand without a thumb was really not very effective. He shared from Judges, chapter one, that in the Old Testament, in order to yield their enemies ineffective for battle, they cut off their thumbs and big toes. It would then be impossible for them to hold a weapon against their enemy. And so, the thumb on the Word Hand was to be MEDITATION. Joshua 1:8 says: *"This book of the law shall not depart out of thy mouth; but thou shalt meditate therein day and night, that thou mayest observe to do according to all that is written therein: for then thou shalt make thy way prosperous, and then thou shalt have good success."*

In this busy, fast-moving age, this was one of the most difficult things to do—to take time for MEDITATION, to be still and know that He is God. God had wonderfully created the thumb to work with any other finger, and it was only through meditation that they could grasp that which they had heard, read, studied and memorized. With all five fingers on God's Word, no one could take it from them, and only then would they be in the position to *"do and teach it."*

Warren asked them to consider all five points and determine which was their weakest finger. That, he said, is where to start. Later, as Larry went before God, he came to these conclusions:

> *In the hand illustration, with fingers denoting hearing, reading, studying, memorizing, and meditation on the Word of God, I find the study finger to be my weakest.*

> *This finger is easy to neglect and hard to readily strengthen without some real workouts. New methods, ideas, or systems may be employed and accepted, but the vital factor in this is to be found in the sweat of time in study. This is extremely hard for me. I think my only solution is to ask God to change my attitude and heart for study and to set aside a specific time each day for some study, whether extensive or not.*
>
> *Also, I have decided to begin a reading program to create a greater interest and familiarity in the Word. Reading four chapters per day, I can finish the New Testament by the end of the summer.*

In regard to the area of meditation, Larry sought answers as to "How to do it" from the Glen personnel. They had several suggestions, all of which he began to incorporate at one time or another during that summer and on into the coming years. One suggestion was that he do a verse analysis on a part of his reading and then share that verse with someone that day. A verse analysis consisted of: 1) Look at the verses before his verse; 2) look at the verses following his verse, so that he could better understand the context of his verse; 3) paraphrase the verse itself, putting it in his own words; 4) record any other verses that would come to mind that spoke of the same things; and, finally, 5) write down any questions that came to mind in the study or that he could foresee might come to someone else's mind in such a study, and to seek to find the answers.

Another idea was to find a verse that especially stood out to him and then read and re-read it, emphasizing a different word each time.

Another approach was to think about Jesus Christ as he read and look for what it said about Him, what others said about Him, and what He said about Himself. He was to record his findings.

Larry was filled with wise counsel and many ideas and good intentions but, as the summer went on, it seemed that, unlike Maranatha, protracted time in prayer and Bible study and meditation were just impossible. His work detail, plus classes and his natural interest in other people, seemed to consume every moment. He was often frustrated and disappointed in his own ability to rise above the situation like his friend, the soaring eagle.

God knew his intentions, as well as his abilities or inabilities, and He saw to it that Larry had friends on the kitchen and grounds crews, on the staff, and even some from back home, who passed through that summer to encourage and strengthen him.

Bud Wiuff, a businessman from Ankeny, Iowa, who was active as a layman in the campus ministry, stopped by the kitchen one hot afternoon. Bud was eagerly welcomed by Larry, whose smile lit up the whole kitchen, he was so glad to see Bud. Bud had brought Jim Sparks to meet Larry, so Larry offered to get them both something to eat. They had to decline because they had just brought some boys down to the Eagle Lake boys' camp, but Larry pointed out they still had to eat sometime. So Larry fed them while they told him about the young men they had just deposited at camp. Bud and Jim had the equivalent of lunch and dinner while they shared with Larry the events behind getting eight young men to camp, including Bud's twin sons, Brian and Bruce. Larry was so thankful for the time they had together that afternoon and looked forward to putting on his magic show for the boys' camp that coming Saturday night so he could see his friends.

Another time, Charlie Johnston stopped by to say "Howdy." Charlie had come to Ames for about two weeks during the winter, and they had spend a lot of time together. Everyone back home was Charley, but this was a real one. While Charlie was there at the Glen, they decided to pray together as they had done often back in Ames. It was during a daily cloudburst, so Larry suggested that Charlie come down to his little room in the basement of the castle. Larry explained that he had a special "closet" under the stairway in the King James room at the end of the bowling alley. He assured Charlie they would not be disturbed there.

Larry led the way to the tiny room with a desk and chair and they spent the next half hour praising God for Who He was and what He was doing in the lives of men.

All of the Glen Eyrie staff were available, helpful and encouraging as Larry asked questions concerning the decisions that lie ahead. Although these were primarily matters between him and the Lord, the staff offered helpful guidelines from God's Word to discover God's will. Larry began to finally realize afresh, it was going to be a matter of not only looking to God for the answers but PATIENTLY doing so.

During his less busy or less serious moments, it became a familiar sight to see Eb and Larry dashing across the green lawns to play tennis in the courts behind one of the buildings named Eagle's Nest, or to see Larry horseback riding along a trail. Those moments only made him miss Carla, whom he longed to have riding beside him. He had finally gotten a letter from her, in which she said she had been writing to him all summer but had been sending them to the wrong address. How relieved Larry was to be in touch again. In fact, that night he wrote to Carla, part of which said:

"Although it's 11:00 p.m. and I'm on breakfast duty at 6:00 tomorrow—I felt like writing to you. I guess it's the night—cool breeze, quiet and peaceful,

full moon, and we're separated by 800 miles of road. I'm glad my mind and thoughts can transcend miles. Sure wish we could be together tonight out on the side of the mountain, lackadaisically enjoying the peaks and hills silhouetted against a star-studded sky, in the light of God's beautiful moon. Psalm 8 cannot begin to express the reality of experience in seeing these views. I trust that a few precious moments might be spent together when I get home, enjoying these picturesque arrays of God's universe. I wish we could just be together and praise God, thank Him for all this and knit our hearts and thoughts together in prayer."

During the week of July 18-25, Larry got to attend the Leadership Conference at the Glen as a conferee. He enjoyed the week off from trainee duties, and he appreciated most the good food from the kitchen. Again, in August, he had a break coming so he wrote to his family.

Howdy, Folks!

That's the cliché that is as popular as chewing gum around here. (This suited Larry just fine because he had always loved wearing a cowboy hat, jeans and cowboy boots.) *It was really exciting to be called Charley again and talk with you people.*

Today we really had a terrific downpour—heaviest I've seen while I've been here. It washed quite a quantity of mud, rocks, etc. onto the lawns. In the last week we have had some refreshing rain to sort of cool and clean things, but this was the hardest. Really nice to sleep in the cool freshness of mountain air and be forced to pull up the covers.

At present there are four conferences left this summer, with a break between the couples and collegiate. I hope you don't give up the idea of coming out—it would do you some real good, and I would really like to see you all. Let's figure out the timing, okay? Why don't you bring Carla out with you? I am going to suggest that she come out since she will be home about August 12. How about leaving the 14th, Friday, driving to Maranatha Bible Camp (North Platte, Nebraska) and staying overnight there? Then Saturday, drive on out here and be here for August 16-19. (We have a break during that time which might give us an opportunity to do some sightseeing together.) Think about this and let me know as soon as you can so that I can arrange things. Get set for a thrilling time!!! Be sure to talk to Carla about coming.

Time for bed—Good night!

Your son and HIS,
Larry
Ecclesiastes 11:9

Their visit turned out to be very enjoyable for all.

After the two-week college retreat at the very end of the summer, Larry rode back to Iowa with Dennis Munch in his '47 Chevy. Larry shared with Denny that a whole summer of fellowshipping with men who really know God had deepened his own spiritual life. He couldn't help but think how exciting it would be when they could all sit down in heaven and share with Moses and David and all the great men God had used to accomplish His work. But, best of all, he was looking forward to talking and listening to the Lord Jesus Himself.

Their minds were temporarily blown away with the reality of that thought and that privilege. Then Larry said that, in a lot of ways, he was tired of this world and kind of homesick for heaven. But he also stated that he knew there was a job for them to do right then; that was to tell others about Christ, and he really wanted to be found faithfully doing that.

What Larry didn't share, however, was his concern that it seemed so few of his goals for that summer had really been accomplished. He felt dry spiritually, as dry as the yellow hills on the way back to Ames.

CHAPTER 9 - CARLA

Iowa, Ames, and Carla never looked so good! There were still several weeks before University classes began and, although most of Ames was sweltering in the hot Indian summer, Larry found the farm weather absolutely perfect. One afternoon when he arrived at the farmhouse he found no one at home, so he walked over to the barn. The sweet smell of hay and the farm sounds were so different and so beautiful, he thought. If only things could stay this peaceful forever. He remembered his trip with Duane to Maranatha in '61 and how horrid the alfalfa had smelled. What was wrong with him; it smelled like a sweet perfume.

He swung himself up on the rail fence, poked a piece of straw in his mouth, and began to mentally review his times here on the farm and especially with Carla.

She was young and playful and maybe even a little spoiled. But then, he'd contributed to that last characteristic. He seldom came without bringing her something, and he pulled the rosebud from behind his ear. Somehow that seemed to be what he brought to her most. They came from his mother's rose garden in the spring and summer and from the florist's the rest of the year.

He glanced back at the farmhouse. They had done so many things together. On the cold winter days, they had played ping pong and pool in the basement or pulled taffy into heart shapes or made caramels better than he'd tasted anywhere. On the evenings when Carla would play the piano, he'd lie in front of the fireplace and drift and dream of the music and laughter that one day might fill their home. He chuckled as he thought of her clomping around in his cowboy boots, her delicate feet in his big clodhoppers. It was so much easier to catch her at times like that—to wrestle and tickle and then to lie down and let her put her foot on his chest like a champion. Of course, she knew he really was stronger.

The swing under the tree brought back memories of her laughter, almost musical he thought. Her whole life was the melody of his heart. He hadn't really realized it until those long weeks at the Glen when he hadn't heard from her and thought he'd lost her. His feelings were stronger than he'd ever imagined.

The sun was getting hotter, so he went to lie down under a tree. He decided that he even loved her when she was angry, or maybe especially when she was angry. Her dark eyes would flash, like the evening he had brought his friend over to meet her and had expected to arrive at 7:00. It was after 10:00 when they finally got there, and she had already started for bed. When she came into the living room, she threw her shoe at him and it left a dent in the wall. Larry laughed at the memory, and the old cow grazing nearby gave him a peculiar look with her big brown eyes.

He apologized to Bossy and explained that he had another girl in his life. Then he recalled a canoe trip with her folks. Again, he had arrived late, and Carla was pacing the floor when he came in. Then, like a sparkler on the Fourth of July, she flared up in all her beauty. She accused him of being late again as her fists had pounded away on his chest. All he had been able to do was grab her arms and laugh as she struggled to release her frustrations. Soon they were all laughing and enjoying their trip with the canoes to Soaper's Mill, where the river was up after a heavy rain.

Larry and Carla were the best canoeists, so they went first and shot the rapids without a problem. Then came the SOS from Mom and Dad Switzer. They had gotten hung up on a large stump protruding from the water. Larry jumped into the swift current, which was up to his waist, and got them loose. Poor Dad. He'd probably never hear the end of that one. Then they had gone back to the farm for hot chocolate and Carla's delicious chocolate chip cookies, his favorite and her specialty.

The best country food came from that kitchen. Farm people didn't eat like city folk, at least not when he was there. There was always country steak and hot, homemade rolls, smothered in pure butter. It was enough to convince him that the old adage, *"the way to a man's heart is through his stomach,"* was true.

But, Larry thought, whether Carla could cook or not, she had found her way into his heart. The sky was never so blue; the birds never sang so sweetly; and the earth never seemed so filled with God's goodness. There was only one thing that seemed like a little cloud off in the horizon. Carla was still young and didn't seem convinced yet that Jesus Christ needed and wanted her whole life, not just part of it.

Carla Switzer and Larry

Since their first date four years before, Larry had always made certain that they at least prayed together, even if they hadn't spent time in the Word as well. How he longed to see her thrilled over God's personal dealings with her. Perhaps he had pushed; perhaps he had expected too much too soon. After all, he couldn't treat her like his college friends. She was four years younger and those particular four years, from, a high school senior to a college senior, brought about an unbelievable amount of growth and maturing that she had not yet had the privilege of experiencing.

Larry thought back to his own senior year in high school and how, with some personal help from Don McDonald, his Christian life had begun to really take on new meaning. That was it. It was the personal time, and Carla hadn't really had that yet. He'd poured his life into guys and the ministry, and it had become a kind of competition to his time with Carla. No wonder she wasn't all fired up! Well, it was going to be different, he told himself, and it seemed that one little cloud was already beginning to disappear as Mom Switzer drove in, her car loaded with groceries for more delicious farm cooking.

Larry went right over to help unload the car. He handed Mom a box of cereal off the top and carried all the rest into the kitchen for her, where he waited for the homecoming of his girl from Nevada High School.

In the meantime, back in Ames, the guys were tying in with their new Navigator representative, Chuck Hunt. One of the decisions reached that day by several of the key guys on the team was that they would be 100 percent sold out for Christ this year, and their ministry on campus would take priority over anything else. So they laid their plans. There would be a kick-off rally at the Whatoffs', and the word went out.

They had a good turnout that night but, to the consternation of some of the team leaders, Larry brought Carla. Instead of talking with new contacts there, he had just talked with Carla.

Finally, Duane, who was really concerned about his buddy, took him aside. Duane explained that the team had decided that their ministry for the coming year was going to come first in their lives. He called to Larry's attention that it didn't look like that was his goal for that year.

Larry defensively asked him what he meant. He was there, wasn't he? With a concerned look on his face, Duane agreed that he was there physically, but mentally he seemed not to be there at all. It looked to the team like Larry's thoughts and attentions were focused on Carla exclusively.

Even more defensively, Larry told Duane that he loved Carla and he wanted to see her grow and get involved. Duane, however, did not back down. He asked Larry that if she wasn't sold out for Christ by then, what made him feel she was the right one for him. He told Larry he thought he was trying to work things out on his own and that it was sidetracking him from the objective of raising up laborers.

Larry tried again to help Duane understand that he didn't look at this as Carla OR the ministry. He saw Carla as a PART OF his ministry.

Duane shook his head, but Larry told him that the team wasn't being realistic. Men do fall in love, and that is no sin.

Again Duane attempted to help Larry see that Carla wasn't right for him, at least not yet. To this, Larry asked him "How would you know that?"

Finally, Duane spelled it out to Larry that as far as the team was concerned, Larry was going to have to make a decision—the ministry or Carla, but not both.

Larry lost no time in telling Duane that his decision then was Carla and that he was sorry, but that was the way it was.

Larry felt rotten inside. Why couldn't they understand and accept his relationship with Carla? Why must it be an "either/or" situation? Chuck Hunt was married. He had a ministry. Bud Wiuff was married and God was using him.

Carla detected a new seriousness about Larry when he returned from talking to Duane and was not surprised when he suggested that they be among the first to leave. Snuggled up close to him in the front seat, she asked him what was wrong. Larry only said he didn't want her to get too much in one night. Larry knew it sounded feeble, but he couldn't tell her about his talk with Duane. She would feel bad, would resent the Navigators, and that would never do. After all, he was on a campaign to sell her on it. Still, he knew he had to get her home. He was no good at pretending or hiding things from her. After a quick word of prayer together, he jovially hustled her into the house and then took off.

All kinds of thoughts and reactions poured through his mind as he drove back to the campus to have a soda. He couldn't go home until he had this evening straightened out in his mind.

He kept thinking of Bud Wiuff. Bud would understand, so he went to the phone. He could see Bud the next morning. Then he drove home to an unusually hard and lumpy bed.

The next day Larry entered Bud's office in Ankeny. Bud was a contractor and the Lord had greatly blessed his labors, but Larry knew things had not always gone smoothly for Bud either. Larry had heard Bud's testimony one night, about how the wife of his youth had died after giving birth to their twin sons, Bruce and Brian. God had used that tragedy to draw Bud to Christ in a new way. Now he and Betty were happily married, the twins were 13—Tony's age, and God was using it all.

Larry knew that Bud would have nothing to gain or lose from this discussion, so his counsel and understanding would be as objective as Larry could hope to find anywhere. For that reason, he listened to what Bud had to say when he asked the question, "Why did it have to be an 'either/or' situation?"

Bud was careful to sense Larry's feelings and needs. From his own experience, Bud could see both sides of the coin. He could understand why Larry would feel that this ultimatum had been shared as a fact, "this is the way it should be," and that they had not taken into account that Larry might already have found his life partner.

On the other side of the coin, however, Bud explained that the Navigators had some very strong ideas about the necessity of a young man equipping himself for a life of service to Christ, and Bud had to agree that it was most difficult to do this if one had his head in the clouds over some doll.

Larry recognized the description aptly applied to him.

Bud reassured Larry that he was not unique. Other guys experienced this, too. He told Larry he was a good-looking young man, and he was responding in a very normal way in his sphere of influence. But, Bud said, he thought that, to the Navigator team, he seemed to have stepped out of character. Larry had to agree that that was the way they felt.

Bud asked Larry to think about what his behavior would mean to the team. If they made him a part of the team while Carla was still the most important part of his life, others would begin to question: "What about this guy with different standards? Why was he always bringing a girl? Why didn't he talk to the new guys anymore? What was going on?" Looking at it from their side, Bud was sure Larry could understand the dilemma this had introduced.

Larry was now at a total loss as to what he should do.

Bud hesitated for a moment and then told Larry that he felt he should keep it all spread out before the Lord and maybe cool it a little bit. Maybe he shouldn't put too much emphasis on one person.

Larry had much to think about after that talk with Bud and after the many more that followed. It always seemed that the question before him was "the ministry OR Carla." So he finally decided Carla would be his ministry. With that question settled, he began to devote more and more time to her and to the church. Between her high school schedule, his University schedule and Campus Baptist, he was caught up in a whirl of activities with Carla the pivotal point.

In all of Larry's visits to the farm, he and Mom S. continued discussions about his finding God's will. Larry kept lamenting that he wanted to know what the Lord wanted him to do. He had gotten a "no" to his inquiry about the insurance offer. What he desperately wanted to know was what was the "yes" God had for him. He was reading his Bible and praying, but he couldn't find out where or how he was supposed to serve God. He felt like he had wasted four years at the University, when he could have been doing something else.

Mom Switzer, after hearing him out, would always say that he just needed patience. She reassured him that God had a plan and a place just for him. In his heart, Larry would respond, "I know, I know, only why does it take so long to find it?"

It was important to Larry to know that during these hard days of indecision and turmoil, he had not shared a lot of it with his folks. He knew they would be as emotionally involved and concerned about his dilemma as he was. He wanted to spare them that. However, knowing that they would be praying for his life and walk daily, anyway, helped to reassure him that the answer would come.

Another confidant during that time was the new Navigator representative, Chuck Hunt. Larry could not divorce himself entirely from the gang that had become such a part of his life. When he talked with Chuck and Bud, things looked so simple. Yet, when he got back in the nitty-gritty of his daily experiences, his heart cried out for the joy of his salvation and the peace for which he thirsted.

December 8, 1964, was a Tuesday night, and Larry had gone down to his room early. This was something he almost never did. His Mom was concerned that he might be sick, but Hi said that he thought Larry had some things on his mind that had been coming to a head for some time. To Mom's suggestion that he might go talk to Larry, Hi sensed that it would be better for him to wait. He didn't feel it was advice that Larry needed or even wanted then. They decided he did need to talk things out, but they'd better give him time to talk it out with God. So, Hi and Lillian went up to their room and lifted their son up to Jesus to guide and direct him in the way he should go. They had done this so many times for their children, and God had never failed them.

Meanwhile, Larry lie staring up at the ceiling. The sounds of the busy household upstairs did not even penetrate, as he was reliving those past few months. Finally, he rose and went to his typewriter. His thoughts always seemed clearer if he could write them down, and so he began.

> *This last quarter has been one of hard lessons and frustration in myself.*
>
> *At present, I am a Christian, having asked Jesus Christ to be the Lord and Savior of my life in 1960; however, in returning to school this quarter, my mind was set to do certain things in my way and find my own answers. With counsel of all sorts, I was*

confused as to what I should do. Consequently, I decided that I would have to make my own decisions, since God's will didn't seem clearly evident from the counsel I had.

In my own mind, some of the things that I had decided to do were: keep myself free from involvement in <u>*any*</u> *program; seek my own leading from only God (no counsel); do what I felt in my own heart was right; spend time with Carla, setting aside my previous experience in Bible study, Scripture memory, prayer, evangelism, etc.; and seek to experience these things with Carla, (thus having the same heart with her in these things).*

Unfortunately, instead of finding real happiness and joy, I have experienced aloneness and loneliness, emptiness, and a separation from the intimacy of Christ. I wanted to find the answer to this emptiness and was determined to work it out on my own. Unwilling to admit defeat to God and ask His help, I turned more to myself and tried to find satisfaction in possessions, popular music, experiences, abuses, and even rebellion—but nothing had any lasting satisfaction.

Right now, I face the decision of choosing to go on, on my own, or admit my defeat and unhappiness to God and allow Him to straighten out the entire situation. To let God do this means a complete surrender to Him, letting Him call the plays and decide for me what I should do. This is a hard decision, because it means dying to myself and believing in God for the best solution. At one time, I knew the joy and happiness of this type of commitment, and my heart will not let me disregard this solution.

The cost of this decision is high. It means becoming so God-conscious and God-centered, that I will be considered a fanatic and a nut. I'm not happy now, and I'm willing to come back to God and humbly ask His forgiveness for my selfishness in trying to please only myself. God promises to give us joy, peace, happiness, fullness, etc., and I know that these things can be experienced. So tonight, December 8, 1964, I am going to ask God to forgive me and to take over the entire situation of my life (physically, mentally, emotionally and spiritually) and ask Him to work out His solution in all of this.

I want God to help me forget the past and to burn the bridges behind me. I am asking that He restore His joy and happiness to me and make me again aware of His presence with me.

In regard to Carla, I don't know what God has in mind, but I am willing to let Him have His way in this matter. I won't try to force this situation to work as I alone want it to and fight for my own way anymore. The interest that I now have, I want God to remove if it is not of Him. If the timing for my interest is wrong, I want God to set it aside for now. If God allows my interest to remain, I want Him to take care of my life in this and keep me from seeking my own selfish desires. Right now, I want to establish my relationship with God and Jesus Christ, and I desire that all of these other relationships would take secondary importance.

Thank you, God.

God had a special plan for Larry, and all of this would work out according to His plan. God and Larry rejoiced that night and, for the first time in many months, he had a really good night's sleep and an exciting Quiet Time the next morning. Psalm 51:12 seemed especially appropriate because God had indeed restored the joy of his salvation: *"Restore unto me the joy of Thy salvation; and uphold me with Thy free spirit."*

Larry was relieved, as Christmas came and went, that God had not taken Carla out of his life. She was still there and she was still special, as he was sure she would always be. But he also knew she no longer occupied that place in his life reserved only for God. Instead, she was in God's hands now to protect and guide and love. If it took a new commitment on his part, daily or even hourly, that was where she must stay, wonderfully cared for by God Himself.

CHAPTER 10 - OOPS, ANOTHER YEAR TO GO

Winter quarter Duane had been especially glad to have Bleek back on the team, with a new heart for men and his ever-contagious zeal and enthusiasm. Even Carla had sensed a new purpose in his life and in their dating, for which he still found time although not nearly as often as before.

One snowy evening as they were putting the finishing touches on a snowman outside the farmhouse, Larry commented to Carla that she had probably noticed that he was frequently late. That day, he told her, it had turned out for the good. Carla wanted to hear what he had to say.

Larry explained that he had gotten to one of his classes late and found a student pacing back and forth outside the room, wearing out the marble hall. He had asked him if he, too, had a speech to give. The young man responded with "No, I'm just late." Then he had told Larry that everything had been going wrong for him. His girl had jilted him, he was failing a couple of courses, and he was about ready to find a high cliff and end it all. Carla's compassionate heart was stirred as Larry continued to relate the conversation that followed. Larry said he really felt bad for the guy, but he was also happy that he had a solution to offer him. He told him he could be sure of One Who would never leave him or fail him. This really sounded good to the fellow, so Larry had gone on to share the difference Christ could make in his life. God really loved him and could fill the emptiness in his life. The young man was wide open to responding to this message and, there in the hall outside the classroom, he invited Jesus to come into his life. Carla was as delighted as Larry at the news and had to agree with him that, in that one case, it was pretty wonderful that he had been late. She let him know, however, that most of the time being late was not okay, and for that she got a handful of snow dumped down her back. Not to be outdone, Larry got his, right in the face.

In February, Campus Baptist got its new minister, Dr. Paul Tassell, and the college group of 43 strong invaded the new pastor's home for a housewarming. Larry, Bill Mullen, Ray and Roger Vogel sang some comical, as well as sacred, songs accompanying themselves on guitars and Larry's gut-bucket—a washtub with one string attached to a pole from the center of the tub and played like a bass viol. Dr. Paul and his family felt very welcomed and encouraged by the whole tone of the evening.

When he talked to Larry later about how much he had enjoyed their quartet numbers, Larry explained the rules the four of them had set up for their performances. They would sing only when asked; they would always give at least one testimony; and they always had prayer before they sang. Then the pastor asked about the other quartet to which Larry belonged. He explained that it was coming along pretty well. They called themselves the MOO-U-4 and consisted of Ron Bennett, Scott Morton, Larry, and a fourth guy that kind of floated in and out. Larry had always enjoyed music and saw it as a real tool for getting the Gospel out in a fun way.

That spring quarter break, the Navigator bunch went to Bloomington, Indiana. Their goal was to contact as many people as they could over the telephone about a great debate that was going on there between a Christian and the local atheist on campus. It was with one of these phone calls that Larry talked to a girl and led her to the Lord over the phone. She still had many problems and, although he faithfully answered her letters, he arranged for one of the young women in her area to get together with her on a consistent basis.

With spring came preparations for Mom and Dad's silver wedding anniversary, and the whole family became excited and involved. Friends and family gathered and Pop, without much coaxing, shared with them in his strong enthusiastic way how the Lord had worked in bringing them together. He set the stage by recalling the depression years and how after his dad's farm dried up and he had a little over three years of college as a chemistry major in South Dakota under his belt, he had hitch-hiked all around the States getting jobs here and there. He had finally settled in Algona, Iowa. His voice took on a more quiet and reverent tone as he continued.

He came home from prayer meeting one night in Algona. On the way to his rented room, he carried his Bible under his arm and did some window shopping. As he was looking in a hardware store window, he said he saw a young woman with two pieces of luggage and about a three-year-old girl walking toward him. The lady, who of course was Lillian, stopped to ask him if he knew where the Baptist parsonage was. Hi said that he did because he had just come from there. He started to tell her how to get there when he decided it would be much better if he would show her the way. He offered to either carry the luggage or the little girl. Hi explained that he didn't know the lady from a load of hay. He proceeded to walk her back to the church. When they got there, they discovered the pastor and his wife had already left. Hi called around to see if they had gone someplace for coffee. The pastor's wife was Lillian's aunt, and the little girl was Lillian's cousin. When the little girl's mother had passed away, Lillian had gone to help take care of her uncle's three children. Lillian had a boyfriend somewhere east of Algona, so she had made arrangements to bring this little girl with her, drop her off at the pastor's home, and then continue her trip to visit her friend. Hi finally found the pastor and his wife. They came to get Lillian and the little girl, and that was the last that Hi saw of her for a year-and-a-half.

Lillian & Hiram during courtship days

The next time when she came to visit, Hi hadn't recognized Lillian at all. While she was there a party was planned, but Lillian couldn't go because she had come down with yellow jaundice. So Hi had gone over to the parsonage and played Chinese checkers with her to keep her company while the rest of them had all gone to the party. And that, he said, was the beginning of the end, as he winked at Lillian.

This was during the depression days, and Hi hadn't felt like he wanted to get married because he wasn't sure he could support a wife. He had been working 75-80 hours a week in a chain grocery store for $12.00 a week. Well, when the economy picked up, they married. By then he was making $20.00 a week, and things just kept getting better. He added that he had never been sorry he made that decision, and he reached over and patted Lillian on the knee. She blushed and said that she had never been sorry, either. This was a fact which no one there could doubt.

A very good time of visiting followed. Out on the patio, Larry struck up a conversation with the Furmans, just back from their farm where they had moved three years before. Soon others joined in that conversation as well. On the way home that evening, Sandy Furman commented to her husband that Larry had impressed her with his ability to express himself and his ideas. Her husband, Dan, agreed that Larry had matured during the three years they had been away. Sandy said that not only did he give his ideas, but he expressed them so that she found herself questioning her own ideas. She looked at Dan for understanding. He asked her to go on. She said she found herself not being converted to becoming a Baptist but questioning not only was she going to be a better Presbyterian, but was she going to be a better Christian as well. Dan remained quiet and thoughtful. He knew she had a talent for talking things out and coming up with some pretty good conclusions.

Sandy said she had no feeling that Larry was judging them or saying they ought to look at it any certain way or to read their Bibles or do good to their fellow man or even live a good life. It wasn't like that at all. It was that he had expressed his views, they had expressed theirs, and they hadn't all been alike. It was a healthy discussion. And yet, as she looked back on it, she realized that it caused her to evaluate herself, not because someone told her she should but because she suddenly wanted to. Dan nodded his head and she continued.

She told her husband that she came away with a new realization as she listened to Larry, clowning around and telling jokes, that for the first time in her life she was able to envision Jesus as having a sense of humor. She could now believe that He could have sat down and laughed heartily, and it didn't seem out of character for Him any more. That whole evening had showed her that Christians could have a ball and be happy and clever, could tease and be funny, and laugh a lot. Her final conclusions of the evening were that Larry had so much fun and yet he remained dedicated and sincere to his purpose. He hadn't gotten so wrapped up in it that he had shut everything else out that was frivolous. He enjoyed frivolity as much as the rest of them. And yet, where others tended to take something and tear it apart, Larry seemed to pull all the living together into one meaning.

As Dan pulled up to their home, he reached over to kiss Sandy. He told her that he agreed that it had definitely been a good evening and that he'd better shape up and get some pointers from Larry at the store. This he did, although Larry was never aware of it.

When Larry registered for spring quarter, it became evident that he still needed some particular subjects for graduation that were not offered any more that year. In the process of all his personal times with students during the past four years, he dropped a course here and there to add a Bible study or some concentrated time with someone. Consequently, he still had another year as a senior at ISU when graduation time rolled around. Instead of his graduation, he got involved with Carla's graduation.

He took her to the most important event to a high school senior—the senior prom. It was a formal occasion and Larry, in his white dinner jacket, was proud to be her escort. She wore a white dress with a black panel in the back and long, black gloves, and he brought her red roses. They made a striking couple, both at the prom and a week later at the church banquet in honor of the graduating seniors. They were the only ones who came dressed formally that year, but they set a new precedent for the years to come.

Another school year had come and gone. It had been a hard one, so Larry looked forward to the summer. He recognized that he needed to get away for awhile so he looked into spending time out at Timberline, a Navigator training camp near Vancouver B.C. However, with the help of Chuck Hunt, he felt God would have him at the Servicemen's Center in Long Beach, California. This would help broaden his vision of the Navigator ministry and might even help give direction to his still unknown future beyond graduation in another year. God knew the end from the beginning and in that, he would rest. Jeremiah 29:11 best expressed his faith: *"For I know the thoughts that I think toward you, saith the Lord, thoughts of peace, and not of evil, to give you an expected end.* Or, as the RSV translation says: *"to give you a future and a hope."*

CHAPTER 11 - LONG BEACH

It was about 4:00 in the morning when Larry knocked softly on his parents' bedroom door. His dad awoke immediately and invited him in. Larry explained it was about time for him to leave. He expected his ride to arrive in the next few minutes. Pop asked him how he was getting to California. Larry explained that he would be stopping at Glen Eyrie on the way, but that wasn't the answer Hi was looking for. He questioned Larry about money for the trip. Larry assured him that he had money and then turned to leave the room. Hi told him that he was getting up and getting dressed and wanted to discuss this trip a bit more before he left.

Over a cup of coffee, his dad asked Larry to look him straight in the eyes and tell him how much money he had.

Larry stuttered a little. He was always amazed at how quickly his Pop could get to the facts. So Larry told him, sheepishly, that he had $7.00.

Hi set his cup back down and told his son he couldn't even get out of the state of Iowa with that, and California was a long ways away. Larry tried to assure him that he knew that Long Beach was where God was calling him to and, therefore, whatever he needed to get there was going to be provided. He wasn't worried, and his dad shouldn't be either. A few minutes later, when the car pulled up to the house, Dad put some money in Larry's pocket and sent him off with his blessings. After a short stop at the Glen, they continued on to California where Larry was dropped off for a week with Gary and Millie before going on to Long Beach. The very night that Larry arrived, Gary got word to report to his ship, the USS Braine. Two days later at 0800, he would be leaving for six months. So they quickly put in a call to Ames, and arrangements were made for Ron to come out so he could drive Millie and his two little nephews, Todd and Troy, back to Ames. Larry stepped right in to help them get their car in shape for the trip and boxes gathered up for storage of their possessions. Two days later, right on time, Gary left for Vietnam.

On Sunday morning, Millie took Larry to the church she and Gary had been attending. That night was the last one before Larry left for Long Beach, so he and Millie talked until quite late. Larry was concerned about their walk with the Lord and whether their church was really meeting their needs. As he shared some of the ways God had been working in his own life, Millie became convinced that her walk with Jesus was not all it should be. And yet, she felt encouraged and challenged to pick up the pieces and take advantage of the spiritual fellowship she could get back in Ames and at Campus Baptist Church.

On Monday, Larry went down to Long Beach with plans to return on the weekend to help Ron and Millie get everything in storage before they drove back to Iowa.

As Larry's bus turned down West Ocean Boulevard, it stopped right across from a series of bars and clothing stores, and the bus driver turned to Larry to tell him he had arrived at his destination. There, along the top of the two-story building housing the bars and shops, were the clean white letters spelling out LONG BEACH SERVICEMEN'S CENTER. Larry crossed the street and found the door with the arrow pointing up, and these became his 27 steps to home for the next three months.

Long Beach Servicemen's Center, 1965

That Monday, as on all Mondays, the Center was closed to the military. This was the day to clean things up and enjoy some free time. So Larry and the guys at the Center had time to get acquainted. That evening, he and Tommy Adkins, the director of the Center, talked together at Tommy's home about the history of the Center that had become a true home away from home for so many young men.

Sue, Tommy's wife, was as interested in the Center as her husband was and after their children, Ricky and Janet, were in bed, she joined them in the living room. Tommy, with his southern drawl, explained to Larry that it was Dawson Trotman who first got the businessmen together in 1939 as the CBMC. Their purpose was two-fold: 1) to encourage Christian fellowship between businessmen and 2) to provide a local Christian Service Organization (CSO) for military men. In the early 40's, Daws challenged the businessmen to get something for the servicemen where they could witness to them, give them free chow, recreation and sleeping quarters. This was a crying need in June of 1942, and the very next day the men found a place to rent for this purpose. Tommy explained that they moved four times during those last 23 years, and they now had 9600 square feet that God had been continuing to bless.

Larry was fascinated as he listened to Tommy recount the blessings that God had given. Tommy said that in the first five years of the CSO, 65 men and women who had initially met Christ at the CSO went into full-time work on mission fields or into pastorates. Larry was very impressed and asked what exactly was the objective of the CSO. Tommy said it, too, was two-fold: 1) to provide a clean, decent, Christian atmosphere where their fighting sons could relax, rest, play and pray, all at no cost to themselves; and 2) to provide a place where they could preach Christ to those who did not know Him and, thus, win them to life eternal before they would go to the battlefields of the world.

Tommy Adkins
Director of the Long Beach
Servicemen's Center

Larry thought of his own brother, Gary, who had just shipped out for Vietnam. How he wished Gary could have gotten involved in the servicemen's center before he had left.

Tommy shared that their oldest son was currently in Vietnam, too, in the Marine Corps. Tommy was very aware about how much it meant to guys over there, or who were going over there, to know that there were folks back home praying for them.

When Larry asked, Tommy said he was just starting his third year at the Center. Before him, Bill Haskell had been there and before Haskell, Sanny who had since become the Navigator president. Loren Sanny had been their first director. This gave Larry an even better idea of how much God had used Loren and Daws to make an impact on lives!

That night, as Larry, Bill Randall (or Randy as they all called him), and Charlie Lofman retired to their room off the kitchen in the northwest end of the Center, Larry had a deep confidence that he had stepped into the very center of God's will for his summer. This was to be a very important truth as the days slipped into weeks and then months.

There were supposed to have been six or seven men like Larry who would spend that summer at the Center for training but, since Larry was the only one who actually came, Tommy worked him right in with the rest of the guys. There were Randy and Charlie, who were in and out, and Rich Reed, who was Tommy's full-time maintenance man since his discharge from the Air Force the year before. Ron Elliot and Larry Graham were also part of the staff. By the end of the first week, when Larry went back up to see Millie and Ron off, the guys all felt his absence.

Ron had arrived on Wednesday so by the time Larry got there, things were pretty well packed and ready for storage. Larry had a great time with Todd, his two-year-old nephew, and even little Troy, only a few weeks old. The beach was close, and Larry and Ron did what every mid-western man craves to do; they went surfing in the ocean. In fact, they got so involved that Larry missed the bus he had intended to take back to Long Beach. As Larry said his goodbyes that night to go back to the Center, his heart ached. He was aware that neither Millie nor Ron were experiencing, to the same degree at least, the wonderful knowledge that a sovereign God had them in the very center of His will.

At 4:00 on Tuesday afternoon of the next week, the doors of the Center were opened to the military men. One by one, they made their way up the steep flight of stairs to the canteen or the recreation room for a game of pool or shuffleboard or ping pong. Always, if there were guys around, Larry would be seen talking to at least one of them and often times to several. He was genuinely interested in each one, and they knew it and needed it. He was older than most, and he had a kind of maturity they respected. At the same time, they felt he was very much one of them because he could understand from where they were coming. He got involved in their lives whether the road led there through a ping pong game or a glass of punch.

One serviceman, with whom Larry spent many hours, was a young man of French descent from Louisiana. His name was Joel, and he was having some real battles in his life. As a new Christian, he longed to know how to have victory but found the way difficult. Larry found a real ministry of encouragement necessary for Joel, and he spent literally hours sharing with him some of the new things he himself was learning that summer about God.

Since all the men working out of the Center knew Christ personally and had a fairly strong walk with their Savior, Tommy decided to really gear in on that part of the Navigator Wheel called the Hub—Christ the Center. So, in their Bible studies on Tuesday nights and any other times they could, they read and listened to all they could get their hands on about the fact that Christ was Adequate; that He was to be Center; He was to be Lord; He was to be Master; He was to be Ruler. In short, this was about the Christ-controlled, Spirit-filled life.

One message that really stirred all their hearts was one they listened to early that summer by Major Ion Thomas of the Torchbearers in England. His tape was entitled, "The Exchanged Life." It had really answered some unsolved questions in Larry's life, and he eagerly found himself sharing many of the principles he had learned from Major Thomas's talk with all of the men, but Joel in particular.

Larry talked with Joel about how easy it was to become legalistic in their Christian walk. They had to get so many verses memorized every week; they had to get their Bible study done; they had to … on and on. When they did that, they got their eyes on the tools and off their Maker and Master. It made a real difference whether or not they were motivated because they had to or because they wanted to. If they were motivated because they loved the Lord and were seeking Him, then the other things would become tools along the way and would accomplish what God intended for them to accomplish. It boiled down to a "faith-love-relationship."

During the first weeks, Larry spent much of his time pounding the streets looking for a job. Tommy helped, as they followed up on all the leads he could get from his business friends. Local students had about exhausted the summer jobs, and the doors were continually closed to Larry. This was a concern to him because he felt a real responsibility to come through for his rent and meal expenses. This turned him to God for an area that had never before been a concern for him. There had always been his dad's furniture store, where he could earn any extra money he needed; or if he had an immediate need, his dad had always been there to come through. Now he wanted to put this same kind of trust and faith in his heavenly Father, Who, after all, owned everything everywhere.

In the process of emphasizing Christ, the center of his life and the One adequate for his every need, he found his heavenly Father directly encouraging his heart through the Scriptures. He had not wanted his parents to worry nor to feel he was depending upon them to support him for that summer. So it was not until the 19th of June, the day before Father's Day, that he sat down, confident that he could communicate on a tape how richly his heavenly Father was blessing his own heart through the experiences He had placed in his life. These words served as a real encouragement to his folks when it arrived a week or so later.

FATHER'S DAY TAPE

> *Howdy from southern California! I do greet you in the name of Jesus Christ and praise His name for you all back there. I thank you for your letters, for your prayers, for your thoughtfulness and your help. I really do appreciate all you do for me. A lot of men, whom I've met here in the service, left home because they got in a fight with their folks and are not on good terms with them back home. They have nothing at home to which they want to go back, nothing at home for which they can be thankful and happy. I regret that they don't! I'm praising God for what I have at home to be thankful for, and I appreciate everything you've ever done for me.*

Tomorrow is Father's Day and I realize that, at this late point, I haven't gotten anything in the mail and I'm sorry, Dad. I appreciate all that you've done and I hope that you'll take this tape, even though it's late, and accept it as my thanks to the most wonderful dad in all the world. And I really mean that! I think of Paul when he said of Timothy, "For I have no man like-minded, who will naturally care for your state." (Philippians 2:20) and I know of no man like-minded like my dad, who will naturally care for my state.

I'd appreciate your words to the rest of the folks there at church and around. Please mention my hellos to them and greet them for me. I hope I can correspond, as much as the Lord will give me the chance, and that I would be faithful in God's Word. I pray that God gives me the time and the discipline to sit down and do it. I would like to share a verse from Matthew 7:7. It says, "Ask and it shall be given you, seek, and ye shall find;, knock and it shall be opened unto you." God asks us to ask Him for things that we need. He's given us a promise in Philippians 4:19, "But my God shall supply all your need according to His riches in glory by Christ Jesus." I thank Him for that! But I also thank Him for the message of Matthew 7:9-11. "Or what man is there of you, whom if his son ask bread, will he give him a stone? Or if he ask a fish, will he give him a serpent? If ye then, being evil, know how to give good gifts unto your children, how much more shall your heavenly Father which is in heaven, give good things to them that ask Him?"

I know a lot of times I haven't asked for things that I've needed but I appreciate, Mom and Dad, the things that you've done, and I thank you that you've known how to give good gifts. It encourages my heart, because God knows how to give good gifts, and I believe that God has put in your hearts the same spirit.

I would like to share a challenge that God has brought to my own heart since I've been here. It's a challenge concerning returning to school this fall and some principles around that. It comes from Jeremiah. As I was reading Jeremiah, this seemed to strike me from the Word. Jeremiah was speaking to Judah, and you know the leaders of Israel, prophets and priests and the pastors, and the people, had kind of turned their backs against God. Jeremiah 22:1-2 says; "Thus saith the Lord; Go down to the house of the king of Judah, and speak there this word, and say, Hear the word of the Lord, O king of Judah, that sittest upon the throne of David, Thou and Thy servants, and Thy people that enter in by these gates."

Then Jeremiah continues in 23:1-2: "Woe be unto the pastors that destroy and scatter the sheep of My pasture! saith the Lord. Therefore thus saith the Lord God of Israel against the pastors that feed My people; Ye have scattered My flock and driven them away, and have not visited them; behold, I will visit upon you the evil of your doings, saith the Lord."

Without realizing the evil that was in Israel and particularly in the city of Jerusalem, He said to the people, "I've given you two choices." And these two choices are in verses 8 and 9 of chapter 21: "...Thus saith the Lord; Behold, I set before you the way of life and the way of death. He that abideth in this city shall die by the sword, and by the famine, and by the pestilence: but he that goeth out, and falleth to the Chaldeans that besiege you, he shall live, and his life shall be unto him for a prey."

So He gave the people a choice. They could either leave the city and be captured and serve the Chaldeans, or they could stay in the city and die, because of the wickedness in the city. I think God still challenges us today, to separate ourselves from wickedness or die. Go out and be captive of the world and be surrounded, this kind of thing, but live; OR die and perish in your wickedness. And then to those people who leave the city, He says this in 24:6-7: "For I will set Mine eyes upon them for good, and I will bring them again to this land; and I will build them, and not pull them down; and I will plant them, and not pluck them up, and I will give them an heart to know Me, that I AM the Lord; and they shall be My people, and I will be their God: for they shall return unto Me with their whole heart."

Now, I'd like to draw the Old Testament application and then share with you how this applies to me. In verse 5, God is speaking to those captives who left Judah and were taken captive by the Chaldeans. I believe God has led me out here away from Iowa State, not particularly captured, but out to Long Beach where I'm surrounded by servicemen and places that are unfamiliar to me. But God gives the promise that "He will set His eye upon us for good." He will promise to look after us and keep His eye on us. And I believe God cares for us, and He watches out for us and keeps His eye on us. This is an encouragement to my heart because I don't have a job right now. I know that God is concerned, He knows and He cares, and He can provide in His time the things that I need. He watches out for me, and He's going to watch out for me this summer. I am convinced of that.

I Peter 5:7 says, "Casting all your care upon Him, for He careth for you." And, Matthew 10:29 says, "Are not two sparrows sold for a farthing? and one of them shall not fall on the ground without your Father." God knows when even a sparrow falls to the ground. Then He continues in Matthew: "But the very hairs of your head are all numbered. Fear ye not therefore, ye are of more value than many sparrows."

We're more valuable to God than the sparrows, but God watches out for them. So that's an encouragement to my heart. God is going to set His eye upon us for good, and in Jeremiah 24:6, He says He will bring them again to their land. He's going to cause the people to return. He was going to bring them back to their original land, to their city. This speaks to my heart about what God is going to do this fall. He's going to bring me back to Ames, to Iowa State, returning me to the place where I've been. He's led me out here this summer, and He's going to cause me to go back.

Then He says in Jeremiah 24:7: "I will build them up and not pull them down."

God will build and this speaks to me. God is going to build in my life this fall at Iowa State. He's not going to pull me down, but He will cause me to grow and become built up in Him. So, "Except the Lord build the house, they labor in vain to build it: ..." (Psalm 127:1). I can't trust myself to build; I can't trust anyone else to build; but God will build in my life and cause me to be established. I

Corinthians 3:12-13 says: "Now, if any man build upon this foundation gold, silver, precious stones, wood, hay, stubble; every man's work shall be made manifest: for the day shall declare it, because it shall be revealed by fire; and the fire shall try every man's work of what sort it is." Verse 10 says: "...I have laid the foundation, and another buildeth thereon. But let every man take heed how he buildeth thereupon."

I think there are some things that I can help God with in my own life, but I need to be careful and cautious that I let Him do the building so that it will last and be established. Then He says that not only will He build them and not pull them down, but "He will plant them and not pluck them up."

Out here in California, there are all kinds of fruit. I went to Tommy Atkin's house, the director of the Servicemen's Center. He has an orange tree, a lemon tree, a grapefruit tree, a plum tree and an olive tree in his backyard. Fruit is so plenteous. When people plant trees out here, they plant them not for the beauty, particularly, but for the fruit. Well, God builds people, and He plants us to be fruitful for Him.

I think that next year at Iowa State, God is not only going to build in my life and in the lives of others; He's also going to plant. He's going to plant me and cause me to be fruitful to Him as He has purposed. Jeremiah 17:7-8 says, "Blessed is the man that trusteth in the Lord, and whose hope the Lord is. For he shall be as a tree planted by the waters, and that spreadeth out her roots by the river, and shall not see when heat cometh, but her leaf shall be green; and shall not be careful in the year of drought, neither shall cease from yielding fruit." I want to be fruitful to God and Jesus Christ back at Iowa State and wherever I go, for that matter. I want to continue to bear fruit.

In John 4:35,36 Christ says, "Say not ye, there are yet four months, and then cometh harvest? Behold, I say unto you, 'Lift up your eyes, and look on the fields; for they are white already to harvest. And he that reapeth receiveth wages, and gathereth fruit unto life eternal: that both he that soweth and he that reapeth may rejoice together.'" That's fruit unto eternal life. When we go back: when we proclaim Jesus Christ and see guys come to know Him, that's eternal fruit. That's building and causing fruit for eternity. That excites my heart, eternal fruit that God has given. And it says when this fruit is reaped, it encourages the person who planted it, and it encourages us because we've seen the fruitfulness of God.

Not only will God plant them and not pluck them up, but He goes on to say "I will give them a heart to know Me." God will give us a heart to know Himself. This thrilled me because I think I need a new heart for God. You know it's easy to become routine or to become systematic in what we do, and I want God to give me a new heart for Himself.

Ezekiel talks about this in 36:25-28. "Then will I sprinkle clean water upon you, and ye shall be clean: from all your filthiness, and from all your idols, will I cleanse you. A new heart also will I give you, and a new Spirit will I put within you: and I will take away the stony heart out of your flesh, and I will give you an heart of flesh. And I will put My Spirit within you, and cause you to walk in My statutes, and ye shall keep My judgments and do them."

God is going to put in my heart a new heart for Himself. I think He's doing that this summer. Just in the times that I'm spending with Him, He's given me a new heart for Himself. Not only will He give us a new heart, but a new attitude, a new look of Himself. What kind of look? "I will give him a heart to know Me, that I am the Lord."

God needs to be our Lord and Master. James 1:8 says, "A double-minded man is unstable in all his ways." I need to be single-minded for God and let Him be my Master. John 3:30 says, "He must increase, but I must decrease." That's what God needs to be in my own life. Then He says He will give them a heart to know Him, that He is the Lord, and they shall be His people and He will be their God.

Look at the promise. I will be His and He will be mine; He will be ours. Isn't that great! We'll belong to Him and He'll belong to us.

I John 1:3 tells us: "That which we have seen and heard declare we unto you, that ye also may have fellowship with us: and truly our fellowship is with the Father, and with His Son Jesus Christ." Our fellowship is with Him. A fellow here at the Center shared these verses with me, and it has been very encouraging. It is Revelation 21:3 & 7. "And I heard a great voice out of heaven saying, 'Behold, the tabernacle of God is with men, and He will dwell with them, and they shall be His people, and God Himself shall be with them, and be their God.'" In verse 7 it says: "He that overcometh shall inherit all things; and I will be his God, and he shall be My son."

We are His and He is ours! We belong to Him and He belongs to us. We've been bought with a price and that price is Jesus Christ!

Then, finally, He says He will do all these things, why? Jeremiah 24:7 says it's because: "they shall returned to Me with their whole heart." And I must return to Iowa State, not half-hearted, not slack, but expecting great things with my whole heart. I want to come back, challenged, on fire, spiritually keen to do God's work next year in my final year at Iowa State.

Luke 10:27 say: "And He answering said, 'Thou shalt love the Lord thy God with all thy heart, and with all thy soul, and with all thy strength, and with all thy mind; and thy neighbor as thyself.'" I want to do that! I want to love God with all my heart, not half my heart, but all my heart. Psalm 42:1 says, "As the hart panteth after the water brooks, so panteth my soul after Thee, O God." I want to pant after God. Let me read Deuteronomy 30:2 to you: "And thou shalt return unto the Lord thy God, and shalt obey His voice according to all that I command thee this day, thou and thy children, with all thine heart, and with all thy soul;"

I want to return with all my heart. And then, do you remember what was said of Hezekiah in II Chronicles 31:21? I want this to be the testimony of my life. "And in every work that he began in the service of the house of God, and in the law, and in the commandments, to seek his God, he did it with all his heart and prospered."

When I come back to Iowa State, I want to come back with all my heart and prosper as God would prosper.

Well, I'd just briefly like to bring a challenge. Millie, I challenge you to get in the Word of God; go to Bible Study. Don't take my word for it; try it yourself. Ron, there are lots of preparations you can give to your own heart in spiritual things for this fall. Tony, I want you to really stick in there. Write me and let me know what you've decided about Eagle Lake. And Marlene, I've picked up some shells for you. I'll send them to you. The seashore's full of them out here. And so, greet the people for me back there. I thank you for everything that you've done and everything that you are.

Larry

CHAPTER 12 - A CALL TO MEN

Much of what Larry was had been a real challenge to the men at the Center as they worked, studied, and witnessed together to the military personnel. For instance, they were all memorizing Scripture. After an especially full week, one or two men would come up with memorized verses like John 11:35, "Jesus wept." But it seemed Larry was always excited about a new portion of Scripture he had learned. For many of them, it was their first time to ever see anyone memorize Scripture just because he wanted to.

Larry and a sailor from the USS Topeka, named Doug Olson, spent a lot of time together that summer. Doug would often have his weekend free and would come in to help around the Center. They had some good times in the Word, working and playing together. On a very cold July 5, they all went surfing. Larry stayed out long after the others had frozen and come in, so intent was he to stay standing on the board. He did not give up easily on anything.

Midway through the summer, Larry finally got a job selling photographs for a Jewish man at Underwood Enterprise. It was a package deal; you buy a photo and get a number of years of film. It was not a full-time job, but it did provide enough to take care of Larry's needs that summer and bring him in contact with people. One of his prayer requests one morning with the crew was, "Pray for me; half the doorbells are answered by bikinis."

During that summer, Larry was invited to speak at Larry Montgomery's church. Montgomery was one of the local businessmen who did some of the public relations work for the CSO, along with Holly Moore and George Seifer. Larry ended up speaking two weeks in a row. After one of those times, Larry was in the Montgomery home, and he shared with Mrs. Montgomery how a person could find God's will. This was a subject in which she was vitally interested.

Larry told her that when he was seeking God's will in a matter, he would look for four things to line up. Those four things were circumstances, counsel, Scripture, and prayer that brings peace. If any one of them did not line up, he would be very cautious about moving ahead. BUT, if all four lined up, then nothing could stop him because he would know for sure it was God's will.

Larry often gave the illustration of the captain of a ship who had to take his vessel into a very difficult harbor. When asked how he did it, he pointed out three lights along the shore. When the captain got those three lights all in line so they looked like one, then he knew he was on course. That is how he recommended people find God's will. Get all four points to line up. The Montgomerys never forgot those four points.

Another means of real growth and challenge to Larry's spiritual life were the trips he and Rich made up to Pasadena once or twice a week. They would meet with Warren Meyers and his Summer Training Program or STP as they called it. Warren explained it like this. "It's guaranteed to put fire in your engine, and it cleans out the sludge." These times brought back good memories from the Glen Eyrie days as, once again, he sat under Warren and worked on the basics in his life.

Sundays were always special at the Center. The staff would take turns on the Friday and Saturday nights, when servicemen would come in at any hour looking for a bed. Sunday morning, all who had slept there Saturday night were given a free evangelistic breakfast, usually involving about 50 men. There were skits (for which they greatly depended upon Larry), and they all took turns bringing a message.

These mornings especially brought a problem to Larry's mind, at least the way he saw it and referred to it. He enjoyed being the center of attention, and yet, he wanted Christ to be the One he revealed. So there was a constant battle with pride for he was an extrovert; God had blessed him with a tremendous amount of showmanship and the ability to communicate in a way that made guys sit up and take notice. In one of Larry's messages he said, "It's hard to get a man into heaven with talcum powder or a shoehorn." Larry told them it took "scores of praying, believing saints of God bound together to give and to serve."

In August, they sold Rich's green '57 Chevy station wagon and bought a '66 Volkswagen bus to transport their men to churches in Long Beach after the Sunday morning breakfasts. There were 29 different churches in the Long Beach area that came to the Center from 4:00-9:00 on Tuesdays through Fridays and from 2:30-9:00 on Saturdays and Sundays to serve free sandwiches, coffee, punch, cakes and pies. On Sundays, the Center had a wide variety of churches to which they could take the servicemen to worship. Then, from 2:30-9:00 pm, the Center was opened for ministry once again.

Anyone who had ever been in the Center on Sunday afternoons knew a dear saint named Miss Taylor. Miss Taylor had been a missionary in Africa and had been sent home to die. That had been 25 years before, and she was in her 70's that summer. Every Sunday afternoon, she would climb those 27 steps and pause a moment to chat with one of the crew while she recovered her breath. She was there for one purpose and, even in the middle of a friendly chat, she might break off her conversation to go to talk with some young sailor or even a whole table full of men. She had a quality about her life that spoke of the Lord, whether she had opened her mouth or not. Although she was only five-feet-one inch, she knew she had the power to single-handedly tackle a whole table full of men and keep the whole thing in control and centered on her Lord and Savior, Jesus Christ.

All through the summer God had been working, as Larry had hoped He would, in directing his thinking in terms of his military service. He had been looking for specific answers ever since he wrote his goals back at the Glen the summer before. Now the draft faced him, and he knew he must make a decision.

His father had been in the Army during World War II, and Gary was now in the Navy in Vietnam. After talking with Chuck Hunt back home, he came here to the Center believing he would probably become a Naval officer when he graduated from ISU. But during the course of the summer, Larry not only talked with many Navy personnel, but also with Rich who had been in the Air Force, and Larry had prayed a good deal with Tommy about his son in the Marines in Vietnam.

He had many helpful discussions there in the Center and at the Adkin's home. Sue was a great cook and Rick and Janet, ages eleven and eight, were a joke-and-riddle teller's idea of a perfect audience. Even before those last days there, Larry had reached the conclusion that, during the next couple of years, God was calling him to concentrate his life entirely on men. He had confidence that for one more year, they would be the men at ISU. But, then, would it be the Navy? He knew God would make that clear, too, when the time came. In the meantime, for that particular summer in Long Beach, he had some immediate decisions that had to be made.

During that summer, Larry's boss at Underwood Enterprises had become very impressed with Larry's salesmanship abilities and his genuine love for people. He did not want to see Larry go back home, so he approached him with the possibility of his sticking around and working full-time for him. He made Larry a good offer, and it was tempting to a college student who was broke. But God had made it very clear what He wanted and, with all his heart, Larry did not want to give his life to photographs, but to men.

Still, as the day for departure came closer, more and more decisions faced Larry. It wasn't simply to go back to ISU. There were still the questions of: how to travel, when to leave, where to go first, and on what resources could he draw? So, he made a list and began to pray over it. This is how it looked:

Plus	*Minus*
A. Go to Conference at Glen Eyrie	
1. Sessions on basics.	*1. Need $40.00 remaining*
2. Help out with conference.	*2. Need to get to Glen by Sunday*
3. Get heart for fall.	*3. Would leave one week for seeing draft board*
4. Get with Jim North	
B. Go Home	
1. Square away draft.	*1. Decide on transportation*
2. Finalize details for fall	
3. Prepare for school	
4. Possible ride for Tony	
5. Time with the guys	
C. Stay for additional week	
1. Call once or twice for TPC.	*1. Be trusting the Lord anyway*
2. Ministry at Center.	*2. Already planning to leave*
	3. Be more personal
	4. Work out transportation

Larry was careful not to share any of his financial needs with anyone all summer. This seemed to be the area that would determine when and how he should go. As an added test, he received $50.00 from his dad about this time, but felt

God was speaking to his heart about Tony going to Glen Eyrie. So he sent the whole $50.00 off to Tony for camp expenses. Finally, all signs except the circumstantial ones of money and transportation, seemed to point to August 20 for his departure date, and he had until then for the circumstances to agree. In faith, he gave his boss his notice. Again, his boss questioned him about the wisdom of passing up such a good offer. Larry was sorry to disappoint him, but he was certain that God wanted him back at ISU. His boss had asked him if he had enough money to get there yet. Larry answered honestly, "No," but that he was sure he would have it by August 20 and explained that he was trusting God for that.

More days slipped by and still with no money in hand a week before he was to leave, but Larry went down and made his bus reservations for August 20. On August 19, when his boss left the shop, Larry told him he'd see him first thing in the morning with enough sales to get him home. Larry was learning to put feet to his faith. His boss said that for Larry's sake he hoped he would make it but, for himself, he would miss him.

That morning, August 19, Larry had asked his buddies at the Center to pray for a specific problem that had to be resolved that day. It was close to midnight before Larry got back to the Center, his sales completed at last. Late as it was, all the crew were still up waiting for Larry's return. They weren't aware of his financial need for his ticket the next morning. All they knew was that Larry was to leave that next day, and they all wanted to show him in some way what his time with them had meant to them that summer. Since he had only one suitcase, they decided a money gift would be easiest to transport home, and he could use it on whatever he wanted or needed.

So, when he climbed the 27 steps, tired but happy, he was greeted by his buddies who handed him white envelopes with money inside. There were more envelopes in his room and still more in his mailbox the next morning. Larry fell asleep that night, amazed at how it was impossible to out-give God.

The next morning, August 20, 1965, the total reached from even unknown sources was $50.00. At breakfast, Larry couldn't say enough about their sacrificial giving and generosity. He felt his "thank you" was so inadequate. Then one of the guys asked about the request he had given them the day before and had everything worked out okay. Larry told him it sure had, thanks to them. He told them that he hadn't had the money to buy his bus ticket yet so he had told his boss he would sell enough that last night to get home on. God answered that one, too. When Larry put their gifts of $50.00 together with the money he made on this job, he had $170. He praised God Who had proved to him once again, that He is never late in answering the needs of His children.

Larry's boss had been watching for Larry's arrival that next morning; one look at his face and his suitcase told him that God had honored this young man's faith and his work. He found himself rejoicing that Jehovah had seen fit to use his business to help Larry. He still hated to admit, even to himself, how much Larry had come to mean to him, but found that he couldn't help it. This young man, so full of life and goodness, had captured his heart.

A few minutes later, Larry boarded the Greyhound, found a seat beside two foreign students, and headed once again for Colorado Springs with a new love and confidence in his heavenly Father and a new heart for men.

CHAPTER 13 - TRUSTING GOD

When Larry got back to Ames, the first order of business was to report to the draft board. Much to his surprise and concern, he had received word to report on September 13. He was sure God wanted him at ISU. He and Jim North had talked in great detail about that year ahead and what God had laid on their hearts on their way back from the Glen. The Army just didn't fit into the picture. Larry was convinced that this was one of Satan's tactics to keep him from fulfilling God's will for his life.

So Larry prayed, *"Father God, I confess I am guilty of procrastinating. I should have turned my schedule in long before this. But I didn't, and now I thank You that I must completely rely upon You to work out this year for me. If You want me in the Army, then close all the doors to ISU; if You want me at ISU, please release me from the Army."* With this matter in God's hands, he set out for the draft board office.

When the secretary called his name and looked at his records, she said matter-of-factly that it looked like he ought to report. Larry said he didn't understand because he still had one more year to complete his B.S. at Iowa State. Her next matter-of-fact statement was, "Well, according to our records you were supposed to have graduated last year. That's why you were classified 1-A." She told him that, unless he could show them proof that he would graduate the following June, signed proof at that, he would have to report on September 13.

Larry knew that the "unless" was in God's hands to work out, so off he went with a prayer, to the campus to set up his schedule. He had planned his classes in the spring, but had forgotten to turn them into his departmental office. His advisor had never understood his dropping courses during his four years to take on another religious thing like a Bible study, so Larry was certain he would have to do some real talking. Larry set up the entire degree program for the year, and his advisor signed the copies of his degree program before he had even finished filling them out. This was highly unusual, and Larry knew God's hand was at work on his behalf.

Next, Larry went to the registration line greatly encouraged. All went well. Then came the classification line, and the lady looked at his schedule. She said she was sorry but he couldn't have three of the courses he had written down. They were mandatory courses in his degree program, but they were full.

The circumstances certainly looked like a closed door, but Larry made a conscious effort to get his eyes off the circumstances and on to the God Who had promised in Romans 8:28: *"And we know that all things work together for good to them that love God, to them who are the called according to His purpose."* So Larry stepped out in faith and asked her if there was any way he could get into those courses. She flatly told him that it was impossible because they were full. There was no way he could change that. Larry persisted and asked if he could speak to the instructors and explain his situation. Finally, there was a ray of hope. She told him that "if" he could get them to okay it he was in, but not to get his hopes up.

Now the "if" was in God's hands, and Larry was more and more convinced that God wanted him in those classes. With another prayer in his heart that if God wanted him at ISU that God would *"set before him an open the door that no man can shut (Revelation 3:8),"* he went to see each instructor. He explained the situation with the draft, and all three instructors signed his approval. Really praising God, he returned to classification where, surprised and even a bit upset, the lady signed his program.

Jeremiah 32:17 ran through his mind. *"Ah Lord God! behold, Thou hast made the heaven and the earth by Thy great power and stretched out arm, and there is nothing too hard for Thee."* Only God could have gotten him in the courses, gotten his degree program set up and signed at this late date. He took it to the draft office, and the lady told him to come back on September 13 or he would be inducted. If he came back that day, they would release him from his draft notice. You can be sure Larry was there on September 13, and on time!

As a result, he shared the experience with the guys out at Long Beach on a tape. He said he thought that John 10:29 was appropriate, where Jesus says, *"My Father, which gave them Me, is greater than all; and no man is able to pluck them out of My Father's hand."* Larry told them that no one could ever pluck them out of God's hand, despite how circumstances might look, and despite whatever might occur.

That fall, Larry's University load was especially full, with 24 contact hours per week. After four years, he still did not feel confident as a student and knew his only hope was with Christ Who could make graduation possible. So, he did the best he could and left the results to God.

In the meantime, the campus ministry continued to be Larry's real major. He took time to set down some objectives for that year, asking God to change any that were not also His objectives. He shared these objectives with other men on the team and found God was working in the same or similar ways with them. The most exciting of all was that God had been putting the same things on the hearts of each of them, whether they had been at the Summer Task Force (STF) in Washington D.C., at Maranatha in the

Midwest, out on the West Coast, or anywhere in between. God had been giving them the same promises from the Word saying, "This is for ISU this year" or "Believe Me to do this."

In another part of Larry's tape to the Long Beach gang, he said that he thought God was going to do something by His mighty hand that year, because the men and women on campus were believing God to do the things He had promised. They had already seen God begin to work in the hearts of others. They had already seen a band of men who, although they were not yet numerous, were willing to walk with God and give their all for God. Larry felt sure mighty things would happen at ISU as they looked to God to accomplish them.

So the objectives and the people fit together for that year of 1965-66.

Objective One was to get the Word out by AGGRESSIVE EVANGELISM: to present the Gospel to men and women and let them know that Jesus Christ died for them and that, right then, they could know abundant life. This objective was carried out on Tuesday nights at 7:30, as they met in a man's room in either the New University Towers or Fryly Hall to share a promise or a portion of Scripture. Time was also spent in prayer, claiming God's promises: for provision; for the words to share; for the confidence they needed in the Lord; and for His promise to go before them and work in the hearts of the people with whom they would share. Then they would pair off and go see a buddy from one of their classes or a person with whom they had made an appointment. Sometimes they would just knock on a door and ask the one who opened the door if he was interested in talking about practical Christianity and the person of Jesus Christ.

These opportunities for Larry showed themselves in many ways. While Ron had been in California to pick up Millie and his nephews, he had dated a Mormon girl and she, in turn, had asked some Mormon missionaries to look him up. So, as fall quarter began, Ron joined a fraternity at ISU and a couple of Mormon fellows began calling on him. Ron came to Larry with his problem. He hadn't really known what to say to them, but he knew he didn't agree with them either. They were going to come back that next Wednesday evening, so he asked Larry if he could be there when they came.

Larry agreed and, in the meantime, he brushed up on the ways they agreed and disagreed and went to the Scriptures for his answers. When that evening came, Ron introduced his brother, and Larry picked up the ball as he asked them what Jesus Christ meant in their lives.

To their remarks that, "Well, He was a good man," Larry went on to explain personally, from Scripture, the difference this "good man" had made in his life. The young men sat and listened and, finally, when they realized that what they had come to share would never be agreed upon, they took their leave with verses of Scripture still ringing in their ears. Ron never saw them again.

One afternoon, as Mom had been getting ready to put Larry's lunch on the table, she heard him drive up in the "Dead Rabbit" and quietly walk through the front door. He wasn't even whistling. He asked if lunch was ready, and she assured him that it was. Larry asked her if she would mind going ahead and eating because he would be back shortly. He went out, got back in the "Dead Rabbit," and drove off.

Mom, who had a hard time keeping up with him these days, shook her head and put his grilled cheese sandwiches back in the open oven. About 20 minutes later he returned, whistling "How Great Thou Art," and she knew he had gotten something settled.

She invited him to sit while she made some fresh sandwiches for him, but he took the ones she had already made and told her about what had just happened. Larry explained that he had stopped to pick up a hitchhiker at school, had let him off on 20th Street, and Larry had driven on home. Then God had reminded him that he had failed to witness to this man. So Larry said that was why he had left. He had driven back down the highway until he found the young man, picked him up again, and this time had talked to him about Jesus. Larry said the fellow seemed shocked that he'd come back, but he thanked him for that, and Larry felt that now God would be working in the young man's heart to water the seeds Larry had planted.

One of the evangelistic tools they used a lot that year was called the "Bridge Illustration." Doug Sparks, a Navigator in the Orient, had developed this illustration to communicate it to the Chinese people to whom he ministered. Larry had first seen it at the Glen in 1964 and now just about all the areas were using it. Any person who went on evangelism with Larry became completely sold on its effectiveness.

The "Bridge Illustration" could be drawn for the listener on any piece of paper that was handy and then be sent home with them to further contemplate the verses of Scripture and the truths stated. Larry's illustration would have looked something like the image on the following page.

Once Larry had the two cliffs drawn with the great bottomless chasm between them, he would explain that all of mankind was represented on the Man side, and all mankind was sinful, meaning we all lack perfection. No one is perfect. Romans 3:23 says: *"For all have sinned, and come short of the glory of God."* Romans 6:23 states, *"For the wages of sin is death ..."*

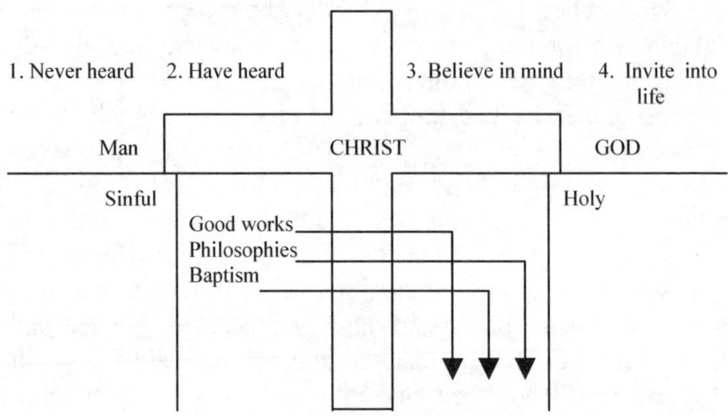

On the other side, however, is God. He is perfect and holy. Then Larry would ask them, *"How can we get from the side of sinful man to the side of the Holy God?"* He would record their answers in the chasm. They would offer ideas like: doing good things, going to church, or being baptized. With each suggestion, Larry would write it down and draw an arrow toward God's side, but the arrows were never quite able to reach the other side. He would say that "if you almost fly over a mountain top, it is just as deadly as if you crash near the bottom." To almost reach the other side was not what they wanted their lives to accomplish. Then Larry would tell them that the only answer that could bridge that deep chasm successfully was the cross of Christ. To prove this was not just his opinion, he would show them verses like John 14:6: *"Jesus saith unto him, I am the Way, the Truth, and the Life: no man cometh unto the Father, but by Me."*

And I Timothy 2:5, in the Living Bible says: *"God is on one side and all the people on the other side, and Christ*

Jesus, Himself man, is between them to bring them together, by giving His life for all mankind." He would also show them John 1:12, which says: *"But as many as received Him, to them gave He power to become the sons of God, even to them that believe on His name."*

To help explain what the key word "believe" really meant, Larry would tell them of the man who strung a tightrope across Niagara Falls and proceeded to walk across it from one side to the other. Of course, a crowd started to gather below. Once on the opposite side, the man took a wheelbarrow and pushed it in front of him as he returned to the first side. The crowd had now gathered from everywhere to watch. This time he filled the wheelbarrow with three or four sacks of sand and, once again, traversed the rope. The crowd was silent as they held their breath and watched, expecting any minute that the man would fall or the rope would break under such a weight. Instead, he had no problem at all reaching the other side. Now, he had their attention and he shouted out the question, "How many of you believe I could wheel a man, instead of the sand, across this chasm?" It was not surprising that everyone raised their hand. They believed he could do anything. Then came the question, "Who would like to be the first to crawl into my wheelbarrow for the ride of your life?" Strangely enough, not a hand remained raised. They had all said they believed but, when it came to committing their whole life to this man by crawling into his wheelbarrow and being carried to the far side of the chasm, their belief came up short.

Larry would then explain that when they were asked if they "believed" in Jesus Christ, the question meant, had they ever responded to His invitation to come to Him by stepping up and giving their whole life over to Him, to steer them down their life's pathway to God?

At the top of his Bridge Illustration, Larry would place the numbers from one to four. He would explain that number one represented all the people in the world who had <u>never heard</u> of Jesus Christ. Number two represented all of those who had <u>heard</u> at least something about Jesus Christ. Number three were those who had <u>heard</u> and <u>believed in their mind</u> that what was said about Jesus Christ was Who He said He was. Number four were those who not only <u>believed</u>, but had acted upon their belief by <u>inviting Jesus to come into their lives</u> and take over. The fourth option was the <u>only one</u> that could take them safely to God's side through the cross.

The final question Larry asked them to consider was to which group did they belong? Had they ever heard of Jesus before? Had they heard a little about Him? Had they heard and believed in their head what they had heard? Had they heard and not only believed in their head but taken the step of faith to invite Jesus into their life?

Then he would ask them which number best represented them? Depending on their answer, he would gear into their particular need. By using an illustration, it was much simpler to stay on the subject and, at the end, each person was aware, by their own evaluation, just where he or she stood with the Lord and what the person needed to do.

A fellow student named Jim Nelson had tried the "Bridge Illustration" once or twice, but not until he watched Larry run through it in his natural enthusiastic way was he impressed. He told Larry, after the illustration had been shared, that he had never cared for it much before that evening. He could then see what a good tool it was. Larry was eager to get Jim even more convinced of its worth, so he invited him to share the "Bridge Illustration" at the next place they went. Jim quickly explained that that wasn't what he had meant; after all, he was still just learning. However,

Larry reassured him that he believed that Jim would do a good job. Larry knew by experience that the very best way to learn was to do it, so Jim knocked on the next door. They were invited in and Larry let Jim go through the illustration, only helping when a verse slipped Jim's mind. By the end of the evening, Jim had new confidence and boldness because Larry had instilled confidence in him, had been available to pull the argumentative ones aside, and had let Jim have those who were interested.

One evening on the way back to Jim's room, Larry asked him how he might make his presentation more effective when he shared the "Bridge Illustration." Jim liked it just the way it was, but Larry was constantly on the lookout for clearer answers and ways of communicating the Gospel. The other men knew this and often came to him for advice.

Scott Morton had been talking with a guy named Joe who had invited Christ into his heart three or four times. Scott walked back to the dorm one night with Larry and said that he couldn't seem to give Joe assurance of his salvation. Scott wanted to know what might help.

Larry shared what he had found most effective. He had needed assurance, too, in the beginning. Larry suggested that Scott ask Joe if he had asked Jesus into his life. If he says "yes," then he should read Revelation. 3:20 which says: *"Behold, I stand at the door, and knock: if any man hear My voice, and open the door, I will come in to him, and will sup with him, and he with Me."*

Then Larry would say, "Joe, if you asked Christ into your life, what does Scripture say would happen?" And Joe would respond with, "He came into my life." Then follow that with, "Okay, Joe, on the basis of this verse, has Christ come into your life?" And his answer should be "Yes." Then ask, "How can we know for sure?" The answer according to that verse is that "He said He would and God never, never lies about anything."

The next day Joe found his assurance.

Another night in one of the lounges, Mike came over to talk with Larry. He said that he didn't have the boldness that Larry had and he couldn't witness. Larry quickly assured Mike that he understood how he probably felt. Larry said sometimes before he would get together with the men, he would pray all afternoon that his heart would be right and that he would have what it took to spend time with them. Mike was surprised at this. Larry was so outgoing, how could that be? But again, Larry said that he wasn't always outgoing and, when he wasn't, he prayed that he would be. God was faithful to answer his prayers.

Even in his University classes, God gave Larry boldness. He shared an incident with Carla, who was now in nursing school, and finding it difficult to witness. Larry told her that a few days earlier, a professor in his advertising class had asked, "What motivates people? What makes people tick?" Then the professor waited for an answer. When nobody said anything, Larry couldn't keep still. He said, "I don't know about other people, but I know what makes me tick. It's the person of Jesus Christ."

Carla asked him what the professor's reaction had been. Larry grinned and said that it hadn't been what he was expecting so the professor had cleared his throat, thanked Larry for sharing, and asked if anyone else had an answer.

Tuesday evening in the dorm was evangelism night, and it accomplished several things. It was a training ground where they could learn to talk to people about Christ, where they could learn to share their testimonies, and how to help another person invite Christ into his life. It also helped spur evangelism for all the other days of the week. These things were happening at ISU.

Objective Two for that year was to REACH OUT to other campuses with weekend trips. Part of what Jim North had shared with Larry on their trip from the Glen to Ames that fall had been some verses God had laid on Jim's heart for ISU. One of those verses was Zechariah 8:21

"And the inhabitants of one city shall go to another, saying, 'Let us go speedily to pray before the Lord, and to seek the Lord of hosts: I will go also.'"

Several weekend mission trips were taken that year to colleges and universities. They went to Cedar Falls in the middle of October; to Iowa City at the end of October; to Columbia, Missouri, in November; and later, to Mankato State, Hope College, and Lincoln, Nebraska. These weekend trips involved leaving Ames after school on Friday afternoons and traveling to their destination in three or four cars. Saturday mornings were spent praying and seeking the Lord for boldness on their part and preparing the hearts of the students in the dorms they were going to be talking with about Christ. Men from two or three campuses would meet together on one campus and share the Gospel with as many students as possible that weekend. On Saturday nights, they'd gather everyone together for fellowship, have something like a pizza party and present Christ again, so that those who had made a decision that day would have clear in their minds what they had done, and so that any who had not completely decided for Christ might have another opportunity to decide and invite Jesus into their lives.

On Sundays, they would take the new babes in Christ to church and begin to establish a contact and a follow-up to help these converts in their new walk with Christ. Before one of these weekend trips, Vern Bundt, Duane's brother, asked Larry if one of his friends was going on the next evangelism trip. Larry said he had just talked with the man, but Larry said he still wasn't sure he could go. Larry said he had suggested that he pray about it. Vern's friend had just looked at him and asked if Larry bothered God with every little thing. Larry said he had answered, "Yes, I guess I do, and you could do the same. God really cares about everything concerning us."

They also had two longer trips that year. During the Christmas break, Glen Eyrie had what they called a "Whing Ding"—meaning "Big Thing." Collegiates from all over the States met for one week of challenging, life-changing messages and testimonies of what God was doing throughout the world. Larry piled seven guys into the '48 Dodge and drove to Dresden where they boarded the train. There was Larry in bibbed overalls, a fellow from Liberia named Uti Kallu, Tim Kuntz, Dave Jahr, Doug Koenigsberg, Ron Bennett, and Scott Morton. They had a great time singing, telling jokes, and quoting Scripture—ingredients for all their trips. The Moo-U-4 performed at one of the meetings. Larry's comment to Scott later was that he was sure glad that they didn't have to major in singing and performing.

Quartet at the Glen
Larry on the "gut bucket"

While at the Glen, Larry was delighted to spend some time with Rich Reed in prayer, about the gang in Long Beach, and with other friends like Jim and Jan Airensmeir, with whom he seldom got to see or talk.

During the spring break, the team took a ten-day trip to New London in Ontario, Canada. The Navigator representative there had opened up a new ministry at the University of Quebec and invited the gang to come up. Five women, eight men, and three cars made the trip. They drove through Detroit and on up to New London and Galt. While they were in New London, the Navigator representative from Kalamazoo said his team was spending a weekend at Kent State, so the ISU gang decided to meet them there on their way back to ISU. Just before Larry left New London, he sent a card to his folks which read:

> *Having a spiritually top time—exciting to be sure!!! Have been doing evangelism since we arrived, and three fellows have become new Christians. Many contacts made and interested hearts. Staying with a lovely Christian couple with three boys, great!!! Will be going to Niagara Falls tomorrow. Then to Toledo and will return Sunday night, late. Thanks for your prayers. Praise God.*

As planned, on the way back they would stop at Niagara Falls, but the closer they got, the thicker the fog became. Finally, with only a few more miles to go, Larry said that since they would like to see the Falls when they got there, why not take some time to pray about it. He acknowledged that God had made the Falls and He had made the fog, so he asked God to please lift the fog so they could behold His handiwork.

There was a moment of silence as not all of them were used to taking this kind of thing to God in prayer. But they did join him in that prayer request, and God did answer! When they got to the Falls, the sun was shining with no fog at all. Then, as they were getting back into their cars, the wind came up, and it rained and sleeted all the rest of the way to their destination.

Larry and Cal Johannes teamed up on the Kent State campus and then went on to the campus of Penn State in Kalamazoo. From there, they stopped at the University of Wisconsin at Madison. Here Doug Koenigsberg and Larry shared the Bridge, and Doug gave his first presentation—the first of many.

Objective Three was that their ministry on campus and in the lives of men would be BIBLE CENTERED. The discipline learned at Maranatha and Glen Eyrie, to get into the Word regardless of how busy he was, had finally become a strong reality in Larry's life. He knew the Word was absolutely essential to knowing and being in God's will and being used by God.

Larry was involved in seven Bible studies during his last year at ISU. The team got their new contacts and converts involved in the new Navigator books 1-10, called "Studies in Christian Living." Book One was especially good for those who were still interested in learning more about Jesus Christ. It covered "Who He Is," "What He's Done," and "What that Can Mean to Me."

Book Two picked up with the New Life in Christ and how we can begin to have meaningful fellowship with Him. Book Three was about "Walking with Him." Larry had gone this far with Carla and the men the year before and, in his last year, he led many more through those books. At the same time, he was involved with the men under Jim North, going through Books Four through Seven. Here are some examples of how God used the Scriptures to work in Larry's own life and to enable him to better help others.

Book Four involved the "Character of a Christian." One Sunday afternoon in November, for the application question at the end of Lesson two on "Demonstrating Christ," Larry had written:

> *The area of biggest need in my life is in humility and getting myself out of my own eyes. Just dying to myself. I need to become completely wrapped up in Christ. I need to become insignificant to self and alive only to Christ. I am going to study Colossians and ask God to really saturate me with Jesus.*

During December, he went through Book Five on the "Foundations for Faith." In Lesson two on the Holy Spirit, his application was:

> *I need to be sensitive, moment by moment (that's hard) to know that I am letting the Holy Spirit have complete control so that my life fulfills God's perfect will. I am going to use Galatians 5:22-23 for my check list.*

Lesson three of Book Five was about "Know Your Enemy," and Larry wrote:

> *I need to be more than just aware of the fact of Satan; I must believe that he really wants to destroy my life. Therefore, I cannot afford not to be always alert and in close fellowship with God. When Satan attacks, I am going to declare the blood of Jesus Christ that was shed for me to make me God's child and not Satan's. Only then can I resist Satan.*

Lesson five in Book Five had a section on "Will Christ Return?" On January 20, 1966, Larry wrote:

> *It is very easy for me to say, "The Lord is coming back" but I don't think I'm living it. I need to be concerned about His coming and less concerned about things like my reputation, grades and position. I'm asking God to make me alert and alive to the fact of His coming so that with urgency, I do those things that are eternally most important. I John 3:2-3 "Beloved, now are we the sons of God, and it doth not yet appear what we shall be: but we know that, when He shall appear, we shall be like Him; for we shall see Him as He is. And every man that hath this hope in Him purifieth himself, even as He is pure."*

Book Six entitled "Growing in Service," continued to speak to Larry's heart. In the chapter on "Helping Others find Christ," he was reminded to pray daily for the men and women at Cedar Falls.

Book Seven was a study on I Thessalonians, and Larry came to this conclusion that spring as he studied it; the Thessalonians came to Christ, intending to follow. Operating in God's power, they became examples in life and in the Word of Christ to the places around them. That, coupled with Paul's challenge to Timothy in I Timothy 4:12-13, is the kind of Christian Larry wanted to be. *"Let no man despise thy youth; but be thou an example of the believers, in word, in conversation, in charity, in spirit, in faith, in purity. Till I come, give attendance to reading, to exhortation, to doctrine."*

Larry was still consistently memorizing Scripture. By spring, he had decided to tackle the book of Colossians since God had been showing him so many good verses about Jesus in it.

One morning at 6:00, he came walking into Clark Wallace's room in the dorm for their Bible study. Larry really looked tired. They finally got him to admit that he'd been up all night studying for a test. It was not easy to fit studying in with his active ministry to others, but he was determined to graduate.

Objective Four was conserving fruit, also called FOLLOW-UP. This was one of the things for which the Navigators were known. Just as a newborn baby is not handed a milk bottle and told to drink it when he gets hungry, so new babes in Christ must learn how to get into the Word, how to pray, and how to talk to others about Jesus. Along with Bible studies and the personal times with men on campus, Larry's heart also went out in a special way to Tony and his friends who had gone to Eagle Lake Boys' Camp. Larry saw them as keen young men, full of vitality with the potential for reaching the world for Christ. He was the first person in many of their lives to take a real interest in them spiritually and "show" them how to do all the things they were being told to do.

Twelve of them would pile into the Dead Rabbit on Saturday evenings and go to the YMCA for some swimming or basketball, or they'd go bowling or skating. Then they'd drive over to one of the guy's homes in Ankeny or Des Moines, where they would have refreshments and spend some time getting them grounded in the basics. Larry had perfected his magic tricks to deliver a spiritual application, and these men got to watch many of these demonstrations. He also spent personal time with students like Tom Jorris, helping him establish a consistent Quiet Time, or Dave

Powell, who found in him someone with whom he could talk things out without worrying about what Larry would think of him. Larry was a good combination of a big brother and one of them. He really enjoyed watching them grow in Christ and giving them a good time while he was at it. The Dead Rabbit contributed a lot to their fun. Larry loved to pile it full of students and then joke about its ability to get them to their destination. One night, with ten in the car, someone asked Larry about his speedometer.

Larry's reply was that the speedometer wasn't hooked up, but when he hung on to the cable he could judge how fast it vibrated. That was how fast they were going.

One of the girls that had met Christ the first Sunday in the fall at Campus Baptist, found Larry a real help as he worked with her to find solutions to some of her problems. He explained how to have a Quiet Time and later helped her determine her priorities based on the Word of God. He could find answers to everything, it seemed, within the pages of the Bible.

Also, a part of "conserving the fruit," was developing new Christians to the point that they could begin to reproduce. Larry had listened countless times to Daws's tape on "Born to Reproduce" and had given men and women his booklet with the same title. He would explain that all Christians are born to reproduce, and that was the only thing that would bring real joy and fulfillment to their lives. They knew that Larry was giving his whole life to doing just that.

Much prayer went into "conserving fruit." God would work where no man could. There were morning prayer meetings at 7:00 on Mondays and Fridays in Fryly Hall and the Towers, plus other additional times throughout the week. God was knitting their hearts before His throne, for the hearts of other men and for their own needs. One day as Larry stopped by Jim North's to pick up Jay Pritchard and

Doug Koenigsberg, he got to talking to them about prayer. Larry said he was becoming more convinced that prayer was the avenue by which they could touch God's heart for men. He said that God didn't tell them to go and get the laborers for Christ. Instead, Matthew 9:37-38 said: *"Then saith He unto His disciples, 'The harvest truly is plenteous, but the laborers are few; pray ye therefore the Lord of the harvest, that He will send forth laborers into His harvest.'"*

They must first PRAY. So, they needed to talk to God about men before they talked to men about God. He shared Luke 18:1: Jesus told His disciples that *"men ought always to pray, and not to faint,"* (or give up.) They all needed to pray and not faint and that, he assured them, required work. Larry was impressed with David's life as recorded in Psalm 55:16, 17: *"As for me, I will call upon God; and the Lord shall save me. Evening, and morning, and at noon, will I pray, and cry aloud: and He shall hear my voice."*

Larry told them that David prayed evening, morning, and at noon. Larry was convinced that David knew something about touching the heart of God in prayer, and that he had known where God's power and His strength were to be found—in God Himself.

When they got to the campus, but before Larry had even turned off the motor, they decided to bow and have some time in prayer. They had many things on their hearts. But suddenly there was a knock on the window. Larry looked up and then rolled the window down. The young man outside looked a bit embarrassed as he explained that he was concerned that maybe they were in trouble from carbon monoxide or something because they all had their heads down. Realizing they were fine, the young man quickly left. Larry turned off the motor, and then the young men in the car also prayed for that fellow who had shown his concern.

Objective Five had to do with RALLIES, which were planned to specifically lift the spirits during those times of the quarters when spirits tended to be the lowest, when a student would think he or she was the only Christian on the whole campus. They'd pack fellows and girls into someone's home and share some of the things God was doing that would encourage hearts and strengthen them in unity together before God.

Objective Six was that God would make them MEN WITH A VISION. Larry could still remember Bob Foster talking to him at the Glen about VISION. He told Larry that *"Vision without work is visionary. Work without vision is mercenary, but work plus vision is missionary."* Their objective was to produce missionaries who could go forth into the world as laymen or professionals, to be personal representatives and ambassadors for Jesus Christ.

As the school year progressed, Larry spent more and more time praying about men and how he could best reach them with his witness for Christ. He was convinced that men were God's vision and must be his as well. By spring quarter, God's vision for using Larry began finally to fall into place.

That spring he took a course called "Military Strategy and Tactics." This course was taught by Major Casey of the United States Marine Corps, and Larry was impressed. God had shut the door to Larry's flying jet fighters because his vision was not 20/20. The Army and the Navy were okay but, as the quarter continued and he prayed and spent time in the Word, Larry began to see the Marines as the men who really put their lives on the firing line and the ones who needed to be reached before it was too late.

Larry read Marine: The Life of Chesty Puller and saw in this man the kind of determination and drive that helped finally to convince him that God was, indeed, calling him to the Marine Corps for His glory and for the service of his country. God used all these things to burn a desire deep into his heart "to be the best Marine officer he could be, or die trying."

So, on a rainy May 26, 1966, John Voss, a sophomore at ISU with whom he had spent much time in the Word, drove Larry into Des Moines to enlist in the Marine Corps. Later, when his mom asked him, "Why the Marines?" he told her "because they need the Lord the most." Two days later, on May 28, 1966, Larry received his Bachelor of Science degree in Industrial Administration from ISU. Larry's only comment about graduation, when they got back home, came as he handed his diploma to his mother and said, "Here, mom. God and I finally made it!"

CHAPTER 14 - TIMBERLINE

Larry was not to report to Officers' Training School at Quantico, Virginia, until January, 1967. Therefore, in the summer of '66, he accepted Elven Smith's invitation to be on the staff at Timberline Training Camp in British Columbia for the summer. There were a few details to work out for that trip since he would also be counseling at the High School Conference at the Glen on the way. It was not surprising, therefore, that Larry, Tony, Dave Powell, Vern Bundt, Cal Johannes and Curt Siemers arrived at Glen Eyrie three days late.

They were a welcome sight to the staff at the Glen, because almost all of the staff was down with bad colds. Larry pitched right in to help lighten the load. He took a bus load of high school young people into Denver for evangelism; he ran the athletic program; he entertained by leading songs, and delighting them with magic acts and skits. The skit the conferees seemed to enjoy the most was the night they got to pick three counselors, lined them up against a brick wall outside the kitchen of the castle, and threw pies at them. Larry was one of the counselors chosen for that honor, and he had a great time throwing back all he could.

At one of the meals, Larry was sitting at a table with some young men and there were still two empty places. When he saw two pretty girls looking for a place to sit, he motioned them over and said he'd be glad to have two of the most beautiful girls in camp sit at their table. Kathy and Ann blushed a little, but they did sit down and enjoyed themselves because, as usual, Larry's table was one of the liveliest in the dining hall.

Larry was soon known for his humor, as well as his devotion. The day they all went up to Eagle Lake for canoe races, Larry wore some crazy swimming trunks with suspenders, a cowboy hat and cowboy boots.

When the high school conference came to an end, Larry continued to search for transportation farther west. There were eight conferees from the Billings, Montana area so Kathy Robbie, one of the two girls he had invited to sit at his table, invited him to ride as far as Billings with them. Nine people climbed into the eight-passenger station wagon with all their luggage, and Larry drove most of the way. Almost all the discussion on the way home was about the Lord. They arrived back at their home church late Saturday afternoon.

Arrangements were made for Larry to stay overnight in Billings before continuing his trip to Seattle. That evening, the group got together with some of the young people who had not gone to Colorado. Kathy was eager for her older sister, Barb, to meet Larry, so she invited her to come, too.

Barb, who had just gone through an unhappy experience of a broken engagement, was definitely not interested in getting to know any more young men, but the get-together sounded like fun so she went.

When they arrived, Larry was in the kitchen talking with the hostess about the Lord. As Barb and Kathy went through the refreshment line, Barb was impressed with what she heard. She told Kathy that she had never heard a person so enthusiastic about the Lord. Kathy reassured her that he was always like that.

Larry was intent on what he was doing, but later in the evening Kathy introduced him to Barb, who was a senior in college. Larry had already noticed her quiet beauty. Now, as he talked with her, it seemed almost as though he were talking with a more mature version of Carla. He quickly dismissed those thoughts but did agree to see Barb and Kathy in church the next morning.

Larry's contributions to the group that night caused a crowd to gather around him on Sunday morning. It was Kathy and Barb's invitation to dinner that he accepted, however, even though he had been planning to begin hitchhiking to Seattle following the church service.

Mrs. Robbie made a lovely dinner, which they enjoyed on the patio. After the meal, Kathy, Barb, their brother Wes and his fiancée, Judy, all helped Larry make signs for the side of his suitcase—BOZEMAN, HELENA, MISSOULA, SPOKANE, and SEATTLE.

It was getting toward late afternoon when Wes suddenly got an idea. He suggested that they help Larry hitch a ride on a private plane from Billings to Seattle, either that night or the next morning. That had worked for Wes once before, so they set out for the airport. They were all disappointed to find that there were no flights scheduled to Seattle in the next week.

Barb suggested that since it was getting late in the day, that he stay over at their place and leave the next morning. He might stand a better chance of getting a ride more quickly. Her brother heartily agreed, convincing Larry that his folks would love to have him stay. Then, teasingly, he looked at his two sisters and winked.

So, it was settled. Then, with more afternoon and evening ahead of them, Wes and Judy, Larry and Barb went horseback riding. Somehow, Larry and Barb's horses were old plugs who could hardly move, so they had a lot of time to visit. It was getting chilly as they headed back, so Larry gave Barb his jacket. They all laughed when she got off her horse, because the jacket came down to her knees.

On Sunday evening, the Methodist Youth Fellowship (MYF) held its meeting up on the Rim, a big wall of rock that extended along the north side of Billings. They were feasting on watermelon when Wes, Judy, Larry and Barb arrived. Then they had a chapel time on the rocks, and Larry led them in some singing. Those back from camp shared what the week had meant to them. Larry was thrilled to hear how God had used that time in their lives. It had, indeed, been a most profitable week.

The next morning at breakfast, Larry turned to Barb and asked if she had had her Quiet Time yet that morning. Barb poured him some coffee as she explained that she was up early but, was making sandwiches for his trip. Larry told her that he had tried "thinking her awake." Wes quickly chimed in that it would take more than that to wake Barb up but was quickly stopped from saying more.

After breakfast Larry, armed with his suitcase and a big brown bag of sandwiches and fruit, climbed into the Robbie's car, and Barb drove him to the outskirts of town. Just as Larry was leaving the car, he asked Barb to get on home and get into the Word. She assured him that she would, and that they would all be praying that he have a safe journey to Timberline and a great summer.

As Barb turned the car around and headed back toward town with a final beep, beep, Larry found himself walking along re-evaluating his first impressions. She really wasn't a mature replica of Carla at all, and he was glad for that. Barb was Barb, and there was something about her that was different from any girl he had ever known.

* * * * *

The setting for the Canadian Summer Training Program was 75 beautiful acres of the Fraser Valley, nestled in the foothills of the Garibaldi Mountains of British Columbia. Since it extended into that area where the mighty Douglas firs and virgin timber stood tall, it was appropriately called "Timberline Ranch." Located in the Fraser Valley, it was affected by the Fraser River, especially when the winter snows began to thaw.

Larry had hitch-hiked 1,000 miles from Billings to the small Canadian town of Haney, and then on down the road to the point where it disappeared beneath the flood waters of the Fraser. Now the Timberline motorboat came into view and Dave McIntyre, whom Larry had phoned from Haney, shouted a friendly welcome as the boat pulled up and they loaded Larry and his gear. They exchanged greetings, and Larry commented that this was the first time he'd had a boat pick him up, and it wouldn't have been complete without it.

Dave told him that there was only about a half mile of water and that the ranch itself was dry. Flooding was a common occurrence each spring. They had even built an old car up on stilts back at the ranch so they could pick up their trainees, but it didn't happen to be working that day. Larry assured him that he didn't feel disappointed at all; he loved the boat ride.

As they headed back to the ranch, Larry asked what he had missed so far. Dave filled him in on their "getting organized" to this point. Dave knew Larry had been to Maranatha and assumed it was pretty much like the first couple of days at any of the training camps. They would have campers all summer, and the staff was there to help in the maintenance and operation of the grounds as well as to see that the trainees got some real, concentrated, spiritual training. Dave said that, so far, there were 11 young men and eight young women as trainees, plus the seven of them on staff.

When they pulled through the gate, banked on either side by a white wagon wheel, Larry's cowboy heart let out a yahoo. This was going to be fun! The men's cabin was up the road past the horse barn and corrals. It was built up on stilts against the side of a slope. The room was filled with army cots with just enough room for the men to swing out of bed and get dressed. There were holes in the floor and only a mesh screen over the windows to let in plenty of Timberline air, with no stove to warm it. It certainly was different from Maranatha. Bleek was always ready for a challenge and this one looked great!

The training director had waited for Bleek to arrive before holding the staff meeting, so Dave and Larry hurried on over so the meeting could begin.

Timberline Crew, 1966

Larry Blake was the director. Bleek had met him once or twice at the Glen in 1964. That was when Blake had just gotten discharged from the Navy. Larry had been impressed with this man's sharp appearance and friendly manner. He was the kind of a man to whom men would respond, and the couple of years since that time had made this even truer. Bleek already had confidence in him as the camp director for the summer.

While they passed the word that the meeting would begin in 15 minutes, Larry and Larry spent the next few moments getting caught up on each other's lives. He filled Bleek in on the week of staff training in Seattle, and the Navigator part of the program that Bleek had missed. Larry told Bleek that most of the staff had little or no training before a group and that, with his experiences on the campus and in the servicemen's work, Bleek would be a real asset to the team.

The others began to arrive, and Blake introduced them as they came. The girls' team leaders were Nancy McRae and Sissy Gates. The men's leaders, besides Blake, Bleeker, and McIntyre, were Jeff Kemmerer and Keith McGuire.

Bleek could remember meeting Sissy back at Glen Eyrie a few years before. Since they were old friends, he spent most of that summer teasing her because he knew it made her furious. She was a city girl from the east coast who never knew quite what to think of his farm-boy sense of humor, especially his comments about her big feet which he overemphasized. He also threatened to cut her beautifully thick, naturally curly, auburn hair since he was the Timberline barber. He told her she could lose 20 pounds with one haircut!

When Larry Blake had written Bleek back in April about coming to Timberline and being on the summer staff, he had suggested that he bring lots of good skits and some fresh ideas as to how to make this a life-changing summer for those for whom they would be responsible. He had suggested that Bleek give the teamwork principle some thought because he wanted a real team emphasis for them. He had also asked him to be ready with a message on any and all of the "basics" and to get in some kind of good physical shape.

Those proved to be words of wisdom. During the next two months, Bleek was grateful that he had heeded them.

Jokes and funny stories were a natural for Bleek, and gales of laughter continually emanated from his table. The Arab-Israeli War had just ended and so he took his dinner table companions by surprise as he, very seriously and yet enthusiastically, asked them if they had heard that the Egyptian rifles had gone on sale for half price. They looked at him to see where this had come from or where it was going. Larry continued to explain that the rifles had never been fired and had been dropped only once. He had taken another bite before they realized what he had said, but once the laughter came, he continued with more until their cheeks and sides ached.

In the process of all his storytelling antics, Bleek was forever breaking one of the table etiquette rules which was: "elbows and wrists off the table during meal times." He would sheepishly "fess up" at each staff meeting and drop some more coins in the penalty box. One day, he even hinted at the impracticality of such a ruling by saying that "all his life he had most enjoyed being able to rest his arms on the table during meals." They all laughed with him over that. It was, indeed, one of his warm, human frailties.

Bleek was a "must" in every program and was either behind or in every skit. It was always interesting to see what role his big straw hat would play. One time, it would assume the posture of a "special forces" man in Vietnam and, the next time, it would be that of an old sour-dough panning for gold. The skit everyone laughed the hardest over was when he dressed up in his bib overalls stuffed with a bed pillow, blackened his teeth, and sang about his tall girlfriend. The more laughs he got the funnier he was, until every fiber of his 190 pounds was involved in making people happy. This, in turn, always made Bleek happy.

As much as he loved to laugh and clown around, however, Bleek could not forget the seriousness of living 100 percent for Christ. He had spent a lot of time in the Word and praying over Larry Blake's comment on "fresh ideas for a life-changing summer for the trainees." Bleek knew his own life had been changed substantially at just such a training program, as guys had spent personal time with him helping him with the basics. Also, he had seen his own personal time with others pay off time and time again.

During those first five weeks, Bleek was team leader for three men, and he poured his whole life into them. Art Tyree, Bob Magistrelli, and Dave Kraft were his men and his responsibility. As interested as he was in everyone and everything, these three guys were uppermost in his thinking. He was constantly looking for ways to serve them and encourage them. Working or relaxing, they had a great time. Bleek had a way of drawing more out of his men than most leaders did, and yet, not building up resentment in the process. He never asked his men to do anything he wouldn't do. And anything he would do, he would do with his whole heart. So Art and Bob and Dave even went through the pre-Marine training that Bleek put himself through. They ran farther, worked harder, and laughed more than anyone else.

One afternoon, Dave McIntyre was out in the section of timberline that the Canadian National Forest had given the ranch and was enjoying the tall firs and the quietness of the land. Suddenly, he picked up the sounds of distant singing floating down from the trail above. Dave thought immediately that it had to be Bleek and his merry men. In another moment there was no doubt, as Bleek came into view at the head of the procession carrying one end of a 10-foot hand saw. Dave, Art and Bob were coming along behind with the other end of the saw and carrying their axes over their shoulders. They'd been up blazing trails for horseback riding and were coming back down for supper, happily chanting a gospel song. McIntyre could only chuckle and wait for them to pass. As they kept singing, Larry smiled and saluted. They all filed by with big grins, never missing a word of their song all the way back to their cabins. Bleek's lack of inhibition was rubbing off on the others and he had, obviously found a way to create real team spirit. This was not to say that it was not difficult to be on Bleek's team. He set high standards for young men, some of whom were very new in the Lord.

Five fifty-five a.m. was reveille six days of the week, and to rise at such a time was not easy. It was a drastic change for those used to sultry summer nights and lazy vacation mornings to awaken to a freezing cabin filled with 10-15 groggy roommates who had just five minutes to get down to the road for calisthenics. On rainy mornings, the fellows and girls would meet together in the shed, an open area with a roof and a sawdust floor. Rain or shine, there was the old 1,2,3,4 each morning. Following this, there was time for getting cleaned up and spending personal, individual time with the Lord.

One morning Magistrelli commented to a couple of his buddies on the way to breakfast that he had seen Bleek down in the shed, kneeling in the sawdust, and praying his heart out to God. Magistrelli had decided that was the secret to his tremendous heart for men. He really knew how to pray. Kraft agreed that their team leader was a good example of what he was talking about a couple of nights before. His message had been about "Setting the Pace." Kraft said that if "pace" is the length of a step and "setter" is one who establishes the length of the step, then Larry was certainly qualified to be a pacesetter. Kraft felt Bleek knew where he was going and how he could get there.

Magistrelli appreciated that Bleek knew it cost something to mean business for God. He seemed always to be the last one to bed and the first one to rise. None of his team could figure out when he slept or how he kept going.

Meanwhile, back in the girls' cabin as they were freshening up for breakfast, one of the trainees mentioned to her team leader, Sissy Gates, that she thought Bleek was sure tall, cool and collected. Sissy smiled as she agreed that he did give that impression, but she said that once they got to know him, he was really a crazy nut. They discovered that Sissy had known him back at the Glen, several years before. Sissy said she couldn't help but notice him. Not only had Bleek been big, but he had worn high-heeled cowboy boots, blue jeans and a funny looking hat, similar to the one he wore there at Timberline. It had become sort of his trademark. Sissy told them she thought he looked great here, but back then he and another guy from Texas had looked like cowboys in a castle, so they had really stood out.

Another girl commented that she thought he really looked sharp in his blue jeans and the baby blue shirt that matched his eyes, the shirt that laced up the neckline with rawhide. They all agreed. Then another said she thought he knew how to make a girl feel special. Another said that he was so funny, that when she sat at his table she could hardly eat because she would be laughing so much.

Finally, Sissy broke in with the statement that she could see the makings for a Larry Bleeker Fan Club. They all agreed again as they headed off for the dining hall, each secretly hoping he would sit at her table.

Had Bleek known their feelings, he would have better understood the significance of the Quiet Time in the lean-to that morning. He had sensed that same gentle reminder from

God that he had heard before, *"Go easy, Larry, with my girls."* And then the familiar verse from II Timothy 2:4: *"No man that warreth entangleth himself with the affairs of this life; that he may please Him Who hath chosen him to be a soldier."*

Bleek had been thoughtful as he prayed: *"God, I'm not entangled with any of them, am I? You know my weakness for girls, and that I've given this area to you. I'm certain that, for now, men and the service are where you want my efforts and, if and when the time is right, You'll bring the girl."* He looked at the others around him and his heart cried out, *"O God, I have no favorites. They are all special."* God knew he meant every word.

Larry decided in his heart anew that he would not be entangled with anything that would get him off the course God had set for him. So, he continued to purposefully joke with, tease and counsel anyone and everyone who needed it but, for some of the girls there were more heart problems ahead. They kept wondering, "Does he or doesn't he like me?" Gradually, as the summer wore on, they each one discovered that he truly did have the capacity to like and be interested in them all. As one girl commented, "He's just like a big puppy dog. You can't stay mad at him or not like him for long."

During the middle of the second week, each team was assigned two days a week to go to the towns near Timberline for evangelism. Those towns were Port Coquitlam, Haney and Mission. Members of the teams paired off and did mostly "cold turkey" evangelism, calling on people they had never met before. As time went on, follow-up appointments were also set for the evangelism time because there was a need to help those who had just received Christ to grow. They also followed up with those who had expressed an interest to know more.

One afternoon, just before they were to go into Port Coquitlam to share Christ, McIntyre discovered his Bible was missing. It was nowhere to be found. He was hesitant to go to Larry Blake, who was out on a tractor pulling in newly cut timber to be used for building the new cabins for the men. Therefore, he went to Bleek, whose team was also going into town that day. McIntyre told Larry he felt like a soldier without his weapon. Without the slightest hesitation, Bleek reached into his attaché case and gave him the Bible he found there. Dave thumbed through it and found a number of verses that were special to Larry neatly marked, so he told him he would give it back as soon as his own showed up. Larry told him that wasn't necessary, to just make it his own. Then McIntyre asked another favor. He wanted Larry to inscribe it with a word of encouragement for him. Even though it was close to time to leave, Larry, sensing that Dave needed encouraging then, took time to pen the following inscription on the flyleaf.

Dave:

Determine to do as God would have you do. Follow Him; that is whether anyone else does or not. Apply I Timothy 4:12, 13 and stay in the battle; we can worship our Lord Jesus forever together in heaven.

Larry Bleeker
"Bleek"

Then the two of them rounded up their trainees for the ride into town. Once there, Bleek learned about a party for young teens to be held at the football field that night and that everyone was welcome. So, when he got back to the ranch, he went to find Blake to see if they could send a team over there to witness, but Jeff found Bleek first.

Jeff told him that Larry Blake had gotten hurt that afternoon right after Bleek's team had left. Blake had jumped down out of the tractor and landed on a rock hidden in the weeds. He had really messed up his ankle. Blake was in the lounge with his foot up and wanted to see Bleek.

Bleek lost no time in getting there and was really concerned when he saw the mess Blake had made of his ankle. Blake told him the doctor said he had chipped a bone, and he was supposed to stay off of his ankle for several weeks. Blake asked him if he could help during that time, and Bleek was more than happy to make himself available. He also encouraged Blake to take it easy while he could. Then he told Blake about his idea of joining the football players at the party that night. Blake gave it his blessing, suggesting that he take about four other men along with him.

As they drove up to the field, the other four wondered how in the world they could witness to a bunch of kids like they saw gathered there. Larry was reminded of Tony and the guys back in Ames, so he felt right at home with these young people. He led the way and soon they were all right in there with them, showing them plays. Before long, Bleek had them gathered around to learn about the Man, Christ Jesus, Who could fill their lives with all the excitement and thrills they could ever hope to find.

Bleek was really busy because he tried to anticipate ways to help Blake out before he did too much. Unfortunately, he was not entirely successful because Blake's ankle got infected, and he was confined with his leg up for three more weeks.

One afternoon, a couple of weeks before the end of the first session, Blake asked to see Larry. Blake had been doing a lot of praying, and he felt certain that Bleek would be just the man that God wanted to head up what they called "The Leftovers." Larry was excited, but somewhat awed, at the responsibility. He knew they had been selecting trainees who could stay over for five more weeks for a special advanced program in evangelism and follow-up. Blake made it clear that it would be a tough job working with five men and three women and he couldn't spare a girl leader. But he told Bleek that he knew he could handle it, and it was all his if he wanted it.

They talked about how to tie in with the rest of the trainees. Blake could see them being the "servants to the servants" by finding ways to help the trainees with their Quiet Times and man-to-man times and to free them occasionally for special activities. When the men's cabin was completed, the guys could all move into that, but the girls would have to stay with the rest of the girl trainees. At the end of their conversation, Bleek thanked Blake for his confidence in him and said he would be happy to give it all he had.

His answer was a tremendous load off of Larry Blake's mind. He told Bleek to do what he wanted with the trainees. He'd be glad to talk to him about anything, but the decision making would be basically up to Bleek.

That was all Larry needed to send ideas cascading through his mind. The preceding Sunday Larry had talked to Don Lawrie, a man who was working with college students in the Vancouver area. He had told Larry that there was a new university in Vancouver called Simon Frasier. It had classes all summer. Since Larry was just about sure that he would be staying in the Vancouver area after Timberline, he decided it would be great to send a crew in to survey how it looked as an evangelism project for the "Leftovers."

The plans for the second session and his "Leftovers" found their way into Bleek's thinking whenever he had a few moments to himself, which wasn't often.

The biggest event of the first session was now looming before them. It was called the "Vancouver Maneuver." This was designed to give all the trainees experience in group evangelism, to trust God in a thing not yet tried by them, and most importantly to bring people to Christ.

The day in Vancouver began at the Navigator home of Don and Shirley Lawrie, where they all gathered to unite and strengthen their hearts in the Word and prayer. Then they were off to the campus of the University of British Columbia (UBC), to talk to men and women in the dorms and cafeteria about Christ and to invite them all to a hootenanny on the beach near the campus that night. One trainee on the way to UBC asked how they could spend all afternoon in evangelism? How could they find enough people? After being on the campus for only a short while, he remarked, "How can we talk to all these people; there are so many?" His eyes, like the rest of them, were being opened to seeing the multitudes and feeling concern.

Sixty to one hundred gathered that evening on the beach to listen to Bleek on his gut-bucket, and Dave Kraft, Rich Sundahl and Bart Walker on their guitars, sing some special numbers and lead them all in song. Several testimonies were shared by the trainees, and a life-changing message was delivered. At least one person came to Christ that night; another did two days later; and still another, three weeks later. Several more were interested and seriously considering the claims of Christ. It was a fitting closure to five weeks of learning to operate as a team and yet function as an individual and watch God use them to bring people to Himself.

Larry expressed the feelings of all of them that night when he turned a cartwheel as they walked down a sidewalk in Vancouver to their cars Elven Smith, from the Navigator home in Seattle, came to the rescue of the much-wearied staff at the end of those first five weeks. He had a friend in Seattle who owned a 37-foot yacht named the Glama Paka. They took four of the staff at a time on a two-day salmon fishing break. It was a wonderful time to relax and refresh themselves, both spiritually and physically.

Bleek welcomed that time away to think through the details for the remaining weeks, and he spent concentrated time with God praying for his eight new team members. This would be his first time to head up such a program. He was more than ready to meet the challenge as the new trainees began to arrive at the ranch, and the second session began.

CHAPTER 15 - LEFTOVERS

Word reached Larry that Tim Kuntz, his friend from ISU, had arrived at the bus station in Haney. He would be participating in the second part of the training at Timberline. Larry was excited to hear Tim had arrived. He borrowed the car keys and took off for the station. He had met Tim back at school and, on the trip to the Whing Ding that Christmas, had gotten to know him even better. So he was eager to welcome him to the great Northwest.

Buddies from Timberline
Art Tyree, Larry, Mick Van Zandt

Tim didn't recognize Larry at first, in his big straw hat and bibbed overalls, but his excited, enthusiastic welcome gave him away. During the whole five miles back to Timberline, which was now all dried out, Tim got filled in on how God was blessing so he, too, arrived at the ranch all fired up. Bleek rustled him up some sandwiches in the kitchen. He and "Cookie" had become the best of friends; his heart always went out to the kitchen crews since his days in the Glen kitchen. Then Tim got settled in and, even though he was not a member of Bleek's Leftovers, they did spend time together during those next weeks.

On one such occasion, Tim thanked Larry for praying for his parents. He said he had never heard anyone else pray for them before. And it was very encouraging for him.

Things really got underway on August 1, when Bleek took his Leftovers on a special trip into the Simon Frazier campus to scout out the land, in order to determine the possibilities of ministering there.

During the afternoon, Larry talked with a young man named Ralph Johnston, who was Student Body treasurer and their special tour guide of the campus. During the course of the tour, several of the Leftovers shared their testimonies with Ralph and he seemed very open and encouraged. Their conclusion at the end of the day was that the land looked great and they should move ahead!

That evening they all met at the Vancouver Navigator home with Don Lawrie to discuss their objectives and to do some brainstorming. Don explained that one of the purposes of this venture was to spearhead the initial phase of starting a work among students that were enrolled during the three remaining weeks of the quarter, which could then tie in with the Navigator ministry in the Vancouver area in the fall. They discussed their objectives and agreed upon the following:

> *Primarily, to find about two men and two girls who were interested and eager to get some personal help and training in their Christian lives.*

Secondarily, to gain an understanding of how to begin a new work: finding out where to start, what to do, how to solve problems that occur, etc. Also, to put into practical application some of the principles learned during the first session of training.

A Vancouver BC Bible study in 1966

Then they headed back to the ranch to get a good night's sleep. The next day, Tuesday, they brushed up on their testimonies and the Bridge Illustration. The following day, Wednesday, they prepared to get into the battle. Bleek's enthusiasm was contagious and, as long as he was leading them, they'd agreed to follow him anywhere.

Nevertheless, as they were returning to their cabins from that first day at Simon Frasier, the reality of their mission began to sink in. The Leftovers wondered if they had learned enough as trainees to do it. Did they know the

Bridge Illustration well enough, etc? Tuesday was busy. The Leftovers began their days 20 minutes earlier than the trainees, so they got some extra time in on calisthenics. Bleek conditioned his men, as well as himself, for pre-Marine training. Part of their work assignment was to survey all the ranch work projects and put them in priority. Then those projects were done as a team with different individuals in charge during the session. And now, a new emphasis was put on the Leftovers in the area of details. Not only were the girls to dust and clean the cabin of one of the staff members, but it was to pass the white glove test. The guys, as well, had to shape up. The steps that were painted, the nails that were pounded, the infield that was raked, were all to be done to the very best of their ability and with their whole hearts as unto the Lord.

The hour before lunch was spent in either preparation of or discussion of, a chapter analysis in I John. As Leftovers, the men and women met together and created a real bond as they discovered they had some of the same problems and fears. God took each chapter and gave them answers to their needs.

Following lunch they got together in pairs, sharpened their weapons for the following day, and prayed for one another, since they were all a bit nervous as well as excited. Then came a challenge from the trainees that they could beat the Leftovers at a game of softball. The challenge was accepted.

That night following dinner, the trainees and "Garbage Crew," as the Leftovers were now fondly called, met together. Bleek spoke to them on "Witnessing," since they were all preparing to do some evangelism during that week. His message followed this outline.

Witnessing

We hear about it—few are involved in it.

What God sees:

Ezekiel 22:30 No man to stand in the gap
Isaiah 41:28 God looks for a man (or woman)
Isaiah 57:1 He finds no man
Isaiah 59:16 There is no man for God
Isaiah 63:5 He finds no man and no help
Isaiah 64:7 There were none to take hold on God
Isaiah 66:4 God repays the ones not helping
Psalm 107:2 God wants us to share and He will use any that are willing

What kind of a person is God looking for?

I Corinthians 1:26-31 Not many wise, or mighty or noble, in the flesh, are called, but those who depend on God for everything, and glory in Him

Why does God use men and women?

God has enlisted us in a battle, going out to capture the enemy

*What is **witnessing**?*

Sharing with others the message of Christ

*What is **evangelism**?*

Sharing the message and bringing people to a logical decision for Christ

Why witness or evangelize?

1. *God commands it.*
   Matthew 28:19-20-GO!
   Mark 6:15 "Go into all the world"
   I Peter 3:15 "Be ready always to give an answer"
   Acts 1:8 In the power of the Holy Spirit, begin where you are and increase your ministry to reach the world

2. *We should see that people NEED Jesus.*
   Matthew 9:36-38 The harvest is great, but the workers are few. Pray that God will send workers into His harvest fields
3. *It is key to our spiritual health.*
   I Samuel 17:20-54
   It keeps us keen and sharp
   It keeps us expectant
   It keeps us refreshed
   It keeps us advancing
   It brings about victory for God

How does one prepare?

1. *What is my heart situation? Am I sure I really belong to Christ?*
   I John 5:11-13 Assurance of salvation
2. *Is my relationship with God pure? Psalm 51, Malachi 2:6*
   I John 1:9 Confess and be forgiven
3. *Do I believe God will do it?*
   John 14:12 If you ask in my name, I will do it

What do I need to do?

1. *Win a sympathetic hearing. God wins them, He's alert to them*
2. *Present the gospel of Jesus Christ (sometimes we are so tactful we never attack)*
   Romans 1:16 Be not ashamed, go in His power
   Romans 10:17 If we don't speak, they will not hear
3. *What is the Gospel?*
   I Corinthians 15:3-4 Christ died, was buried and rose again, for us
4. *Give them an opportunity to respond*
   Acts 26:27 Do you believe?

5. *Leave the door open.*
   Mark 12:28 Let them ask questions
   Remember, things that bring the greatest joy are the hardest to do!

Then Larry told the following story about Charlie:

There was this guy named Charlie who went into the Marines, and he was always doing things wrong, always fouling up. Well, he finally got through basic training and went out to the front lines. They were overrun, all the enemy was coming at them, pouring over the hill and somebody yelled "Retreat." So they all retreated.

Then they said, "Okay, who is here?" They figured out who was there; and one guy was missing. It was Charlie. They thought, "Oh no, poor old Charlie, poor guy, he's probably lying out there in some foxhole in a pool of blood. Poor Charlie. So they were lamenting Charlie and, all of a sudden, somebody yelled, "There's somebody coming." They all got down behind a little knoll there. Over the hill way off on the horizon, they saw three guys coming, so they aimed their rifles and were ready to fire. Pretty soon they noticed that it was two guys walking in front of one with a rifle. They kept watching and, as they got closer, they realized, "It is; it's Charlie. It's fantastic. It's Charlie and he's got two prisoners. It's amazing!"

Finally they got him back, they took his prisoners, and they were all gathered around Charlie and really happy to see him. Then they asked, "Charlie, how did you do it?" And Charlie said, "Man, it's easy. There are thousands of them out there. Go out and get you a couple."

That's the idea in witnessing. There are thousands of them out there, so go out and get you a couple.

During their 40-minute drive to SFU the following afternoon, they prayed and planned their last minute strategy. They would go two by two, a more experienced person with a less experienced one. Since there were three girls, two would go and the third would pray. They would trade off until they were ready to go on their own. They had noticed on their last visit that on nice days, the campus mall was a place to find students enjoying fellowship and the sun, so they chose that as their place to begin. They would meet again at 5:00 p.m. to share their war stories and the blessings God had given. And God did bless in a number of ways.

One team reported that they had met a guy named Doug Rempel, who worked in the University Theater. He was really a sharp guy. They all felt that God had given them two men who could really be an influence on the campus: Ralph, the student body treasurer, and now Doug.

On the way back to the ranch, Bleek drew them out as to what the day had meant to them. One said that he had never been so scared. But that it was good, because he knew he needed God and He had been right there with him. Another shared that he wanted to spend more time in the Word so he would have more answers. Another, that he needed to nail down references to his verses so he could turn to them quickly and quote them accurately. Still another said she had found herself giving some wise advice that she hadn't been following herself and that she had better shape up. Another felt that all the prayer behind this had made the difference, and he wanted to remain faithful in prayer.

Bleek was confident, as they pulled back into the ranch for supper, that the afternoon had been profitable and that God was pleased. Blake was excited, too, as he listened to their reports that evening and talked with them about world vision.

Thursday was spent at the ranch and, in the afternoon, team played team in the Timberline Olympics. Friday they were back at SFU. This time, they invited those they talked with to go back to the ranch with them that evening for supper. Several responded.

On Sunday morning, an engineer from Seattle named Warfield Munce, came to speak to them about the Person of Christ and, with Him as their focal point, the following week was spent in intensive evangelism on the campus.

One afternoon as they stopped for coffee on the way back to the ranch, they again shared their afternoon adventures. One person said they had a guy who hadn't known much about Christ before and, when they told him all he needed to do was ask Christ into his life, he had said that that was too simple. They just hadn't been able to convince him otherwise.

So Larry turned to the others and asked them what they would say if that happened to them. One volunteered that the Bible says in John 14:6 that *"Jesus saith unto him, I am the Way, the Truth and the Life: no man cometh unto the Father but by Me."* Christ is the only Way to God.

Another agreed and quoted Ephesians 2:8-9 that says, *"For by grace are ye saved through faith; and that not of yourselves: it is the gift of God: not of works, lest any man should boast."* We can't earn it.

The team explained that they had shared all that on the Bridge Illustration. They had pointed out all the ways man tries to get to God, how they all fall short, and Christ is the only Bridge that goes all the way. And, still, he hadn't believed it could be that easy, they lamented.

Bleek continued to ask questions and guide their thinking until they finally concluded that if God, Who knew every possibility, had not made it that easy for us, then it would have automatically eliminated some people. Lack of ability or intelligence, or something else, would have made it impossible for everyone to be saved. It had to be a condition that young and old, weak and strong, could respond to alike, to be really just and fair. Although it was very easy for us, it was a gift that cost God the very life of His only Son. The group then began to pray that they could find that young man again and give him an answer that would really make sense.

Time had sped by, and they were due back at the ranch. The café bill came and they pooled their resources. They had 35 cents, and the bill was $2.15! Everyone had thought everyone else had some money. They were $1.80 short, and the food had already been consumed. Bleek was ready to do the dishes to pay the bill when one of the Leftovers came up with $20.00. Larry was surprised and he showed it. He expressed his feelings, that "they had a common pot. What had he held out for?" Larry later apologized for having been so tactless, but the feeling that they were a team, there to help anyone in need, was still a strong feeling that Larry had, and so did his Leftovers by then.

That Thursday, when they returned to the campus, Bleek talked to a young man in the mall named Colin McKenzie. He, like Bleek, had been reared in a Christian home and felt that he had been a Christian since the age of nine. Larry said Colin's testimony sounded just like his. Bleek told him that his folks really loved the Lord and that he had first responded to Christ when he was about eight. He went on to share that somehow it had taken until he was 17 to really get turned on about the Christian life.

That got Colin's attention, and he asked Larry what had made the difference when he was 17?

Larry explained that one day a young man had come into his father's furniture store. Larry told how he knew this man was interested in spiritual things and as they had talked the guy really put him on the spot. He had asked him, *"Larry, if you were to die right now, do you know for sure that you would go to be with God?"* Larry shared that he had had some close calls that summer but, for the first time in his life, he had really faced that question, and he didn't know for sure. He had been to church and camps for 17 years, but he had never known in his heart for sure that he had eternal life.

He explained to Colin how Don MacDonald had, in a very simple way, told him how to invite Jesus Christ to come in and take over his life and rule it. He then knew for sure that he would go to be with God when he died.

Colin obviously wanted to hear more, so Bleek continued by drawing the Bridge Illustration for him, to explain the things Don had told Larry. Then Bleek shared the verse that he had never known was in the Bible before that memorable day. I John 5:11-12: *"And this is the record, that God hath given to us eternal life, and this life is in His Son. He that hath the Son hath life; and he that hath not the Son of God hath not life. These things have I written unto you that believe on the name of the Son of God; that ye may* ***know*** *that ye have eternal life, and that ye may believe on the name of the Son of God."*

Larry told Colin that he wanted to know, so he had bowed his head and prayed to God, telling Him that he realized that he had done some wrong things in his life, that he needed God to forgive him. He had said he realized that he was not sure of heaven, but he wanted to be sure. So Larry had asked Jesus Christ to come into his life if He never had before. And then he had tacked a special request on the end of his prayer: he wanted to know for sure if his salvation was now taken care of.

Larry told Colin that when he finished his prayer, he hadn't jumped off the floor spitting BBs or sprouted wings and floated on air! Colin chuckled. But, Larry continued saying, in his heart something had happened. For the first time he could remember, his heart was satisfied and he had a peace down inside that he knew would really last, and he told Colin that it had! It was now six years later, and it had been the most abundant and most exciting life he had ever known.

Colin expressed sincerely that this was what he was looking for and hadn't found yet.

When Larry asked him if there was any reason why they couldn't get that issue settled right then, Colin realized that the SFU bell had rung and there were students everywhere hurrying to their next classes and shouting back and forth. But Bleek asked again, '"How about it?" and Colin responded. They bowed their heads right there, in the midst of everything, and prayed.

Colin grinned widely as the new transaction had taken place. The mall, as well as his heart, was at peace. He expressed his thanks that Larry had pursued this. Colin explained that he might have put it off too long had they waited.

Larry had told him that he had the philosophy that if a guy was going to do anything with Jesus Christ, he shouldn't be taken off to a corner or in a quiet spot to accept Christ. Wherever a guy was when he indicated a need, his need could be met.

Colin had witnessed that Larry was so proud of Jesus Christ that he hadn't cared how many people were around. Consequently, Colin had a desire to get to know the Lord like that. Now there was a third solid contact on the SFU campus, and they began to meet regularly to build this relationship with Christ. That same night back at the ranch, they had a pizza dinner, Bleek's specialty, especially for their SFU contacts, and Ralph, Doug and Colin were there for the dinner and the skit night with the staff and had a wonderful evening.

That weekend Larry Blake, who was now getting around pretty well on his sore ankle, had yet another obstacle to surmount. Word came that his father had been killed in a car accident. All the trainees and Leftovers rallied to the occasion and supplied the necessary money for Blake's sudden flight home.

The night before the Leftovers were to drive into town to pick up Larry Blake, Bleek spoke to all of them on the topic of "Discouragement." Bleek was impressed with Blake's ability to cope with the sudden home-going of his father. They were close, and it was not easy, but Blake was encouraged. Larry challenged the trainees to ask themselves, "What about them?" He told them that he was convinced that discouragement was one of the best-used weapons of the enemy to defeat Christians and keep them from victory. They agreed they had all experienced discouragement in their lives. So Larry shared with them the following challenge.

Discouragement

1. *How does God look at discouragement?*
   Deuteronomy 1:21—Don't be discouraged.
   Joshua 1:6,7,9—Be of good courage and not dismayed.
   Isaiah 41:10—Be not dismayed.
   Our doubts bring disillusionment and we can't see God's plan.
   Result—despair and complete discouragement
2. *The biggest thing that can multiply a doubt is other people.*
   I Kings 18,19—Elijah doubted and became discouraged when Jezebel threatened his life,

even though this was just after God's great victory.

3. *When we take our eyes off of Christ and look at the situation, it gets bigger and bigger and weighs us down.*
4. *What to do when discouraged?*
   I Peter 4:12—Expect trials.
   James 1:2-4 (Phillips Translation)—Welcome temptations and problems as friends; realize they come to strengthen our walk with the Lord.
   Romans 14:22—The D.D. Principle—Don't Doubt!
   Psalm 73:26—Look to God.
   Isaiah 41:10—In spite of discouragement, Move Out.

Midway through August, Bleek sent a letter home, a portion of which read:

> *There are about eight guys and gals who stayed after the first session, and I have been given the oversight of these, a real challenge in building and helping these lives for God's use and direction. We, as a team, are asking God to open up a new work among students at the new university in Vancouver (Simon Fraser University).*
>
> *God has already given us contact with some Christians on campus and with some others who are very close to receiving Christ. Pray for Ralph Johnson, Student Body treasurer; his secretary, Denese Gerley; Colin McKenzie and Gillian Lindredge. Have the people at church claim Isaiah 58:10-12 for this work we are doing and pray for these people. Pray for direction for me, too. God*

may be directing me to stay on here and head up the work at this university until January, when I head to the Marine Corps.

God did lead that way. Those final weeks at Timberline, Bleek kept so busy with his team, his contacts at SFU, and with sudden plans for a big evangelistic thrust at Crescent Beach south of Vancouver at White Rock, that Blake feared Larry would burn himself out. He was thankful, for Bleek's sake, that the program was about over.

The Crescent Beach evangelism was in response to a plea for help from the First Presbyterian Church of New Westminster, B.C. They coordinated the day's activities with Doug Carley, the youth minister at First Presbyterian, and on August 25 God truly blessed their efforts.

It began at 9:30 with breakfast at the church and a briefing on the day's planned activities. At noon they paired off, a church youth with a Timberline youth, and spent the afternoon talking with people on and around the beach area. Those contacted were mostly high-school age.

At 4:00, they met again to plan the evening of folk singing, skits and testimonies.

At 7:30, a hootenanny on the beach began. At 8:00, as it began to grow chilly, a unique band composed of ten people—each having an instrument such as pot lids for symbols, a pan for a drum, potato whistles for horns, and a plunger for the baton twirler—began to march. It led the people from the beach to a new location for the rest of the program. They convened in a home about one mile from the beach. Almost all of the 200 on the beach followed the band and 185 were at the second meeting. Even when eight hoodlums showed up with the objective of breaking up the party, they found the program so interesting that they wanted to know what would happen next, so they melted right into the group of enthusiastic onlookers. At the end of the meeting, about ten young people showed a sincere interest in learning more about Christ.

Doug Carley's parting words to the Timberline gang that night were, "Becoming a Christian has been the most exciting time in my life; but this hootenanny was second!"

Everyone's faith was increased by seeing God work in such obvious and unusual ways. Having evaluated the experience, it was not clear why God had chosen to work so miraculously. Some suggestions that were offered were: 1. Specific prayer over promises; 2. A "Prayer Consciousness" that God gave them; 3. Doug Carley's faith; 4. Sharing their lives, not preaching; 5. God-prepared hearts; 6. Due to the short notice (one day prior to the occasion they had been asked), there was no time to be concerned about food, rehearsals, etc., so they were more concerned with praying and presenting Christ; 7. Unity of heart among the trainees; and 8. Because Romans 9:15-16 tell of God's sovereignty. *"...I will have mercy on whom I will have mercy, and I will have compassion on whom I will have compassion. So then it is not of him that willeth, nor of him that runneth, but of God that sheweth mercy."*

Coming down from a "high" like the Crescent Beach evangelism, Larry knew he must spend additional time in the Word. Satan always attacked the hardest after spiritual victories.

Once again Larry turned to Isaiah 45—that portion of Scripture God had given him when he had gone back to ISU the previous fall. From verses one and two, he had, indeed, seen God open the doors for that final year. *"I will go before thee, and make the crooked places straight; I will break in pieces the gates of brass, and cut in sunder the bars of iron:"* This passage spoke to Larry about those obstacles that might, otherwise, stand in the way of getting his B.S. degree.

From verse three, through his Quiet Times he had seen God showing Himself and His will—*"I will give thee the treasures of darkness, and hidden riches of secret places."* God began more and more specifically to lead him to the men of the United States Marine Corps.

As he again read the portion from verses 11-25 and thought of the training just ahead of him, God gave him these verses afresh:

Vs. 11-ASK *"Ask Me of things to come concerning My sons, and concerning the work of My hands command ye Me."* Larry had asked "where?" and God had answered, "The Marines," and Larry had real peace in God's answer.

Vs. 13-JOB *"I have raised him up in righteousness, and I will direct all his ways: he shall build my city, and he shall let go my captives, not for price nor reward, saith the Lord of Hosts."* As a Marine, Larry was convinced he must let Christ live in him so that his Marine buddies who would be placing their lives in harms' way, could see Christ when they looked at Larry. His job was to build a relationship so he could point them to Christ, Who alone could set the captives free.

Vs. 14-MOTIVE That men of stature might respond to Christ and be followed up and encouraged by Larry.

Vs. 24-25-PROMISE These verses gave him a new spurt of confidence in his call, for it would not be by Larry's works that these men would respond, but by the Lord's righteousness and strength. It would be to the Lord that they would come, not to Larry.

To be a Christian Marine was the highest calling God had yet given him and one that was to be the greatest challenge of all.

Just before the Timberline training program broke up, Bleek called together all the trainees who were heading back to ISU, and they prayed for the men and women back home and their impact on the campus that fall. On the very last night for the Timberline gang that summer, they held their banquet.

They all knew Bleek would soon be heading to Quantico for his Marine training, so the Leftovers got together to make a special presentation at the banquet.

They told him that he had meant a lot to all of them there that summer and how much they had enjoyed his humor, encouragement, comfort and patience. They had a little something that they wanted to give him as he anticipated soon becoming a Marine.

Their thoughtfulness meant a lot to Bleek, who felt somewhat guilty taking anything for doing what he had enjoyed so much. But, as he took the beautifully wrapped package, he sensed that all was not serious.

He put the package to his ear a moment and shook it carefully. He accused them of maybe putting a time-bomb in it, because he was sure he had it coming. Then, he opened the box and threw back his head to roar with laughter. He pulled out a toy tank. His response? "Tanks a lot" and he took his seat.

CHAPTER 16 - VANCOUVER, B.C.

Larry with Don Lawrie and two sons in Vancouver BC

Larry was happily welcomed into the Lawrie family the day Timberline training was completed. As Bleek drove the now very familiar and well-worn 35 miles into Vancouver and the Lawrie home, he was anticipating his time with Don, Shirley, and their three sons, Bobby, Scotty and Kevin. Also living with the Lawries were Barry Nerney from Australia, Mac Jardine, and now Bleek. There was never a dull moment, which suited Bleek to a tee. They were all there for one purpose—for training to better equip themselves to reach men and women for Jesus Christ. They prayed and planned, did Bible studies and evangelism, ate and joked and worked together for a real impact for Christ on the campuses of the University of British Columbia (UBC) and Simon Fraser University (SFU).

Sissy Gates and Nancy McRae, the girls' leaders from Timberline, came for a couple of days and went sightseeing in Victoria before Sissy flew back home to D.C. While they waited for passenger loading, Larry commented that he would be pretty close to her home town when he was at Quantico, and he promised to look her up. She said that would be great. Then Bleek just had to add the request that she get her hair cut while she was down there. Sissy swung her purse at him but missed.

On the way back home Scotty, then age 11 and very perceptive of the guys living with them, asked Larry very quietly why he didn't like Sissy's hair? Larry explained to his little buddy that he really did like it, but she was just so much fun to tease. Then he explained a little more. If a guy is attracted to a girl because of any physical attribute, that's not good. Her hair could keep a guy from getting to know her, and Larry knew Sissy was worth getting to know.

Then Scotty got a knowing little grin and proclaimed to Bleek that he liked her, didn't he?

Larry told Scotty that it was really hard to find any girl that he didn't like. Therefore, he was leaving the choice up to God. Only God knew the if's and when's and who's. Right then, he explained, he knew God had called him to men, men like Scotty himself. Scotty sat a little taller all the rest of the way home.

Bleek followed through with Scotty, no matter how busy he got. He prayed with him, had Quiet Times with him, rough-housed, and played games; a real spirit of camaraderie developed during those next three months.

Shirley appreciated him, even in the kitchen. For such a big man with such a big appetite, he really knew how to be helpful. He knew the pressure of getting everything on the table at once, while it was still warm. So whenever he was home for supper, he was there to help dish up, and that was no small task. Even without guests, there were many hungry men to feed, and many were the nights when extra plates and chairs were added.

Shirley found she had not only Glen Eyrie to thank for his kitchen perceptiveness, but Maranatha for his painting ability. He and Barry tackled the front bedroom with paint, and Larry proved to be an a-number-one decorator. Shirley didn't have to do a thing. He took down the drapes and rods, painted, cleaned the windows and mirrors, and put things back in place. All the while, he and Barry were listening to tapes and discussing their meanings.

Shirley was delighted with the end results and praised them for their work. Larry explained that at Maranatha, where he spent a whole summer painting, he hadn't really enjoyed it all that much. So, he had listened to tapes by Dawson or Sanny or Eims to spark it up. It had worked there in Vancouver as well. Plus, just looking at Barry's smile had made the painting incidental to the great fellowship and learning they had experienced.

Larry had no idea just how much fellowship and learning lay ahead for that fall. The second week he was there was packed with preparations for a weekend camp-out retreat at Lake Chelan in eastern Washington on September 9-11. Don had given Bleek the responsibility of getting all the camping gear lined up for everyone who was going from the Vancouver area. He was to go ahead of them and set up camp, since the rest of them would have to get a late start from Vancouver. So Bleek and Colin got to Chelan early Friday afternoon before anyone else had arrived.

Bleek watched Colin as he gazed out upon the clear blue waters of the lake and then up into the blue sky with only a wisp of a cloud here and there. A breeze rustled the leaves, birds sang, and squirrels came to investigate the promise of a meal soon to be at hand. Larry thought about his and Colin's conversation down here and the conversations before that, dating back to their first encounter in the mall at SFU. Larry considered how much alike the two of them were. They both liked sports, gospel music, song leading, eating and, yea, even girls. Then Larry prayed that God would give Colin a single heart toward Jesus, putting Him first. He asked God to give Colin a burden for the men that only He could give. And also to use himself, in every way He wanted to.

It was time for them to get busy and set up a couple of tents before taking a swimming break. Colin agreed wholeheartedly, with Larry's familiar response, "Good Deal!"

Because of the picnic tables and camp stove arrangement, they began setting up the tents where they felt they would be the most conveniently located. The afternoon got hotter, but they decided to stick to it until they were done. Finally Larry called out, "Last one in is a rotten egg."

During that next half hour, as the blue waters supported their strong frames, Larry's "Roman nose," as McIntrye had called it, turned a salmon pink.

Larry had just commented how easy it was to praise God in a setting like this, when the first two cars drove in with some of the gang from Seattle. Ron Jackson, the tall, slender coordinator for the conference, looked the grounds over while Bleek and Colin got back into their work clothes.

Maybe we could help the new arrivals set up their tents, Larry commented, as they walked over to Ron, who was busy giving orders. Larry only got his "Can we..." out before Ron cut in with the orders to take down the tents that he and Colin had just put up and move them to a different location. The tents were standing in the area where Ron envisioned the meetings to be held. With a quick "Sorry," Ron was off to his next duty.

Bleek looked at Colin and then at his watch. It was getting on toward supper time and the gang from Vancouver should arrive soon after that. Larry reflected on Ron's words, "You'll have to take yours down and move them all over here." Okay, Bleek, he thought to himself, he's right. And you knew this would be a possibility, so why fight it—get to work.

Larry tried to be cheerful as he and Colin pulled up stakes and hauled the tents to their new location. He told Colin he felt like a couple of Old Testament Israelites, packing up their tents to move on.

Colin looked a bit puzzled, as well as disgusted with the whole thing.

Larry explained that he was referring to every time the cloud or pillar of fire moved, the children of Israel had to pack up and move, too. They both decided they were thankful that they would probably only have to do this once, where the Israelites did it for forty years! Larry had been caught up short since his comment on how easy it was to praise the Lord here. His initial reaction to Ron had made him a hypocrite. Just let some little thing change his plans and pride had loomed up big and black. His heart had not immediately praised God or given thanks.

As the sun was getting ready to set, Larry went down by the lake away from the others, feasted on God's Word, and confessed his wrong attitude and his arrogant spirit. He prayed once again for a servant's heart, as well as a thankful one. He knew God knew all the details about this, so he just left his case with God. He thanked God for Ron and for the glimpse of his own black heart. He asked God to show him how to praise Him rather than to try to justify himself.

Bleek was back just as Colin finished up his meal, and off they went again to work on the two or three remaining tents. It was getting dark. It seemed like old Satan was working overtime, hiding ropes and splitting pegs, so when Vancouver did arrive all was not ready and waiting for them.

Shirley was the first to greet them and commented, half jokingly and half irritated, that the tents weren't all up yet. Her comment was met without a response, except for Larry's, "I'm sorry" and the pounding of more tent pegs. Don, too, showed his disappointment. He called Barry and Mac to give them a hand and then said to Larry that he had really expected it to be all done.

Again, Larry merely said he was really sorry.

Don and Mac set to work on another tent while Barry helped the others unload and haul stuff to those tents that were done. Colin questioned Larry about why he hadn't told anyone that they had put the tents up twice. Larry said it was because that would have made it look like it was Ron's fault, and it wasn't. Don had every right to be disappointed in him, not in Ron.

Colin tried to protest, but Larry said he felt it was all squared away. He said he was sorry, however, that Colin had pulled double duty out of it. Colin assured him that he was just glad he could help and, once again, Larry heard himself saying with all his heart, "It's not hard to praise God for conditions like this."

That weekend God worked in many hearts and answered some Timberline prayers. Ralph Johnston, whom Larry had met his first day on the SFU campus and who had visited Timberline, could no longer put off his decision for Christ. He gave his heart to the Lord. It also brought about a new commitment from Colin, who went on to become a strong and faithful part of the SFU Navigator ministry.

As the fall quarter began, Larry's ministry schedule once again began to mount. On Tuesday and Thursday mornings at 7:00, Bleek would meet with Colin for a Quiet Time. Once a week, he and Colin and Ralph had a Bible study, and Thursday nights were evangelism in the dorms.

Toward the end of September, Judy Robbins came to the Lawries. She was impressed with the changes she saw in Larry since her last contact with him at the Glen in 1964. She told Shirley she couldn't believe he was the same young man; he had grown so much in his faith. Shirley was a bit surprised to learn that he hadn't always been this way. Judy saw him now as much more stable and mature in the Lord, and he finally seemed to know where he was going with his life. They both agreed it was great.

The momentum of September gathered even more speed in October. Judy and Millie Young moved into their new apartment on Osler Street, from which they would minister to the girls in the area. This got the Navigator home team and the campus teams well under way. Don called the home team together on Monday mornings at 6:00 for prayer and man-to-man principles and ideas. On Friday mornings at 6:00, they had Bible study together. Monday afternoons, Bleek now met with Colin, Ralph and Doug for Bible study at 4:00. Tuesday and Thursday mornings at 7:00 was still time with Colin, and Thursday evenings was evangelism. The rest of the time was quickly filled in with people from anywhere and everywhere he went. He had a God-given magnetism to draw men and to be drawn to men. At a swimming pool one afternoon with Ralph and Colin, he noticed a guy sitting in the bleachers. Larry said, "Let's go get him." Off they went to talk to the young man, and they presented Christ to him.

Another time they met a guy named Tony, and Larry asked him if he would be interested in a personal explanation of how one can become a Christian. He said he would, so Larry shared the Bridge Illustration and Tony said "Yes" to Jesus Christ.

Ralph was especially thrilled when an old drinking buddy of his, named Les Howard, invited Jesus into his life.

And when another drinking friend, Jim Fischer, showed a real interest in finding something to fill his life, Ralph rejoiced when his friend's excitement about hunting ducks changed to excitement about knowing Christ.

As the home team prayed together about their two ministries on the local college campuses, Larry became involved on the campus of UBC as well when it did not conflict with SFU.

On one such occasion, Larry took a young man named Gordy Tansley out on his first evangelism. Gordy was a sharp guy who was married and teaching in a nearby high school. It was the same school in which Mac was also teaching. Gordy wanted to learn to share his faith in Christ, so Don sent him with Larry to learn how.

Bleek knew that his own heart beat faster when he approached a person about his personal commitment to Christ, and he had been doing this consistently now for six years. Gordy, who was brand new at this, could not help but feel the fiery darts of Satan, named fear and doubt, because the enemy certainly did not want to see young men coming to Christ. So Bleek, who was always thrilled to get involved in a battle against the forces of evil, carefully led Gordy into it so he'd become a real fighter and see the fun involved in sharing Christ.

The dorm they were to attack had three floors. As they entered the first floor, Bleek could see Gordy was anticipating them knocking on room number one. So he told Gordy they would be starting on the top floor. Larry explained that the men up there would think, wow, they came all the way up here just to talk to them.

When they got to the second floor, Larry again stopped and they shot up a prayer ahead of them so the guys would be prepared by the time they got there. It's not surprising then that by the time they reached the third floor, even

Gordy's heart was prepared, as Larry's thoughtfulness had taken the edge off of his nervousness.

The first door they knocked on Larry said, "Hi, I'm Larry Bleeker and this is Gordy Tansley. We were just wondering if you were interested in spiritual things."

The young man's response was a flat, "No, I'm not."

Unshaken, Larry smiled and said, "Oh, you don't drink, eh?"

The guy who had been about to shut his door opened it a little wider, scratched his head and, because of the shocking effect of Larry's response, stood and listened as Bleek shared Christ.

By the time Gordy was given an opportunity to share, he was more than eager. He had seen certain questions come up again and again, and Larry had answered them calmly from Scripture, with no panic or defensiveness. Genuine concern flowed from Larry that these men hear and understand that Christ died for them. He wanted them to realize that He wanted to give their lives purpose and fulfillment.

Larry's technique launched Gordy on evangelism that was fun and exciting. It also developed a great friendship that eventually led to Larry going over to Gordy and Mac's school to help get a football team organized and coached. The young people couldn't help but respond to the enthusiasm and wholeheartedness of their new coach, and they put all they had into the practice times and games they played.

One Saturday in October, the Northwest gang met in Seattle for a planning session at the Smith's Navigator home. Then, the following week, a group of them headed over to Pullman. The night before the trip to Pullman, Bleek invited Ralph and Colin's parents and the young men to dinner at the Lawries. He was concerned that the parents get to know the Lawries and what all the trips and activities were about. They had a good evening together, sharing how God was using the Navigator ministry and listening to a tape together. Both Ralph and Colin went to Pullman the next morning.

That fall was special to Larry. He appreciated being able to be himself and to find out exactly where he fit into the scheme of things. Navigators had greatly influenced and changed his life, and he was right at home in the midst of its ministry as God opened doors to meet his every need.

The ministry at SFU was well under way. Colin and Ralph, in particular, were available for Larry to pour his life into. Men were responding to Christ's hand on their lives, and they met young men everywhere who were interested in knowing Him.

On a trip back from Mac's home in Kamloops, they picked up a man on the road. They brought him all the way to the Lawries' home. They got him into a tub, washed and ironed his clothes, gave him good food and a clean bed and, the next day, they found a place for him to stay. He'd never had anyone care for him like that before, and he responded to Christ's love.

The time with the Lawries was special, too. The men on the team—Mac, Barry, Don and Larry—prayed together, studied the Scriptures together, laughed and worked and even cried together.

When ends didn't meet financially, Larry and Don took off together with blacktop to find potholes to fill. They filled paper bags with blacktop and then drove around until they found a driveway or a parking lot with holes. Then, together, they would go out and contract to fill up the holes for ten or twenty or thirty dollars, whatever it would take. One afternoon they noticed a driveway with several bad holes, so Don went to the door. A very nice lady answered. Don offered to fix the potholes in her driveway for $24.00.

She thought that would be lovely, but she wanted to know if the stuff they filled it with was any good. Don hollered over to Larry to fill a small pothole for her. Larry had begun before Don finished his sentence and, in no time, he had the bag out, had whipped it open, and had the pothole fixed. Don told the lady that is what it would look like, and the stuff they used was good. Her immediate reply was that if it looked that good, to go ahead and do them all. They did and found it didn't even cost her $24.00. They left a happy woman with a nice, smooth driveway about a half hour later.

Another time, as they were waiting for a ferry on Vancouver Island to take them back to the mainland, they saw a hole right beside the car. They looked at each other. They still had two bags of blacktop left in the car, so off they went to talk to the ticket taker in the toll booth. They said they could fix the hole for him for $9.00. At first he thought they were kidding, but when he discovered they were serious, he decided to take them up on their offer. So, as the ferry was docking and cars were getting off, they were happily pounding the blacktop into the hole. Then they packed up their tools, put them in the car, and drove on the ferry. That was their ferry ticket.

Young kids were still an important part of Bleek's life, especially the Lawrie boys. Times spent with Scotty in the book of Job were special, as Bleek got to witness this young lad's desire to know and serve God really opening up. He was so much like Larry himself that Shirley gained some real insight into her middle son from her talks with Larry.

God even provided the frosting on the cake through a Timberline Leftover, little Carel Moore. She had a red sports car, and she made it available to Larry whenever he needed or wanted it. This was a far cry from the good old "dead rabbit" back in Ames. He was always careful not to abuse the privilege, and it came back each time with a full tank of gas if not a wax job to boot.

Carel lived in a large apartment building in Vancouver, and Larry would stop by every once in awhile. One night there was a knock at the door, and Carel opened it to find Larry lying on the floor, all out of breath, and a twinkle in his eyes. Carel asked what had happened, and Larry managed to say, "I ran up here." Carel couldn't believe it. She was on the 12th floor, and they had elevators. Why would he do such a stupid thing?

It was a good way to get in shape for boot camp, he told her, as he picked himself up off the floor. Carel was convinced he was nuts but invited him in anyway.

Those times together, whether in the apartment or driving around, always proved to come at a time when Carel needed encouragement from the Word. She'd fill him up with pie, and he'd fill her up with just the right encouraging words from the Bible that he'd been reading.

One night as they rode around, he asked her to check him out on some verses he was learning in Colossians. Carel somewhat half-heartedly agreed. So he began at Colossians, the first verse in the first chapter. He continued through the first chapter, to the second chapter, to the third. He finished at the fourth verse of the third chapter.

Carel was overwhelmed. She accused him of not memorizing it but preaching it to her. She asked him if he intended to commit the whole book to memory. Larry assured her that he would because he was so impressed with the pre-eminence of Christ to be found in its pages.

In Larry's life, few if any, people were aware of problems he had in his Christian walk because Christ was so pre-eminent in his life most of the time. He was genuinely excited about serving Him and seeing men and women come to know Him.

When they picked up hitchhikers, it didn't matter if the man rode a block or ten miles, Larry became an instant evangelist. He would begin as soon as the person got settled in the car by introducing himself and asking him his name. Then he would proceed to tell him that a few years before he had become a Christian, and he wondered if his new friend was interested in spiritual things. The way Larry asked the question and looked the guy in the eye, showing his personal concern that he find the happiness Larry knew, the hitchhiker invariably would find himself truly getting interested.

Not every hitchhiker, not every man in the dorm or person on the street said "yes" to Jesus. But Bleek took his responsibility seriously to at least see to it that they all heard about the greatest gift available to them. Due to that keen and unusual sense of responsibility to win souls and build them up in the faith, Don found Larry more and more involved in the two ministries at SFU and UBC, at the high school, with the team, and getting Ralph and Colin's Quiet Times established and vital. One morning about 5:00, when Don came downstairs, he found Larry sacked out on the living room carpet, obviously too tired to make it up to bed. Larry greeted him with a cheery good morning and asked if Don were ready to hit a new day. They both were, so as soon as Mac and Barry joined them, they enjoyed a Bible study together before Larry took off to contact his next person.

It wasn't until Sunday afternoon that Don had a chance to follow through, and he took Bleek aside for a few moments. Don expressed his concern for Larry. He told him he was doing too much, and he was going to burn himself out if he didn't let up a little. Larry's response was with real seriousness that seemed to have already been thought through to a surprising conclusion. He told Don that his war would soon be over. He didn't have long to go, but he wanted to give his all in the time he had. A phone call prevented any further discussion but, as Larry heard his own words, he felt God definitely wanted those last couple of weeks in the Vancouver area to really count.

The fall Navigator Conference November 8-11 at Warm Beach in Washington, was just such an occasion. An important outreach that Saturday was to send the conferees into the nearby town of Arlington, two by two, to knock on every door and to see if that person would be interested in talking about spiritual things. Larry had the responsibility of selling the conferees on the idea; most of them were scared speechless. Larry shared with them what to do and how to do it. The result was that even the first timers were excited and effective in sharing Christ. Several Arlington residents responded to Christ's provision of bridging the gap between themselves and a Holy God.

All too soon, it seemed for everyone in Vancouver that it was time for God to call Larry on to his next place of ministry. Several of the guys accompanied him as far as the Glen for a Thanksgiving conference. One night on their way, they stopped at a little place in Montana and spent the night in what they all thought was probably the first hotel in the West. The next morning, Bleek went out ahead to scout out a good place for breakfast and joined the others outside the hotel to tell them about a good little place down the street.

One of the other guys spoke up saying that there was a café right in front of them so why not eat breakfast there. Don looked at Larry and knew he had something else in mind. But Larry smoothed over the situation and said his typical "Good deal" and they ate where they were. Bleek was sincere, and the fact that he had been out hunting for a more comfortable place and had found one was really no problem to him.

The trip was full of jokes and rich fellowship. On the last night before they reached the Glen, Larry was driving down the highway through the dark open countryside, enthusiastically talking. As he got more and more involved with his story, his foot seemed to press harder and harder on the gas peddle. Everyone was looking at Larry as he told the story, except for one of the guys in the right side of the back seat who suddenly saw the road make a turn ahead; they were going too fast to make it. No problem. Larry didn't even try; he just went straight ahead, right off the road. They all braced themselves for what would be the inevitable crash, but the car came down in the darkness on an old farming road that came to meet the road they had been on, right on the curve. So, they continued on down the dirt road a few more feet to a pile of gravel the highway department had deposited there. Larry drove around it and back out onto the highway, almost as if nothing had happened. His only comment was that he guessed he must have missed a curve. The guy in the right side of the back seat responded with a "Y-y-y-yes," and they all had a good laugh.

They did arrive safely at Glen Eyrie and, the last day there, Larry and Don got together to pray. Larry suggested his prayer closet at the end of the bowling alley in the King James. The room was small and the two guys were big, so they filled the whole place. They started to read the Bible and pray together; Larry broke down and so did Don. They weren't sad, but they realized that a bond had been struck up between them, similar to that of David and Jonathan. They had to get out of there before they flooded themselves out.

Then God led Don back to his Canadian ministry and Larry, after a few more days at the Glen, continued back home to Ames. It would be good to be back home with his family again.

CHAPTER 17 - O.C.S.

On December 10, 1966, Don McDonald and Laura Bodkin were to be married in Seattle, Washington, so Larry and a couple of other guys from Ames decided to go see old Don tie the knot. On their way through Billings, Montana, Larry called and talked a few minutes with Barb Robbie, but their connection was poor and the others were anxious to be on their way.

After a rather hasty goodbye, Barb stood holding the phone a moment longer. She was thinking that she had prayed that she would hear from him, but now she wondered if she would ever hear from him again. One of the ladies in Barb's church, who had been very impressed with Larry, had been praying that Barb would hear. So when Barb told her that he had called, she changed her prayer to, "Lord, now let her see him again, if it be Thy will."

When Larry and his friends got ready to head back to Ames, the other two got flights out, but Larry felt he should hitchhike back. So on Thursday, around noon, he found himself ringing the Robbie doorbell.

Mrs. Robbie was surprised and delighted to see him standing there, his suitcase in hand, and his latest means of transportation disappearing around the corner. Larry was hungry so, while he washed up, Mrs. Robbie made a huge platter of sandwiches and other good things. They sat and ate and had an interesting and stimulating visit centered around the Lord and the things they had been experiencing over the past few months.

Barb was at a blind lady's home helping her with some music. She didn't return home until Larry had finished off the platter of sandwiches and they had retired to the living room.

When Barb came in and stood for a moment struck with surprise, Larry knew he was glad to see her again. Those short 36 hours at the beginning of the summer had only served to create an interest in getting to know more about her. She hadn't come on strong, like many girls seemed to do, so she held an element of fascination. There was something he couldn't put his finger on that had kept his interest high.

Another hour sped by as he answered their questions about his plans and how the Lord had led him into the Marines. He also talked to Barb about considering going to Maranatha that coming summer. All too soon he was once again being dropped off, this time on the east side of town, by this charming little brunette who still remained an intriguing mystery to him. He now had about 30 hours to go the remaining 1,000 miles to Ames, where he was to emcee a banquet in connection with the showing of a Billy Graham film, "For Pete's Sake."

This time his parting words to Barb were that he would let her know when he got to Ames, and he would send her an application form for Maranatha. Larry reached Ames in time for the banquet, and he did call to let them know of his arrival but Barb missed the call.

About a week later, on Christmas day, as he was setting his room in order for his parents' anticipated move once their house sold, he came across a Maranatha application. His mind focused again on Billings and the family that had become quite special to him. He knew he could just send the application by mail, but by 10:30 that night he had talked himself into calling them to wish them a Merry Christmas. Again, he found himself promising to send her the application and, again, with the holidays and his departure for Quantico, Barb watched the mailbox for a month before its arrival.

In the meantime, Larry was in Maryland and ready to begin the rigors of Marine boot camp, the first part of the O.C.S. program at Quantico. On January 11, he sent a card to his folks saying:

> *Had a good trip out. Got to D.C. and called LeRoy and Sandy Eims in the Navigator home there. Had dinner and stayed overnight with them. Hopped on a bus for Norfolk Tuesday and will be staying with the Navigator representative, Tim Arensmeier.*
>
> *Looks exciting, and I'm eager just being around all these uniforms. The Navigator bunch in D.C. is great—got to see some of the sights.*
>
> *Larry*

O.C.S. (Officers' Candidate School) began the week of January 15. That first day, Larry found occasion to give his personal testimony to several different guys. One of them was Warren Murphy. Larry wasn't sure where Murphy stood with the Lord. He knew Murphy was interested, and a new friendship began to develop. That first night Larry noticed that most of the guys were really keyed up with uncertainty about what lay ahead, but Larry dropped off to sleep telling God how much he loved Him and appreciated His peace for a time like that.

Those next days were busy gearing into a rigid Marine boot camp, guaranteed to separate the men from the boys. In a letter to his parents after two weeks, he wrote:

Dear Mom and Dad,

Just got into class this morning; got about five minutes so I thought I'd drop a line. Things are still good, and I am praising God for His love and care. Isn't our God just the greatest?

We are increasing the P.T. (Physical Training) part of the schedule, but it mostly takes determination in mind more than physical excellence. Seems to give me a real appetite, and the chow is pretty good eating. I don't get any pizzas before going to the rack though. Ha! My rack-mate got some high protein chocolate bars on liberty last weekend. Good stuff.

I got an 80 % on our physical readiness test but didn't do as well on the reaction test (testing ability to coordinate and direct a small team in accomplishing a difficult mission in 12 minutes).

Next weekend I am planning on going to Washington D.C. to see Jeff and Herb (men I was with at Timberline last summer), and I will probably stay overnight with Dean Troug (Navigator representative at the University of Maryland). We get paid Friday, and I'll probably call you Sunday night.

I'm getting to know some of the guys in the platoon fairly well, and now I am looking for the sympathetic hearing for sharing the Bridge and the person of Christ in my testimony and life.

Then he asked for prayer for some of the guys and about the possibility of doing a Bible study with Warren Murphy.

It's hard to be consistent in my Quiet Time, but I have been waking up before we get up at 5:30, so I think I'll try to be regular in this time, then spend some time praying before I drop off to sleep. I got challenged from Psalms 91 and 92 in my Quiet Time the other day.

We get some free time for studying, etc. in the evenings from 1800-2130 (6:00-9:30). I hope to do some Bible study in this time. Keep praying and give my regards to people around.

Your son,
Larry

That next weekend in D.C. Larry felt more like old times. He went to Jeff Kemmerer's apartment in D.C. and spent some time with Jeff, Herb Jarrell and Bob Magistrelli going over Timberline days and getting caught up on each other's lives to date. Then he headed over to Dean and Dottie Troug's in College Park. He was still reliving his summer at Timberline when a girl up ahead of him caught his attention.

He called out her name and broke into a trot toward the girl who had stopped to see who was calling to her. Then she put on a horrified look and asked if he was really Bleek and what had happened to his hair.

Larry laughed and said he would have to get her in the Marines, too, if he hoped to get her hair cut, to which Sissy replied "Ooh, please."

Larry promised not to say another word about it. Sissy asked him if he was headed for the Troug's, to quickly change the subject. She was living with them and Larry had missed talking to her when he first arrived in January.

The rest of the walk to the Troug front porch was spent with Larry giving her a humorous and vivid picture of life in O.C.S.

Dean and Dottie welcomed Larry as part of their family and so did their little son, David. Although he was only a few months old, he squealed with delight each time Larry, like Dean, threw him into the air.

Larry knew Dean from previous retreats. Dean was now working on the campus of the University of Maryland. This proved to be a revitalizing weekend for Larry who, for lack of constant vital fellowship at Quantico, had begun to feel almost like Elijah must have, when he said in I Kings 19:10: *"... and I, even I only, am left; and they seek my life, to take it away."*

Boot camp was a whole new chapter in Larry's life of walking with Jesus and living with men. It had never been so difficult to witness to men about Christ as it was there. Even a quiet testimony of a bowed head at mealtime brought mashed potatoes in his face from a fellow classmate.

It seemed almost that to believe in Jesus was like believing in Santa Claus or the Easter bunny but, for Larry, Jesus was his life and he could not deny Him however rough the way.

Much of his encouragement and strength he knew came from those back home who cared and prayed for him. So he tried to take advantage of every opportunity to shoot a letter off to inform those back in Ames how things were going. Larry had heard from Dave Powell, so he sent this letter off to him.

Howdy Dave,

Appreciated getting your letter and the good word. Sounds like you're having as busy a time as I am; I guess we can be thankful that God sticks closer than a brother and is really faithful to us. Keep spending that personal time with the Lord each day—it's the only way to know the freshness of our daily relationship with Jesus.

After six weeks of Basic, I'm still encouraged and, although tired at times, I'm enjoying the training. We have academic tests every Monday and various sorts of physical tests. We get up at 5:30 each morning, have our first class about 7:30 after chow and cleaning up our squad bay (where we sleep). Generally, we have a couple of hours drilling with our rifles, more classes, and physical conditioning which includes general push ups, sit ups, etc., running an obstacle course, isometrics and then running about four miles. After evening chow, we generally have until about 10:00 to work on our equipment, clean and polish our boots, clean our rifles, study our assignments, wash clothes, etc.

Every fourth day we are duty platoon, and we stand two-hour guard duty, as well as clean up the company office and the Major's office.

The guys I am with are nice personally, but they need Jesus in their lives. Some of them are very hard and have no real experience of spiritual reality. It takes boldness to share Christ with your buddies you are closest to.

On the next page, I have laid out a simple plan which I find useful in doing a verse analysis Bible study. You might try following it and see how it works for you. Remember, Dave, that the secret to any Bible study is the PERSONAL APPLICATION we make in specific areas in our lives.

Keep walkin' with Jesus
Your big brother,
Bleek
Joel 2:21

Larry had a strong conviction that since he was representing Christ in the Marine Corps, he should do his very best. But he found that whatever he did, it wasn't good enough. He knew the Marines were exacting, so he really concentrated on spit-polishing his boots and keeping his things in order, but he drew demerits anyway. Finally, he asked why, and his head officer explained it was because he was spending too much time on his "stuff" and not enough on the men.

Larry switched his emphasis and still drew demerits. Because of his built-in desire to do things right, he again went to his superior and asked what he could do to raise his marks. He was assured that those marks were not the whole story, so not to worry about them. But God did use those experiences to get him thinking more seriously about the need for a balanced life, and he knew he still had much to learn.

It only took another week or so to finish up the boot camp part of O.C.S. As he started his next phase of training, Larry wrote his dad, in part:

> *It's good to talk to you all on weekends; I sure appreciate you paying for the calls on your end. Dad, I can never hope to express my thanks and love for all that you have done for me. You're the greatest dad in the world.*
>
> *The things at the store are busy, I'm sure. I trust God is faithful in supplying needs. I had a good time in prayer for things there and for the whole family last night. The chapel here is open at all times, so I'm going to use it when I can.*
>
> *Tell Gary that there isn't as much harassment as in boot, but the physical and academic are much more demanding. We ran the obstacle course today*

for time. One hundred and thirty seconds is passing. God helped me get a 68 for 100 %. Praise God! The nine-mile hike wasn't bad. We got a speed three-mile forced march and the reaction course Monday. (Pray, I need to do well on the reaction course.) I understand we get Washington's Birthday off next Wednesday. It will be a refreshing breather in the middle of the week. Duty this weekend.

How's Ron doing? Boy, I keep thinking of Solomon in Ecclesiastes, when I think of all the worldly "Mickey Mouse" and its emptiness. God can get to him, even if we can't. Say, has Gary got into a Bible study yet? He was interested and was going to check with Jim North.

Keep praying, Pop, and trusting Jesus.

Your son, Larry

The day Pop received Larry's letter was the day for the three-mile forced march. The sky was a heavy gray and showed no promise of anything but rain and, of that, it was full. The men in Larry's platoon donned their helmets, rifles, packs, cartridge belts, and all their gear and took off running and walking through the pouring rain. The slippery hill trail was the worst, and the drill instructor ran them through the march not once, but three times that day. The third time when Larry reached the hill trail, both legs cramped up and he fell out. To drop out of a forced march was the same as to drop out of the program. But Larry couldn't move. The gunnery sergeant could not afford to be sympathetic with leg cramps. A fundamental principle in the Marine Corps is to learn that you can go on beyond that of which you thought you were capable.

Larry felt the sergeant's boot as he yelled at him to "get going." His whole future hung on whether he would be able to "get going." But the cramps were becoming more intense. The boot kicked harder and the words fired at him, along with the pounding rain, made the whole thing seem like a nightmare. And then, it seemed he could see an eagle circling in the sky back at Glen Eyrie. His heart cried out to God for "wings as eagles, that he might run and not be weary, walk and not faint." He hobbled to his feet, and the pain was severe as he took a step and then another and another; by the time he caught up with his platoon the cramps were nothing more than sore. He made it the rest of the way without difficulty. He found himself praising God for a vivid object lesson he would never forget. Sometimes, you have to push people and even hurt them to get them to do what they need to do.

As the end of O.C.S. drew closer, the weeks got tougher. In a letter to his parents on March 2 he said:

> *Dear Mom & Dad,*
>
> *This, by all degrees, has been our toughest week so far. It began with a 9.2 mile hike Monday at 4.6 mph; about five miles Tuesday to training area #4 for offensive movement training and then back; then today classes and regular P.T. with a three-mile run. Tomorrow is the confidence course and a three-mile run; inspection comes on Saturday. Whew! Can almost make a man tired. I did well with my part in leading a tactical assault on a machine gun bunker in the offensive evaluation—that helps.*
>
> *Hey, Mom, can I twist your arm and ask for a refill for my chocolate chip cookie jar? Boy, those were some of your best. We have good chow, but I'm partial to yours—particularly after 23 years of home training and accustoming.*

As it is, right now, we will have eight days' leave between O.C.S. and Basic. If it isn't too costly, I'll probably fly home the weekend of March 25-26. Our Basic won't pick up until Monday, about April 3. I'll be staying in a dorm-like BOQ (Basic Officers' Quarters), sharing a room with another guy. I need to be praying that God will work this out and give me a guy warm toward spiritual things.

Hope things are good there and that you all keep on loving Jesus.

Your son and His,
Larry

Larry also sent a card to his sister, Marlene, a day or so later:

Dear Marlene,

Thanks for writing. It looks like you are learning how to type pretty well. Just takes a lot of practice.

I asked mom to send some cookies. You might give her a hand just for old "Big Charlie!"

Let's see, you are almost twelve now and beginning to see and understand more and more. I wonder what you feel it means to be a "real" Christian and how it fits into the things you do and take part in. What would you think about going to girls' camp in Colorado with the Navigators this coming summer? I'll tell you more about it later when I'm home. Well, keep on loving Jesus. I love Him, too.

Big Charlie,
Larry

During the middle of that hard week, Larry received a letter from Colin, and a week later he was finally able to answer it.

Dear Colin,

Buddy, your letter was just the encouragement my heart needed. Colin, I'm glad, thrilled inside, to know you're moving ahead and growing to love Jesus more. Remember Buddy, you are the fruit of my labors at SFU and "are our glory and joy" (I Thessalonians 2:20). Praise God!

We are in our ninth week here at O.C.S. now and have only one week left. The hard training is basically over. We have had 3-6-9-10-12-mile hikes, considerable P.T. (physical training), obstacle training, as well as class work and drill. There's a lot pushed into ten weeks and a lot of pressing spiritually, not so much direct as indirect. For instance, my Quiet Time is about nil right now and I feel somewhat weak spiritually. I sure could use a good round of prayer with you and the bunch. Yay! I think Satan has trapped me some by his circumstances—we got to remember that we operate on God's promises no matter what the circumstances. When you read this letter, just get down right where you are and claim Isaiah 45:2, 3 for me, that God's hidden riches would be mine in Jesus.

Sounds like "A" is having a struggle. That's normal. Satan is still out to skin him and wipe out the possibility of reproduction through his life at SFU. If you can't pray with "A," bear down and pray for him. Now might be a good time to get with him if he and "B" broke it off. Something I'm reminded of: "A man in battle sees need for sharp tools." How much in the battle have you been with "A"? Show the Bridge, make appointments, go to the park, or take a buddy to church. Try something. It might work.

From your letter, I'd say, Praise God! We just can't out-give Him, can we? If God is the author of your life and "C's," being one in the years ahead, you might check some little indicators and remember to keep your stake to follow God in this, down deep. 1) Does your interest in her increase or diminish your stability in the basics? 2) Is she one in heart with you?

You are on the right track being willing to see her only a little during weekends. God is going to need some time to build both of your lives in perfect union with Christ (Amos 3:3). Also, begin praying that God would give her a heart to get some training (for instance at Timberline this summer). Keep God first and I'll guarantee, on the basis of Matthew 6:33, that you can't get the short end.

Say, it sounds like March 18 will be a good time at the Glen and good fellowship on the road. Greet the brethren both there and at Glen Eyrie for me, Buddy.

Regarding a man of like mind for me, pray that God will direct my heart as I move into Basic School at Camp Barrett BOQ with a roommate.

Warren Murphy and I are fairly close here at O.C.S. and have talked about spiritual things considerably. Also have gone to chapel together. Pray for further contact with him. I'm praying that God will make you a real man of his Word, Colin. Keep in the ole fight and keep that verse pack hot.

Wish we could be together and tell Jesus just how much we love Him.

In His love forever,

Bleek

Psalm 27:1

Finally, the day came for the men to graduate from O.C.S. and receive their commission. Since Larry was flying home for his leave, his parents had not come down for the commissioning. Tom Abrams, a close buddy through these last ten weeks, had his bars pinned on by his wife, Sue. Sue's mother, Mrs. Delpho, was also there, so Larry asked her if she would help pin his on him; she was delighted to do so. The Abrams, the Delphos and Larry had lunch together to celebrate before they brought the men back to get their leave papers. Then they hustled Larry off to the airport where he barely had enough time to get his bags out of the trunk and board the plane before take-off. He was Iowa-bound.

That next week sped by. There were the Easter services and family and friends to see. One afternoon, Curt Siemers called Larry. He said he would be going down to the Mission in Des Moines that night and, since he'd heard that Larry was in town, he asked him if he'd like to come share his testimony. Larry quickly replied that he would be glad to. He had spent much time down there in the past.

That night Curt did the preaching and, being Easter time, his message was about death and the Christian's hope through the resurrection of Jesus Christ.

Larry listened intently to Curt's words and rejoiced, not only in the truth of his message, but also at how much Curt had grown since the days of Timberline. As he lie in bed that night, he felt that same burning urgency to get the message out before that time when God would call him home. As Curt had said, "That will be a glorious day for the Christian," but Larry thought about the many here, at Quantico, and the world over, for whom death held no good news at all. For some reason unknown to him, Ron's girl friend came to mind. Larry had not yet met her, but that night he began praying for Donna.

When his leave was up, Larry needed a ride to Omaha to catch his military hop back to Quantico. Ron offered to drive him. It was a rainy day and, when Ron suggested stopping in Adair to pick up Donna, Larry was a bit hesitant. He was eager to meet her, but the weather showed all signs of getting worse.

Ron assured him that would be no problem. Donna's mom gave her approval as well. The three-hour trip was fun as Ron and Larry took turns driving, playing the uke or the harmonica, and singing songs Larry had taught Ron from the Navigator rallies. As the roads got more and more treacherous, Larry, who had been talking about the Lord, asked Donna, "What do you think about spiritual things?"

Donna's mouth dropped open, and she looked at Ron helplessly. She told Larry that she really didn't know what she thought.

Larry hadn't intended it to come as such a surprise, so he hurried on to explain what he meant by sharing his own testimony about how spiritual things had changed his life. Donna listened intently to every word. Then they sang the rest of the way to Omaha through the rain.

They stopped first to get a sandwich before going on out to the Strategic Air Command Air Force base for Larry's flight. As he flew back down to Quantico, he had no idea how God had used what, to him now seemed like a blunder on his part, to raise questions in Donna's mind about Christianity—questions that even Ron could not answer.

CHAPTER 18 - T.B.S.

T.B.S. (The Basic School) began on April 5, and Larry was put in Company L, 1st Platoon, which was made up of the men whose last names began with A-Dr, plus one man from Seoul, Korea. Larry's new roommate was Bert Black, and they lived in the part of Quantico that housed the commissioned officers. It was called Camp Barrett.

Larry explained some of this move to Colin in a letter of April 11:

> *After ten long weeks of hikes, physical training, tactical movements, classes and harassment, they made me a 2nd Lieutenant in the Marines! Now I'm in my second week of a six-month tactical training in Field Combat Operations, in preparation for Vietnam. I'm excited; I have a sympathetic roommate and several men who are real interested. Pray that God would give me one man—might be Warren Murphy, a guy who I shared my testimony with the first day of O.C.S. Basic. We spent time together, and I'd like to get DTB (down to business) with him. Pray! Now is the time I begin really leaning on those promises from Isaiah 45.*

That next weekend Larry had leave, so he and Herb Jarrell from Washington D.C. went to Norfolk to a Navigator get-together. Larry was pleased to see an old friend from Grand Rapids who was now in the Marines there, and they had a good visit. Then it was back to T.B.S. for a week of exams and, on Friday, 10-12 hours of land navigation with compass and map.

The next week they went to the rifle range for qualification with M14 and 45 caliber pistols. Never before had Larry been made so aware of the life-and-death business of war. To miss his mark could mean death for himself, but to hit his mark could mean death for the other guy. And yet, it was the cause for which they were fighting and the protection for all that he held dear that enabled him to work hard for precision. Still, Larry knew that the peace they were all learning to fight for and hoping they would gain could only come as men's hearts found peace with God. That was his primary objective. Many of his buddies, he knew, would give their lives in Vietnam, and Larry longed for each one to know God's peace before that time came, however soon or far away it might be.

Not everyone looked at things the way Larry did, however, and Bert, his roommate, made their differences obvious. Bert had never met anyone like Larry and had real difficulty believing any guy could believe the things Larry felt were important. He thought Larry must be some kind of a religious fanatic, and he began to treat him as such. It made having a Quiet Time and Bible study more difficult for Larry, but it also gave him more of a burden and concern for Bert. Although he didn't share their discussions with others, Larry did ask for prayer for Bert from all the gang in D.C. and back home.

It was about this time that Larry felt a real need for a man after his own heart that would be there at Camp Barrett, where he had to spend so much of his time. The guys in D.C. were great but not around enough, and Murphy was no longer in his platoon of 44 men. So, he began to pray in real earnest that God would provide such a man, if indeed it was a legitimate need.

One morning between classes, Larry went to the garbage can outside his room where he had dumped his wastebasket earlier that day. He remembered in the middle of the last class that he had thrown away an address he had not yet copied in his book. Now he began looking for it. Just down the hall, several men were talking. When they saw Larry rummaging through the overflowing garbage can, one of them called his name and asked if he was looking for his Jesus in there? The others had laughed.

A little later that day, someone called him Deacon Bleeker, and that name soon caught on in fine style. Still later that day, while Larry stood in line waiting for chow, a guy standing behind him began a conversation with him. He told Larry he had heard him getting chided earlier and commented that he had sure taken it a lot better than he would have.

Larry hadn't met this fellow before because he had just joined their group when T.B.S. started. Larry explained that these were guys with whom he had gone through O.C.S., and he was getting pretty used to their comments. Then he gave his testimony. When he finished, the young man shook his hand. He told Larry that he was Dan Anger and that he was a Christian, too.

Larry learned that Dan had graduated from Wheaton College. He had taken the PLC program (Platoon Leaders Class, the Marine counterpart for ROTC), graduated, received his commission, and then went on to graduate school at the state university at Buffalo, New York. Dan was now jumping in, mid-stream so to speak. So far, Dan had received thumbs down to all of his attempts to be a witness, so he was delighted to find a brother in Christ and in his same squad.

Larry was delighted, as well, to see how God had again answered prayer. During those next five months, a friendship developed such as neither of them had ever had before. They lived next door to each other, they were in the same squad, they ate and snacked (always snacked) together, they studied together, and what really knit their hearts were the times in prayer, Bible reading, worshiping and general fellowshipping together. They became brothers in every sense of the word.

When Memorial Day was about upon them, Larry wrote his parents:

Dear Mom & Dad,

We are in class now and are getting information on the various MOS (Military Occupational Specialty) fields, duty stations, and probable initial assignments following T.B.S. training. I am planning on listing my preference of duty: 1. Infantry (possible civil pacification program), 2. Tanks and amphibian tractors, 3. Supply. I am going to ask for language training and see what God works out. As I was reading in Psalm 143 the other day in my Quiet Time, I noticed the pattern of David's life in situations. In verse 1, he asked God to let him hear and to let him know what to do. Probably the key to the entire situation is in verse 10 where he says "teach me to do Thy will." David was concerned with action and the actual doing of God's will.

This is a busy week. We will be in the field late tomorrow—breaching and clearing mines. Wednesday is tactics all day in the field. Thursday and Friday, among other things, are our student presentation days. Saturday we're supposed to be in the field, firing the 106 recoilless rifle until 1700.

Then Larry wrote about the possibility of his coming home on Saturday and visiting Uncle Otto before flying back to camp on Wednesday.

> *I've got a lot of work to crank out for tomorrow, so guess I'll sign off for now. Keep trusting God, and I'm looking forward to this weekend.*
> *Your son,*
> *Larry*
> *Psalm 150-There are 13 praises in this Psalm!*

Because most of that Memorial Day leave was spent at his aunt and uncle's in Emery, South Dakota, Larry only heard that Ron and Donna had decided to get married. He had no chance to see them. Pop said they were still trying to decide whether they should get married that June or the next. So, once again, Larry flew back to Quantico with Ron and his new fiancée on his heart.

It was only a week later that word came that they had set the date—June 11. That was only a week away. Larry and Dan got together and prayed for Ron and Donna, and that his CO would give Larry a pass to go to the wedding. He secured the pass with no difficulty and called Ron to let him know he'd be there. Ron and Donna would always remember that he was there when they looked back on that memorable day.

Larry's first surprise for them was a Marine sword that he brought, with writing on it, for cutting the wedding cake.

When they arrived at the church, Larry told Ron that he didn't think he should leave his car parked right across from the church. When Ron said he'd go move it, Larry told him he had enough to do, so Larry asked for the keys and offered to move it for him.

Ron thanked him and told him to be sure and lock it. He didn't really care what was done to the outside, but he knew the guys in his frat house would probably make a real mess inside if it wasn't locked. Larry promised to lock it for him.

Larry's second surprise was enough money to extend their intended three-day honeymoon to Chicago to a full week.

His next series of surprises came as Ron and Donna ran to their car. They couldn't even see through it because it was filled solid with balloons. When Ron looked at his brother, Larry explained that he sure didn't want anybody to get the keys, so he had stuck them in one of the balloons. Ron played along and began popping each one, only to find each had three or four kernels of rice in it which went flying everywhere in the car. But they found no keys. Larry told them there was one more balloon they hadn't popped, but Ron assured him there were no balloons left in the car. Larry grinned and looked toward the hood ornament. Inside that balloon were the keys.

Finally, Ron and Donna were ready to take off but when he turned the ignition something else was obviously wrong. So Ron lifted the hood and his coil wire was gone. While he was hunting for the coil wire, Larry jacked the back end of his car up to take his rear tires off, but he didn't have time to remove them. Ron found the coil wire, got in and got the car started, got out and unjacked his car, and FINALLY got away.

As they drove safely down the highway, Donna asked Ron if he was glad his brother had made it to their wedding. Ron's reply was that he sure was. It would have lacked something without him. They both really did appreciate all that Larry had done for them to make it memorable. They also looked forward to the day when they could return the favors.

Shortly after Larry got back to Quantico, he got a letter off to another young couple he had met in Vancouver and Seattle. Judy Robbins and Bob Magnuson had gotten married the same day as Ron and Donnie, so he wrote:

Dear Bob and Judy,

God's very best to you both now that God has united your lives as one in Him. I trust that these days lay foundations for years to come of ministry and fruitfulness. Remember, "Except the Lord build the house, they labor in vain that build it." (Psalm 127:1). As you build and construct in the lives of others, and some day with your own children, keep the words of Joel in mind. "Tell ye your children of it, and let your children tell their children, and their children another generation." (Joel 1:3).

Much has happened here since your last word. O.C.S. is past and I am in Phase II of training. This includes 21 weeks of tactical (movements, employment of weapons, coordination of military tasks, etc.) training—12 of which are already completed. I'm still at Quantico; however, it's a new address and I'm a commissioned officer. About the fifth week here at T.B.S. (The Basic School), I found out my next door buddy, Dan Anger, is a Christian and has been for years. We are spending some time together and are hoping to see some other men trust Christ. Pray!

We will be finishing this program August 30 and, after about 20 days, I'll probably be in Vietnam DMZ. There is a possibility that I might get to go to language school. We'll wait to see how God works this out. I may be swinging through your area and up to Vancouver in September. I might pop in on you—How's that?

Dan Anger and Larry at Quantico, 1967

Larry and Dan spent their furloughs together whenever they could. Dan had some friends nearby named the McCrory's, and Dan and Larry spent three weekends that summer at their place. Most of the rest of the time was spent at the Troug's and Navigator functions, such as the Summer Task Force Rally in early June.

One day, on their way back from a weekend at the D.C. Navigator home, Larry shared his morning Quiet Time with Dan. He had been really challenged that morning to take a good look at himself spiritually. John 4:14 says that when

Jesus was talking to the woman at the well, He said that *"Whosoever drinketh of the water that I shall give him shall never thirst; but the water that I shall give him shall be in him a well of water springing up into everlasting life."*

Larry found himself wondering what kind of a well of water his buddies saw when they looked at him. A Christian's "water" could be murky or polluted. It could be bitter or stagnant. Only in Jesus could it be bubbling, crystal, sparkling, pure water which is inviting to those thirsty for life and meaning. Larry told Dan he wanted his fountain to flow with that fresh and satisfying water of Christ. The secret he felt must lie in John 3:30: *"He must increase, but I must decrease."*

As the hot summer slipped into July, many weddings took place and dates were set—including Dan's—to a young lady back in New York named Diane. Marriage was still something Larry was looking forward to, but only God knew who the right girl was. Carla seemed less and less a possibility.

In a letter to Colin he wrote:

> *Out here on the eastern shores, it seems like all the guys and gals are getting married. You know it makes me wonder, and yet I remember that God stimulated my heart to leave this area of my life with Him. His promise to me has been from Isaiah 64:4: "For since the beginning of the world men have not heard, nor perceived by the ear, neither hath the eye seen, O God, beside Thee, what He hath prepared for him that waiteth for Him."*
>
> *I pray, Colin, that you are with me in heart in waiting for God's timing and moving. Let's stay on target with reaching this world. Yea!*

Larry was busy now serving as company gunnery sergeant, which meant he was the legs for the company commander and XO. He was responsible for the platoon sergeant and the supply sergeant. They got much more time out in the field in July on raid patrols. Larry spent one whole weekend working out details for leading a combat patrol for their reinforced platoon.

One day, in a letter from his mom, Larry learned that on their way to Glen Eyrie for a conference, they had stopped at Maranatha. And she said, "A girl named Barbara Robbie had said to say hello."

Larry praised the Lord. Barb had gone to Maranatha; his heart rejoiced. He had sent several letters or cards since he'd been at Quantico, to encourage her to go, and then had decided to leave it in God's hands. There had been no communication between them for some time now. With only about five weeks left until he'd be on furlough and make his trip out West, he decided to drop her a line and see if he could stop and see her when he went through Billings. As he licked the envelope, he was confident that he would see her again. Then he got a letter off to his folks, to help get his mind back on things at hand.

Dear Mom and Pop,

With our sixteenth week coming to a close, we only have about five weeks remaining. This past week was busy! Patrol Monday, test Tuesday—a 32-kilometer hike and live fire problems, and we have a southeast Asian village display tomorrow.

Dan and I are going to the Senators-Orioles game tomorrow and then spend the weekend in D.C. with some of his friends. We'll probably go to the Navigator rally Saturday night. I sure haven't been getting my Quiet Times lately. It's like standing God up for a date and losing all the way around.

We're having a Marine Corps reception next Friday night, and guess who they have escorting one of the colonel's daughters? Right, ole Bleek himself! I guess I'll go with John Baker (a buddy in the platoon) since his (the colonel's) *daughter may not be excited about taxiing over. Ha!*

I included the bulletin from last week's service and a picture of the little church here in Triangle, a good little fellowship.

Love you and Him!
Larry

For some time Larry had experienced victory over the pressures of lust of the flesh and the eyes, but Satan had subtly been getting him to slack off on his attention to the "basics." He had begun to feel spiritually dry and experience some personal defeats. He had been walking with the Lord long enough to recognize the symptoms. He wrote to Colin saying that he knew that reality was to be found in one place only, at the feet of Jesus. Jesus—nothing more, nothing less. By bringing his problem to Jesus, he could again feel the joy that comes from a right relationship with God. Even when assignments came through and the doors to Language School closed and the infantry on the DMZ in Vietnam swung open, he had a deep settled peace that that was exactly where God wanted him. He was excited about what lie ahead. He was mentally somewhere in Vietnam, talking with a buddy in a foxhole, when Bert called him back to reality with his favorite greeting, "Hey, Deacon." He accused Larry of holding out on him as he showed him a letter from a Miss Barbara Robbie, whose return address was in D.C.!

CHAPTER 19 - BARB

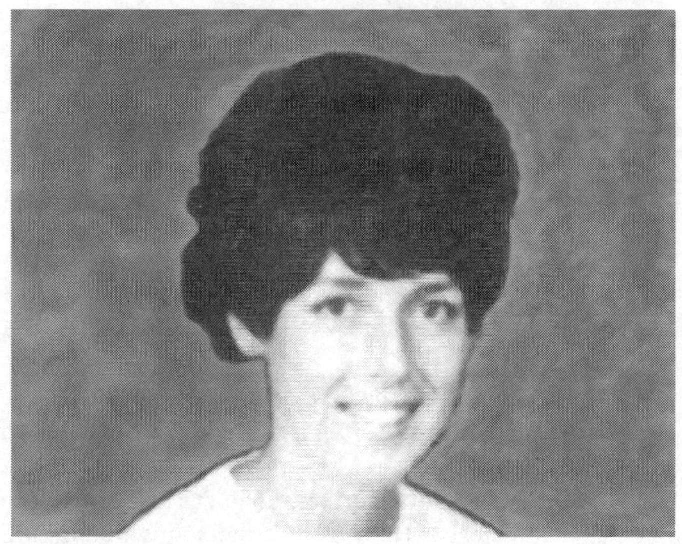

Barb Robbie

That second week of August, though busy, went very slowly. Why had God brought Barb back into his life now? With his future in the hands of God and the Marine Corps, he had felt no ties. But why, too, he wondered, did he wish he'd asked to see her sooner than Sunday?

He had gotten her letter on Monday saying that she was in Washington D.C. working for International Christian Leadership. It had to do with congressmen and senators there in D.C., who were having prayer breakfasts all over the country. She had just started her job on August 1. She said that, although she would not be in Billings during his furlough, she knew her family would love to see him when he made his trip to Canada. Larry had looked up the ICL phone number and called her at work that same day. Since he didn't have a car and he wanted Dan to meet her anyway, he had asked if she would like to go to church and out to dinner with him and a couple of buddies.

There had been a slight hesitation before her acceptance, but when she said fine, a kind of anticipation began to build in Larry's heart. God had been wise in having him put it off for a week, because it allowed the necessary time for Larry to be sure God was in it and would direct it.

That Saturday, August 12, Larry and some of the guys from the base went to the S.T.F. picnic at Lake Fairfax. A good game of football helped to pass the time as he concentrated on one of his buddies in particular who did not know the Lord. That evening he also dropped a card off to Colin. One side said, "My work is so secret...I don't even know what I'm doing!" And the other side read:

> *Dear Colin,*
>
> *Brother, how's the battle? If you're losing ground, you need to hit the offensive more—more time in the Book, in the Quiet Time and in Scripture memory. Ya! Ya! Ya!*
>
> *Say, buddy, I'm going to Okinawa and then to Vietnam, and I plan to see you sometime around September 15. I've been having some tough times trying to maintain the Basics. I guess I need more push and God-given eagerness! I'm asking God for the type of desire David had in Psalm 143:10 to "teach" and "do." Not only to know, but to do.*
>
> *Say "Howdy" to your folks, and give the gang at church my hellos.*

When Sunday came, the skies were gray and dreary. Only with the help of a detailed city map did they finally find the elegant mansion that at one time had been an embassy. It now housed the girls who worked for ICL.

Larry rang the doorbell and was admitted by a young woman who said she would get Barbara for him.

His response to her trailed off as he saw Barb already coming down the spiral staircase. No wonder he'd been looking forward to this all week, he thought, as her eyes met his and her radiant smile seemed to fill the room with sunshine. "Okay, Bleek, enough of this," he told himself. "She's just a very pretty girl, and you've seen lots of them before."

Once in the car, Larry introduced her to Dan and Warren Murphy. Then it seemed there was so much to say, so much catching up to do. Larry began with asking her how she liked Maranatha. Barb told him that it had been great, but that she had almost not gone to it. Larry invited her to explain and, as he listened, he sensed a new kind of stability in her as she related how God had worked. Barb had struggled in the days preceding Maranatha. Why should she go to this horrible place? She had pretty much rationalized herself out of going and was feeling very relieved about it, except for one little uncertainty that wouldn't go away. Two nights before she would leave, if she went, she prayed that if she was supposed to go that God would change her mind. She asked that when she woke up the next morning, if she was to go, when her thoughts turned to Maranatha, God would give her good thoughts and make her excited about going. And that was just what He had done. So she had gone and loved it.

Larry thought back to that morning in June when he had had his last real burden that Barb go to Maranatha and had really prayed that God would give her such a strong desire to go that she wouldn't be able to stay home. Then the burden had lifted and he'd not prayed about it again.

Barb and Larry talked on and on about who was there and what they'd each learned from Maranatha. Now and then, Dan would throw a comment in to tease this obviously very happy reunion.

The church service was very good that morning, but Larry was shocked at his own behavior. As they stood sharing a hymnbook, he could not keep his normally steady hand from shaking. And he knew the words to the hymns by heart, but they kept coming out all wrong.

When the day was over, he felt like he'd acted like some kid on his first date, but she had agreed to go with him when he treated his Timberline crew to dinner at the Officers' Club that next Saturday night.

So, another week lay before him—a week in which he sensed, in a new way, his need for a vital relationship with God. His time in the Word was rich and meaningful, and his heart was truly praising God as he shared some of the things God had been saying to him with the gang on Saturday night. It all had to do with maintaining a balanced Christian life.

The Summer Task Force and the Navigators seemed to have recruited well from the Timberline gang the summer before. There was Sissy Gates, Diane Cooper, Barb Zerman, Jeff Kemmerer, Bob Magistrelli, Herb Jarrell, and Mick VanZant, plus Larry, Dan and Barb, that met for dinner at Andrew's Air Force Base in the Officers' Club.

Larry had especially wanted Sissy to meet Barb. He thought that Sissy would be good to follow Barb up, since Barb was new in D.C. and seemed open to the Navigators. This was really a special night for Larry. He had borrowed money even for cokes at Timberline and, now, God had given him this opportunity to show some of his appreciation in a small way. The girls, in particular, were worried about the bill he would have after all ten of them had eaten all they could hold. But Larry really did want to treat them all and he did.

That evening, after they dropped all the others off, Dan drove him and Barb over to the Troug's where Barb had met them for the first time. This was quite a ways from where Barb was living, so Dan let Larry drive her home.

All the way back to the ICL home, Barb seemed unusually quiet, as she had been all evening. Perhaps she had felt out of place. He had hoped that she and Sissy would become good friends, but they had both been quiet. He walked Barb up to the door and looked down into her almost sad, brown eyes.

He asked her if he might see her again and, after another slight hesitation, she said that would be fine. Larry promised to call as soon as he knew his week's schedule, and they could decide what to do.

Larry felt like he had three feet as he made his way back to the car. And over the miles back to the frat house where he and Dan were staying, he thought about the evening. Had she just been nice? Did she really not want to go out with him again?

That next morning, he and Mick Van Zandt had some time together in the Word and prayer and then joined the guys for breakfast. Larry was beginning to sense what it was going to be like in another week or two when he had to say goodbye to this gang and the others all around the country. It wouldn't be easy, and yet, obviously God could work in lives whether he was there or not. And this was what was on his heart for each of them. Then Larry noticed Sissy coming out of the kitchen and he went over to her. He accused her of being the reason breakfast tasted so good. She was surprised to see that he hadn't returned to Quantico yet. He told her he was leaving that evening, but asked if he had heard correctly. Was she talking about going out to California for ministry? She confirmed that she was and would be living with Elven and Joyce Smith in the Pasadena home. The Smiths had just moved there from Seattle.

As Larry realized Sissy would soon be leaving, he could better understand why God had not brought Barb and Sissy to a greater friendship. God still always knew what He was doing, and he should never doubt it. Larry was happy for Sissy and her new assignment. She would be heading for California right after the East Coast Conference just a few weeks away. They parted with the knowledge that they would see each other in a couple of weeks.

That next morning when he got up for his Quiet Time at the Base, an envelope fell out of his Bible. Larry opened it and read, *"The girls wanted you to have this." Mick.* Larry looked at the money in his hand. The only time he could think of that Mick could have put that in his Bible was during their prayer time the morning before. He was sure it hadn't been there for their time in the Word.

As the new week began, Larry called Barb. He had Thursday night and the weekend off again. Each time he called, there was either no answer, or *"Sorry, she's not here right now."* Again, he began to wonder if she really did not care to date him. Thursday afternoon came and, again, he still had not talked with her. So he talked some more with God: *"Father God, if You are the one closing these doors, then please keep them closed when I call this time. But God, if you ARE in my feelings toward Barb, which even I don't completely understand, please have her be home and available."*

As Larry walked to the phone, he heard someone calling to him, "Hey Deacon…I've got a guy here you ought to talk to. He doesn't have such a good outlook on life."

With his platoon facing Vietnam, Larry had seen varied reactions among the men, and he found this young man truly fearful for his life with no hope whatsoever. Larry spent the next hour explaining to him how he could have peace if he could just place his life in the loving hands of God. The young man left, seriously considering what the Bible said he must do to obtain eternal life; Larry sat a moment longer to ask God to make the way of salvation clear to him. Then he again went to the phone, and this time he dialed.

Barb had just gotten in the door from work when the phone rang, so she was the one who answered. Larry asked to speak to Barb Robbie, and she replied that she was Barb.

Larry tried not to show his feelings too much, as he asked her if she had any plans for Saturday. He had thought, since they were both still relatively new to the D.C. area, they might do some sightseeing together on Saturday. This time she said that would be great, without any hesitation.

Encouraged by this, Larry asked his next question and was even more delighted when he discovered Barb didn't have any plans for that night either.

He hopped into Dan's car and got himself lost trying to find her. He arrived late, as he was so used to doing. He was greeted warmly, and together they looked through the evening paper and decided to see "Thoroughly Modern Millie." Larry got such a kick out of it he had all those around him laughing, too. After the movie, he took her out to eat and then something like a monsoon hit. They could barely see to drive back to Barb's place. Then, with the rain still pelting down on the burgundy Corvair, Larry asked her if she'd like to pray. This was their first time to pray together, and the words flowed freely from them both to God. Then he hurried her off to the door through the still pouring rain and said he would see her Saturday.

Saturday was a beautiful day, but very humid. Larry again arrived a little behind schedule. They had decided to take in everything they could, so they began with Mount Vernon. He took Barb's hand while they crossed the traffic. She seemed so fairy-like, he felt the need to protect her.

There was a line to stand in to go through Mount Vernon itself, and Larry was soon involved in conversation with what turned out to be some Vietnamese men who were standing behind them in line. They had a good discussion together.

On the way back to the busy highway, Larry again took Barb's hand, and he held it the rest of the way to the car.

Next came the Washington Monument. Again, there was a long line of people waiting for the elevator. Larry suggested they take the stairs instead and was surprised and impressed when Barb agreed. There was absolutely no line there! So they began, 1, 2, 3, 4...101, 102, 103, 104...501...602. The closer they got to the top, the curlier Barb's hair got and the more Larry was impressed with her character and spunk. She couldn't be in the kind of shape he was, but she didn't complain even when she needed to stop and catch her breath. He didn't mind in the least, having to take her hand to help her. 701,...803, and finally 898, as they reached the top. It seemed to be the top of the world as they stood there together overlooking the 69 square miles which comprise the District of Columbia. From their vantage point, they could easily see the plan of the designer, Pierre Charles L'Enfant. A perfect cross lay before them, with the White House to the north, the Jefferson Memorial to the south, the Capitol Building to the east, and the Lincoln Memorial to the west. Larry was so proud to be fighting for this "one nation, under God!"

Their next stops were the Jefferson and Lincoln Memorials and all the significant spots around that they could think of. Then they went back to Barb's to freshen up and rest before hitting it again. They spent several hours at the Smithsonian Institute. When they got to the part where there were a lot of weapons and uniforms and things like that, Larry jokingly told Barb that he guessed he'd go over to Vietnam and get himself a white cross.

Barb looked at him aghast and pleaded with him to never say things like that. Larry was used to that kind of talk at the Base but had not realized it was in poor taste with Barb. He felt sorry he had said it.

By the time they left the Institute, it was beginning to get dark. Still, they decided to try Arlington Cemetery to see the Kennedy grave if there was time. It was closed, however, when they arrived, so they just looked through the huge gate, then got back in the car, and drove up to the Marine monument. This was really special to Larry, with his obvious pride for the Marine Corps, and he sensed it was meaningful to Barb as well.

As they sat for a much-needed rest, staring out at the lights of the city, Barb had one more suggestion. She knew of a coffee house where a friend of hers played her harp, and she really wanted Larry to hear her. So off they went again. They ordered sandwiches and waited quite a while before discovering her friend, Pinkie, would not be there that evening. Then, once again, they found themselves outside the big estate that Barb now called home.

Barb asked Larry if he was still hungry and would like some sandwiches. He gladly accepted and smiled as he walked her up to the now-darkened mansion. They were tired and almost slap-happy by now. But the peanut butter sandwiches tasted terrific, and he was thoroughly convinced that Barb was terrific as well. He wanted to tell her that this had been one of the happiest days of his life. But he didn't. Later, as she stood two steps up on the winding staircase, he wanted to take her in his arms. But he didn't. He knew that would be getting ahead of God and, more than anything, he didn't want to spoil this relationship by doing that. So instead, they made plans to hear Pinkie the next time she performed.

Larry said he would check with her the next day about when and where. When he called Sunday after church, the guys in the frat house knew, perhaps better than Larry, what was going on. While he was on the phone, Dan could be heard in the background teasing him that he just couldn't be away from that girl for a minute. Consequently, they invited Dan to go with them that evening to the dinner where Dr. Veradee, the founder of International Christian Leadership would be speaking and Pinkie would be giving a concert. Both Larry and Dan were greatly impressed with the saintly, white-haired founder of ICL and with Pinkie's heavenly music. When Larry had first met the Robbies, George had been the youth pastor in Billings. Since then, he and his wife Carol had moved to Maryland. While Barb now talked with them, Larry found himself cornered by another young lady.

Before the evening was over, Larry invited Barb to meet his folks and go with them to the East Coast Conference on Tuesday evening, the day of their arrival. Then, later that night back at the base, he called home. He told his mom that the young woman she had talked to at Maranatha was now there in D.C., and she would get a chance to see her when they came to graduation. His mom asked if he had been dating her and, as soon as Larry said "Yes," he knew his mom would put two and two together. He never had been quite this excited around them about any girl before.

When Mom, Dad and Marlene arrived, they spent much of their supper time listening to "Barb and I did this" and "Barb and I went there." Then they went to pick her up and head for the evening meeting at the conference.

Larry took all the wrong turns, so they finally settled for ice cream sundaes and a picture taken back at the Bleeker's motel. Before he left to take Barb back home, he asked her if she'd like to come to the graduation with his folks the next day. She said she would.

When they got into the car Larry had rented for his folks' visit, Barb tried to roll up her window without success. When she told Larry her dilemma, he said it was because the weather stripping was off and this was his secret weapon. She looked surprised for just a moment and then asked if he were hinting. To his grinning "Yes," she moved over next to him. He put his arm around her, and they both just sat silently for a moment. Then, on the long drive home, they began to talk as they had not done before. Larry prayed that God would control their feelings and his words. He asked God to let them know what was on His heart for them to know at this stage of their relationship. As they talked, they were aware that there was much more than a physical attraction involved.

Larry told her that God had really used her as a kind of spiritual catalyst in his life. Being with her made him want to be a man that would please God in every way.

Barb was amazed that God was using her that way in Larry's life, mostly because that was the way He was using Larry in her life. She said God had never been so important to her as He had become since she met him. She found herself praying about every move she made and every thought she had.

They continued talking over the miles back to Barb's, and they felt God's hand upon them for His good as they asked each other how they felt about different things. They really did not know each other well, but they were finding that God had made them very much alike in the important things.

At one point, when they had been talking quite seriously, Barb asked Larry if she could tell him something. Larry hesitated a moment. His mind immediately went to the Lord, to check if they were moving too quickly. He asked God not to let that happen. Then he remembered her question and, since he didn't know what she was about to say, he invited her to continue.

Barb began with "Larry, I..." Then she stopped and decided that was not the time to say it, but she would tell him some other time. They both sensed that that was better.

When they got back to the mansion, they turned to God in prayer together. As Larry listened to Barb's words, they seemed almost like his own. "Lord, you know...you know how my feelings have been all this year and three months. You know that I've prayed that my feelings would just be Yours..."

Before they left the car, Larry gave her a copy of Living Prophecies and said he'd buy her a tape recorder in Okinawa so they could send tapes back and forth and not just letters.

When he took her to the door, he knew God had given him a green light to the desire of his heart, and he bent down and kissed her on the lips. There was no doubt to either one of them that God was there and smiling His approval.

The next morning Larry picked her up before breakfast. He had on his white dress uniform, which made him look all the more handsome and strong. As he climbed back into the rented car, he noticed Barb had left a little space between them. He reached over and took her small hand in his strong suntanned one, and they knew the night before had not been a dream.

This was their last day together, but they did not talk much as they drove out to get Mom, Dad and Marlene and then stopped to get a roll and some juice and coffee for breakfast.

The graduation itself was most impressive as 534 of the nation's top young men received their well-deserved honors.

There was just time to get Mom and Marlene over to the commissary for shopping before Larry, Dan and Murphy had to get ready to leave for Dan's wedding in New York. As Mom and Marlene shopped, Larry and Barb stood hand in hand in the background. Larry felt time to be his biggest enemy. One month of furlough and 13 months in Vietnam lie ahead.

Larry managed to put off leaving until he had taken Barb back downtown to work and loaded her down with tapes to take back to Dean and Dottie for him. This would help get her involved. Then, as they stood by the elevator, the only words Larry could find to say were, "Thanks Barb…we'll see you, and keep praying." The elevator was there, he stepped in, and the big iron doors banged shut.

Graduation from Quantico
August 1967

CHAPTER 20 - PREPARING TO LEAVE

Larry rode from Quantico to Buffalo, New York, with Warren Murphy in his Volkswagen. They arrived in the middle of the night. The next morning, August 31, was the wedding practice for Dan and Diane's wedding later that day. Larry was the Commander of the Guard of Lieutenants that assisted in the wedding. Again, Larry witnessed someone very close to him take the vow, "to love, honor and obey, till death do you part." Larry looked at Murphy standing across from him, and his mind drifted back to Quantico and the discussion they had when the assignment had come through for Larry and Dan's platoon to head for Vietnam. Larry had told Murphy that he had joined the Marines because he felt it was God's will for him to share in the responsibility of going to Vietnam. He knew this to be God's "call" to him, and he was looking forward to serving God there. Now, Warren's words came back to mind. Warren had said, "As Christians, we deserve the most to live in God's world, but have the least to lose by leaving it."

Then Larry's heart had responded to God as the wedding procession filed out.

> *Father God, You know how I long to be with You and yet I feel a real urgency to do all You have for me to do while I'm still here upon this earth. Whether You take me home from Vietnam, or Ames, or right here from this wedding, God, I want to be actively involved in the battle of bringing souls to You, right down to the end.*

It was a beautiful wedding, and Larry rejoiced that God had brought Dan and Diane together. He prayed that God would protect Dan for his new bride. On and off throughout the wedding, Larry thought of Barb. The next day he got a letter off to her telling her how much he missed her and wished she could be there with him.

Larry got a flight from New York to Des Moines late Saturday night and, since his folks had just moved into their new home and were not yet settled, he called Ron and Donna when he got in. They came down to get him. He spent the night there and surprised everyone the next morning when they saw him in church.

That afternoon, Larry got to attend Marlene's piano recital. He later told his folks how much he would like to buy a new piano for Marlene during his year in Vietnam. That evening he went to the college youth group, and they asked him to give a sermonette. The message on his heart was to challenge them to really "dig in and serve the Lord with their whole heart." Then, that evening before going to bed, he called Barb.

Larry spent Monday helping out at home with the unpacking and looking up old friends in Ames. As always, he found himself challenging them and himself to hang in there and serve God.

It was during these first couple of days back home that Larry spent some concentrated time alone with God, to really get his feelings about Barb totally yielded to Him and to find God's leading for the next 13 months. He knew how he felt, but the important thing to him was to know how God and Barb felt. As he spent time in the Word and in prayer, God began to reveal His plan, at least in part. Then he wrote Barb what would have been the most difficult letter he'd every penned, except for the fact that he was confident it was just what God wanted him to say, and that the Holy Spirit would be present with Barb to convey the proper message to her heart.

He told her that he felt that God was asking them not to write during his days in Vietnam. He would have the responsibility of 30 to 40 men, and he would have to give one hundred per cent of himself to them. She, too, would have that time to be learning from God in her daily walk and witness. And he said that they must trust God to once again renew the feelings He had given them for each other when he returned. He added that the important thing was that she had peace about this and that she would let him know how she felt about it.

On Tuesday, Larry sat down in the kitchen while his mom put together a pie. He told her that he'd like to go to the Christian Businessmen's Banquet and take his best gal. Mom looked at him. She knew he had been calling Barb, and Tony teased him every time he wrote Barb a letter. Mom said it was a great idea for him to go, since Hi couldn't make it that year. Then, to her surprise, Larry asked her if she didn't know who his best gal was. His twinkling eyes gave him away even before he said, "Yea, you!"

Mom accepted with real delight and was proud as could be to be escorted by her tall, handsome, Marine son, who continued to introduce her as his "best gal."

The rest of that week was spent visiting with family and friends. Jim North was preparing to go to Indonesia, and Don and Laura McDonald were now back to pick up the ministry at ISU. So he had some good fellowship with the Navigator gang that was around.

When he talked with Don, he expressed the possibility of his not returning and that he felt it best that he and Barb not write in case God would soon take him home. There was no sadness in what he said, only a kind of excitement that God was sovereign and His way was guaranteed to be good for everyone!

Larry also spent as much time with those at Campus Baptist as time would allow. He knew they had upheld him in prayer all through those months at Quantico.

On Friday morning, Larry and Mom got some of his clothes dyed a Marine green and others packed, sorted and stored. As he hung up one uniform after another, he said it was too bad they couldn't have given that thousand dollars to missionaries instead of having to buy all those uniforms, when they knew they could only take two of them to Vietnam.

The Music Committee at Campus Baptist had asked Larry and his three brothers to get a quartet number worked up for Sunday evening. Gary, Ron and Tony decided Larry should be the one to represent them all, and they could spend what little time they could get together visiting instead of practicing. This they did until the wee hours of the morning.

On Saturday, Gram arrived at the Des Moines airport at 12:30 and Larry, Marlene and Mom went to meet her. Later that afternoon, Larry stopped by the church. As he walked around the corner, he almost ran right into Curt Siemers. Larry asked how Curt was as he shook his hand eagerly.

Curt said he had just been praying for Larry. He told him he came over to the church one day each week and prayed for guys in the service, and he had just finished bringing Larry to the Lord in prayer. Larry was thrilled to know someone was praying for him. He knew he would be needing all the prayers he could get, and he thanked Curt genuinely for them.

On Sunday evening, there were 13 of his family who sat together in the pew. That brief encounter with Curt the day before had helped to finalize in his own thinking what he wanted to communicate to the congregation. He had managed to put together some words of his own to the song, "I Found the Answer, I Learned to Pray." He had told no one, so when they called on him to minister in song, he gave a short testimony and then introduced the song which many thought they knew. It was not until he reached the second verse that they began to realize that these words were Larry's words and they came directly from Larry's heart to theirs.

I was sad and lonely, All my hope was gone;
Days were long and dreary, I couldn't carry on;
When troubles round me gathered, God put my heart at ease;
I bowed my head in worship, and got down on my knees.
Chorus:
I found the answer—I learned to pray,
With faith to guide me, I found my way;
The sun is shining on me each day,
I found the answer—I learned to pray.

Sometimes I get discouraged, with those I try to win;
They have no peace or gladness, they seem content in sin;
I wonder, "Can I reach them?" They have a distant air;
The Spirit then reminds me, "Now, Bleek, begin with prayer."

I soon will leave my country, to serve in Vietnam;
I'm going with my Jesus, God's Son, the spotless Lamb;
Now this is all I'm asking, if in your heart you care;
For me and all my buddies, Remember us in prayer.

Chorus:
You have the answer—You all can pray,
With faith to guide us, we'll find our way;
The sun will shine on us each day;
You have the answer—You all can pray!

As Larry walked back to his seat, tall and strong and handsome, he sensed God had communicated his feelings to the congregation. After the service, one by one, people expressed to him how God had used it and that they would be praying. Larry felt a real tug in his heart as he already began to miss them.

One lady came up to him and asked him if the Lord should ask him to give his life, was he ready for that? And Larry assured her that he was.

As he thought more about that question that night, he knew he had already done that. His life was God's to use however He wanted, one hundred per cent. And he thought of the verse in Galatians 2:20: *"I am crucified with Christ: nevertheless I live; yet not I, but Christ liveth in me: and the life which I now live in the flesh I live by the faith of the Son of God, Who loved me, and gave Himself for me."*

Then, with the peace that comes only from total commitment to a God he knew loved him, he got a short, but good night's sleep.

That next day, Ron and Donna drove him to the airport in Des Moines for his trip out to Vancouver, Edmonton and Billings. During his stop-over in Denver on the way out West, Larry wrote Barb a letter and told her about his trip that morning to the airport.

Dear Barb,

When we walk with God, something exciting is bound to be happening. Psalm 68:19 says; "Blessed be the Lord, Who daily loadeth us with benefits, even the God of our salvation." This reminds me of the daily things God is doing. This morning Ron and Donna took me to Des Moines to the airport. On the way down (about a 30-minute drive), we purposely began chatting about spiritual things and what changes in attitude they've had since getting married. Donna said that she didn't think she had a relationship with Christ and wanted to know how to be sure of eternal life. Before going into the airport, we prayed and she asked Jesus Christ to come into her heart and life—Man, it was great!!

Barb, pray for her particularly now, as these are important days for a spiritual babe. With the simplicity of a child and tears in her eyes, she and Ron are now in a much closer and tighter union in heart. I'm also trusting God to use this to stimulate Ron and get him underway spiritually as well.

I'm in Denver now and will soon take off for Seattle. I shall bid hello to the fair city and to Seattle Pacific College for you, okay?

I had an interesting chat with the guy next to me regarding life insurance and spiritual values. I shared my testimony, and he wants me to write to him. Maybe I can challenge him to more personally consider Christ. We can't write to everyone like this, but I guess we never know what one letter or a couple of post cards might mean in terms of eternity in a man's life. It is fascinating how God seems to use our time in connection with people around us.

Barb, I am sending the words to a song that I scratched out. They asked me to sing in church last night, and I wanted to say something to the congregation so I used the tune of "I Found the

Answer, I Learned to Pray" by George Beverly Shea and added some of my own words.

After quoting the song to her, he ended by saying:

Barb, pray for the kids there in Billings on Saturday and Sunday. Ask God to give me the right words to share. I wish you could be here. I'm praying for you.
Yours in Him,

When Larry got to Seattle, he caught a bus up to Bellingham to see Bob and Judy Magnuson and had a good visit with them. Bob was working on the campus of Western Washington as a Navigator representative. This was his first such assignment, and Larry did much to encourage him and Judy in their new ministry.

Larry remembered to thank Judy for the fudge she had sent to him at Quantico. She asked him what shape it was in when it arrived. She thought, after sending it in the hot summer, it probably had melted all over. Larry assured her that even though they had eaten it with a spoon, they had eaten it so fast it didn't have time to run.

Their conversation that evening naturally turned to Vietnam. When they asked him if he was scared to go, he replied that he wasn't really. He was convinced that God wanted him there, so he was finding it exciting to anticipate. Then, with the same good humor that helped make him human to Judy at the Lawrie home, he commented that there might be just one little thing that concerned him. That was "digging in" over there when an enemy attacked. He was a big guy and those holes were pretty small.

God really used every conversation on that trip to totally convince Larry that his life was truly God's to do with what

He wanted. God's will was that for which he was looking forward.

Larry went on to spend two days with Colin in Vancouver. They had much to talk about, laugh about and sing about. They prayed together about Vietnam, and Larry told him that he had a job to do over there. He was thrilled to think of all the men he could talk to about Jesus Christ.

He got to see the whole Vancouver gang when he went to the Lee's for Bill's birthday dinner. He took Miriam Lee a bouquet of roses. He was so glad to be able to give anything he could to these who had given so much to him in his "no money" days at Timberline and Vancouver.

Then Ralph and Colin drove him to the airport, and he again took to the air to continue his trip to the Lawries' new home in Edmonton, Alberta, Canada. Since they had been there less than a week, there was still some cleaning and unpacking to be done, much as his own home had looked a week or so before. Larry pitched in on scrubbing the floors for Shirley, who was now kept extra busy with their new daughter, Joann, who was only a few months old. Larry was delighted to get to know the baby and, when Shirley was busy, he thought nothing of changing her diaper or giving her a bottle.

He was especially grateful for the opportunities to go with Mac, Barry and Don to the campuses where they were beginning their new ministry. Bleek was a real encouragement as he was filled with all the excitement and enthusiasm of his own college days.

One morning, Don and Larry went out for breakfast for some special time alone before he left. The waitress that morning evidently wished she could have stayed at home. She was grumpy and cross.

When she came to their table she asked in a curt and sober manner if they were ready to order. Larry knew her whole day would go badly unless she could look at the brighter side so, while she wrote up the orders, he came through with two short but appropriate jokes. Within 30 seconds, he had her laughing. As they left an hour or so later, she still had this totally new outlook on her day.

Scotty Lawrie was, of course, especially excited over Larry's visit. Bleek showed him the military way of making his bed and spit-polishing his shoes, and they had some really good times in the Word and prayer together. All the Lawrie boys enjoyed a rousing football game with their Marine buddy. Somehow, he seemed so much stronger and bigger and, when he put his Marine uniform on for them, he was all that young boys look for in an ideal to pattern their lives after.

Several times during the conversations of those three days in Edmonton, the subject of Vietnam came up. Larry always had the same confidence that he knew this was where God was sending him, and he was ready to go.

The evening before he left, Larry took a brightly-splashed, green and black shirt into Don. He told him he wouldn't be needing it in Vietnam and, this way, when he looked at the shirt it could remind him to pray for all of them over there.

The next morning there were some sad good-byes to the boys as they went off to school, and then Don, Berry and Mac drove him the 180 miles to the airport in Calgary where he would fly on to Billings, Montana.

No sooner had they driven out of the driveway and Larry said he had been working on the book of Colossians as far as memorizing it was concerned. He asked them if they would mind checking him out for any mistakes. They knew he had begun this project while he had been in Vancouver and were eager to see if he had, indeed, mastered it. For the next half hour or so, he quoted the entire book of Colossians. As they listened, it sounded like Larry's own words, from his heart to theirs. They were wide open to anything else he had to say.

He seemed running over with encouraging and challenging comments to the guys to *"keep at their calling, to win souls for Christ, and to deepen their own relationship with the Lord."* Many times in the days to come, Larry's words or a verse from Colossians would stir and encourage their hearts.

The plane was already loading when they got to Calgary, so he just had time to press some Canadian money into Don's hand as he ran for the plane, and he was off to Billings.

Inside the plane, Larry found a seat next to a man who, in that next hour, became a very dear friend. He was a Mormon gentleman supervising youth work among the Canadian Indians. Since Larry, too, had been active with youth on college campuses in Canada and was now headed for Billings where he would be speaking to the youth, they found a common interest and built upon it. Larry had learned to listen respectfully to another man's religious beliefs and then, simply and sincerely, to share what Jesus Christ had done for him and meant to him.

When the plane landed, the man was home but he lingered as long as he could talking with Larry. When he asked Larry for his address, Larry told him it would be Vietnam. Then the man gave Larry his address and asked if he could send him the tape of his message in Billings; Larry said he would be happy to. They shook hands warmly, and Larry waved to the man as he went to meet his wife and seven children.

When Larry arrived in Billings on Saturday morning in the rain, Kathy and Mrs. Robbie were there to meet him. They took him home and showed him his room. The rest of Saturday was spent visiting with Mrs. Robbie about spiritual things and Barb, and talking with Kathy who was about to enter her senior year of high school. She found Larry to have a listening ear and sound advice. On Saturday night, Larry spoke to the young people gathered from various churches in the community. Then, when he and Kathy returned home at 10:30, he suggested he go get some pizzas to eat around the open fire in the living room. So, Saturday very happily drew to a close, and everyone enjoyed a few short hours of rest.

Sunday morning breakfast was served at 4:30, and by 5:00 Mr. and Mrs. Robbie, Kathy and Larry were on their way to pick up two more passengers for the boat trip ahead of them. One was a young man in the insurance business, who had given his time unselfishly for a couple of years working with the young people of Billings to bring them the message of Christ. The other was a young man named John, a sophomore in college, who had accepted Christ but was finding total commitment to Him difficult. He and Larry hit it off immediately and the two-hour drive to Lovell, Wyoming, was a delightful time of jokes, conversations, singing, mouth organ music and laughter, until they arrived at Yellowtail Lake and the launching site.

Yellowtail Lake is a fantastically beautiful lake in the Big Horn Canyon, which is about 50 miles long. It was formed by the construction of Yellowtail Dam, and few people had yet seen its beauty. The canyon itself was a miniature Grand Canyon, with very steep, sheer rock walls along each side, extremely interesting rock formations and magnificent coloring. There were only two or three places, many miles from civilization, where a vehicle of any kind could get near the water. Very few people had put their boats into the water to explore its beauty. Mr. Robbie had had the privilege of exploring it on a patrol boat just a few weeks before with a friend in the office of the Bureau of Reclamation. He had learned of a man who built a houseboat, which he launched on the lake almost every weekend. On those trips he took groups of people, launching at 7:00 in the morning and traveling 50 miles up the lake to the dam and back to the dock by 5:00 in the evening.

At 7:00 that morning, Cecil, the skipper, called out "All aboard" and they were on their way.

They had every kind of reasonable September weather that day: rain, wind, mist, sunshine and clouds. The skipper was a most congenial host, and each of them got to take turns steering the boat. The coffee was kept hot, and there was food available at all times.

As Larry and John talked about spiritual things, Larry challenged him to commit his life totally to Christ, and there was a marked difference in John from that point on. At one time during the middle of the afternoon, while the sun was shining beautifully, Cecil tied the boat up to a dock half way up the lake, and Larry and John spent about 45 minutes diving off the top of the houseboat and swimming in the cold, cold lake waters.

During a rainy time, Larry took his harmonica and played soft, lovely music as his heart, like David's, communed with God.

They got back to the Robbie home around 8:00 Sunday night. In Larry's conversations with Kathy, he had learned that one of the young men whom he had led to the Lord at the Glen the year before was having some serious spiritual battles and Larry felt a real responsibility to get together with him. Kathy took him to his customary hangout; they found him and brought him back to be a part of the family circle, which also now included John, who had stopped by his place on their way back to change his clothes. They spent another hour or so joking, singing and talking about the Lord.

As the evening progressed, Larry excused himself for a few minutes while he put in his usual Sunday night call to Barb, and told her how great her family had treated him and how much he wished she could have been there in more than just spirit.

Then he changed back into his uniform. Once in it, he became a Marine again with a seriousness about his "calling." Just before he left, the young high school senior questioned Larry about his philosophy of taking another human life.

Larry told him that he had given that a lot of thought. He didn't pretend to know whether or not America should be in Vietnam, but he did know that it was where God was sending him. He told him he believed the Bible gives grounds, under certain circumstances, for taking human life. He didn't know what would be required of him in the future, but he was confident that God would lead him in that moment, if that moment ever arrived and he would do whatever he needed to do. For Larry, that was settled and he would not spend his time worrying about it. He knew he was in God's will in his uniform, serving his country, and he had peace down inside.

Larry's flight time was 11:45 p.m. and just before boarding the plane, he pulled from his duffle bag the sandwiches the Robbies had been almost too embarrassed to ask a lieutenant if he wanted. He happily tucked them in his pocket for his all-night flight home.

Because of a severe rainstorm, no planes could land in Des Moines early that next morning, so Larry was held over in Omaha until afternoon, when Mom, Gram and Marlene met him.

Much of Larry's final week in Ames was spent getting things in order for his going. Larry and Tony went to Hill's Studios, where Larry had his picture taken. He asked Ron to pick up the proofs and have his brothers choose the best negative for him to have a picture made to surprise his parents for Christmas. He also visited a piano store to price new pianos.

Lt. Larry Bleeker

There were still some people he wanted to call on personally, too. First, he went to the hospital to see Millie and his new niece, Tammy. He was disappointed that he, being a proud "uncle," did not have the same visiting privileges as proud daddy, Gary. So he made up for it when Tammy and Millie got to come home.

He also called on a dear saint from Campus Baptist who had terminal cancer. Larry was confident he would not see him again this side of glory. Just to talk with a man whose feet were on the threshold of eternity made heaven and God seem so much closer and the need to make Christ known so much more urgent.

As it got closer to the time for Dan and Diane to arrive to pick him up and take him with them to San Francisco, there remained one more important thing to do before he could really feel ready to go. That one thing was perhaps the hardest yet. Larry realized that no matter how long he waited, it had to be done and only God could come up with the right words to say.

When he arrived at the Switzer home, he asked Carla to get her sweater so they could go outside and talk. Then he walked her clear out in the back pasture where the smell of alfalfa brought back many fond memories. With all the gentleness and love that God could show through him, and yet with a kind of solid determination, he told Carla that she must forget him. What they had had, had been beautiful, but now they both knew it was over and she must forget him and look to God for a bright future.

As he drove back home, he knew that only God could help her find understanding and that He could be counted on to do just that.

CHAPTER 21 - THE LAST GOOD-BYES

One by one, the lights had been extinguished in the Bleeker home but few, if any, were asleep. Their minds were filled with thoughts of Larry. What they had tried not to think about now loomed before them like white phantoms in the darkness. "Would he come back safely?"

Only an hour or so earlier, the house had been filled with laughter and fun, and yet, a seriousness had wrapped itself around each heart. Here were two young men—Larry and Dan, who were leaving in the morning for Vietnam. Although it was for only 13 months, it seemed like forever to many there that night. Besides all the Bleekers, including the little ones, there had been Dan and Diane Anger, Bud and Betty Wiuff, and the twins. They had all come over after church for this final night before the guys left.

Once during the evening, when there was a lull in the conversations, Mom could be heard reading one of her child evangelism stories to Todd, Troy and Tammy, about a mother who had a star in her window because she had had a son killed in the war. Other conversations were sparked up immediately. No one could dwell on that—at least not with the lights on and everyone alive and well. But later, in the darkness, the story drifted back into the minds of several of them.

Shortly after the story, Mom had asked Larry if he would record the song he had sung in church the week before, while Betty Wiuff was there to accompany it. They had no music, but Betty was able to play it just fine with Larry's help. Soon they came up with a good rendition which they were able to record.

As Larry left Tony's room in the basement, after a much appreciated brother-to-brother talk, Larry glanced up at the clock on the wall. It was 1:20 a.m. He walked thoughtfully to the recreation room and sat for a moment on his cot. Mom had wanted him in a bed, but Larry had said even a cot would soon be a luxury. He had really wanted this 10' x 12' room for his own during this furlough, and it had been perfect. As he looked around, he knew he had gotten everything in order. He had sorted through all the things in his trunk, and he'd given away a lot of the clothes he wouldn't be needing for awhile. All that remained now was the final last-minute packing in the morning. The past 24 days had gone so quickly. Only a few hours remained, but there was one more important thing to be done.

Larry had the song on tape, but there was so much more on his heart to share with his family. So, with the tape recorder once again warmed up, he sat down and recorded this tape around that song.

> *This is Sunday, the 24th of September, 1967. As I think back from this day to my childhood, the days that have passed and the experiences, the things that God has done, I count it a real privilege to have the Christian heritage that I do. And I find it not surprising that I've come to find a reality in Jesus Christ, because of my parents and their concern and interest, because of my grandparents, and right on back in the ancestor background that I have.*
>
> *I think of something the Scriptures say that God has recorded for us. It says, in Proverbs 22:6: "Train up a child in the way he should go: and when he is old, he will not depart from it."*
>
> *I look back and I think that probably the reason why I'm walking with God today is because my*

parents were concerned in training me in the way that I should go, so that in these years, when I finally came to decide personally in Jesus Christ, it would be a matter of walking in the ways that I had learned.

I can remember, as a very little kid, kneeling down to say my prayers before I hit the rack at night. I can remember the folks praying at the supper table. I can remember spending time praying and just the importance of prayer, although maybe not understood at that time, has come to mean so much to me now. And I think there's an answer in our Christian lives to seeking God's work, and I think God works in response to our prayers. I think people come to Christ, because people pray, and I think people go on, because they pray. I'd like to sing a song now, called, "I Found the Answer, I Learned to Pray," particularly significant to me since coming into the Marine Corps.

(The song was recorded here).

As I think now about not only praying, but soon to go overseas, Mom and Dad, I can only say I go with the confidence of Jesus Christ, Who sticks closer than a friend or a brother. And I think of what Paul was saying to the Philippians and the confidence he had when he said in Philippians 1:6-9: "Being confident of this very thing, that He which hath begun a good work in you will perform it until the day of Jesus Christ: Even as it is meet for me to think this of you all, because I have you in my heart; inasmuch as both in my bonds, and in the defense and confirmation of the gospel, ye all are partakers of my grace. For God is my record, how greatly I long after you all in the bowels of Jesus Christ. And this I pray, that your love may abound yet more and more in knowledge and in all judgment."

Mom and Dad, I think not only of you but I think of the entire family. I think of Ron and Donna, since she's trusted Jesus Christ. I think of Gary and Millie and, in my heart, I hold you before God and I long to see you again. And I trust that God will grant this.

And I just want you to know this, I'm ready to go and I say also as Paul said in Philippians 1:21-23: "For me to live is Christ, and to die is gain. But if I live in the flesh, this is the fruit of my labor: yet what I shall choose I wot not. For I am in a strait betwixt two, having a desire to depart, and to be with Christ; which is far better: nevertheless to abide in the flesh is more needful for you."

And yet, to go to Vietnam, I'm ready to—to live, or to die, and to do either for the glory of Jesus Christ.

I'd like now to take time to pray on the tape for you all:

Father, You know our hearts. And I pray that by Jesus Christ we might with all boldness, approach Your throne. God, we thank You for the position we have in You, through Jesus. We thank You for the life that's possible and for the promise that You've given us, that this life can be and will be abundant. Father, we thank You for the good times, the rough times, and yet the very thrilling times, God, that we have in walking with You. And I pray for the Bleeker household, God, that it might be a testimony in the earth and a praise to Your name. Be with Mom and Dad and keep them in physical strength and spiritual healthiness that they might walk by faith.

Be with Gary, Millie and the little ones. Keep them growing in grace and performing, God, before You, with eager and responsive hearts. Be with Ron and Donna, as they start out and really form this household, and I pray that Jesus Christ might be the very center.

So God, keep the entire family in Jesus' precious name and for His sake.

Amen.

See ya.

The hours hastened on. Monday morning was rather hectic, trying to get all the necessary things packed and loaded into Dan's little burgundy Corvair and still leave room for Dan, Diane and Larry. The goodbyes were particularly hard that morning, as Pop left for the furniture store and Tony and Marlene reluctantly left for school. Ron skipped his speech class that morning so that he and Donna could have an early lunch with Larry before he left. It was now nearing "blast-off" time, the last-minute things were packed and said and felt. Tears brimmed eyes as Larry told his mom he thought it was all the praying here at home that was paying off, so to keep praying. And then, he handed his mom the tape he had recorded for them the night before. Then, with hugs, and "see ya's," the tiny back seat began to bulge as Larry tried to cram in his long legs and arms. Mom, Gram and Donna watched tearfully as Ron snapped pictures, and Larry waved enthusiastically until his home and loved ones had disappeared from sight.

From Ames they drove to Glen Eyrie, just a few miles from Colorado Springs. Larry recalled again to Dan and Diane some of the experiences he had had there while at conferences and a summer training program. His enthusiasm and almost reverence for the place was soon shared by his two traveling companions as they drove through the gate and up to the 67-room castle. During their two days there, Larry took them up to the top of Razorback Ridge overlooking the 1100-acre grounds to the place where Dawson Trotman, the founder, had first claimed this estate for God back in the spring of 1953. There, in a rugged rock, was etched this Bible reference, *"I Chronicles 29:11-14."* Dan knew Larry knew all about Trotman and figured he'd know that passage, so he asked him, and Larry quoted it for them. *"Thine, O Lord, is the greatness, and the power, and the glory, and the victory, and the majesty: for all that is in the heaven and in the earth is Thine; Thine is the Kingdom, O Lord, and Thou art exalted as Head above all. Both riches and honor come of Thee, and Thou reignest over all; and in Thine hand is power and might; and in Thine hand it is to make great, and to give strength unto all. Now therefore, our God, we thank Thee, and praise Thy glorious Name. But who am I, and what is my people, that we should be able to offer so willingly after this sort? For all things come of Thee, and of Thine own have we given Thee."*

Larry went on to tell them how God miraculously raised the $100,000 needed to buy the estate in six weeks! He shared that Daws had lived three more years to watch God make of this place the International Headquarters, Training Center and Conference Grounds of the Navigators, where countless lives had been changed and would continue to be changed.

As they stood a moment longer in silence, Larry saw his eagle friend soaring high in the heavens and, for a moment, Larry felt he was there, too.

Their last evening there, Larry went into Colorado Springs to visit with the Eims family and to ask LeRoy about the possibility of tying in with him when he returned from Vietnam. Larry was sure now that the Navigators were right where he belonged, and LeRoy was glad to hear it. Since LeRoy and Dan Green, who had just gotten out of the service, were both ex-Marines, they talked quite a bit that night. Then, early the next morning, the Corvair continued its trip west.

From the Glen, they drove on to Salt Lake City and then to San Francisco, where they spent the remaining days with some of Dan's friends and took in the sights. All during those last hours in San Francisco, Larry's thoughts were of Barb. He had tried to call her Sunday evening and had missed her. Barb had said that she understood about their not writing while he was out of the country, but now he needed to hear her say it again. He'd be leaving in just a few short hours, and he must get through. Once again he placed a call through to her at her work. As they talked, Larry shared some verses on his heart for her. One of them was from I Corinthians 2:9:

"...Eye hath not seen, nor ear heard, neither have entered into the heart of man, the things which God hath prepared for them that love Him."

Their hearts rejoiced together over those miles, knowing that God had been in their relationship thus far and their future, whether together or apart, was safely resting in their heavenly Father's wise and loving arms. They prayed and then said their good-byes.

In the meantime, Dan and Diane were saying their parting words, so Diane could leave before the plane took off and maybe it wouldn't be so hard. That evening, the huge transport plane took off from Travis Air Force Base as Larry and Dan Anger took *"wings as eagles,"* their destination—VIETNAM!

CHAPTER 22 - "I WILL GO BEFORE THEE"

The huge, silver transport slid through the black skies over Japan to land at Yakota, the United States air base, approximately 30 miles west of Tokyo. It was now October 5. While the plane was being refueled, the men who had slept very little since leaving San Francisco took advantage of the time to stretch their legs and look around the Fighter Interceptor wing. It was still the dark of night. Then, with a few less Air Force personnel aboard, they again took to the skies; next stop—Okinawa.

The sun was rising in flaming splendor, shimmering across the tops of the clouds when the plane again began to lose altitude. Below appeared the islands of the Pacific. One of these, some 64 miles in length and 2 to 18 miles wide, was to be their home for the next three days. The northern part of Okinawa was rugged and comparatively unpopulated, while the southern part was lower and contained most of the population. Camp Doris Hansen, in the central portion, soon extended its hot humid arms and welcomed the tired, restless human cargo.

One of the first things that Larry did after checking in at Camp Hansen, helped him realize that he was out of the states, even if it was under United States Military Occupation. He got a shave and a haircut for 80 cents from a woman barber. Several other things impressed Larry, too. Either he was unusually tall or they were unusually short. These little people, who all made him feel like a giant, were not afraid to work. The maids available in the quarters changed sheets, washed, ironed, scrubbed and polished shoes and boots, and would do just about any kind of work the men wanted at whatever price they would pay.

Perhaps the deepest impression of his visit on Okinawa came from the injection room at Camp Hansen. The flu shot, combined with the malaria pill, about wiped Larry out for a day. He did find time, however, to go shopping to buy Tony his belated birthday present and early Christmas present, a great camera. Saturday night Larry and Dan went to Yaka Beach to spend some time with Ken Metzger, a Navigator staff man working with the servicemen on the many bases on Okinawa. The morale was good among the men, and Larry and Dan were encouraged by their fellowship. That night went very quickly for, all too soon, it was time to again board the plane. At 0115 October 8, they left Okinawa and flew out of Kadena Air Force Base on the end of the island about 0330, arriving in Da Nang, Vietnam, about 0630 in pouring rain.

The glowering skies continued to drench the base at Da Nang as rain hit and ran off the aluminum roofs of the wood frame buildings wallowing in the mud. Those next long hours were spent waiting for assignments. Finally they came, and with them a separation for Larry and Dan. Larry was assigned to the Second Battalion, 4th Marines, and Dan to the Second Battalion, 26th Marines. This meant that Dan was on his way to Phu Bai to meet his battalion and Larry to Dong Ha. They waited that whole day in a crowded terminal with Marines literally all over the place with foot lockers and sea bags. Then late that afternoon Dan got a flight to Phu Bai, and Larry had time for only a passing word of departing because he was telling another lieutenant there about Jesus Christ.

That evening, with Dan gone and still no news about his flight out, he dropped a line to Colin. It read in part:

There are about only two ways to go in this area of the world, walk with God or live in sin. Boy, things are really loose and I'm afraid that without thrusting yourself continually on God, you would soon be caught up in the lust and fornication which is so open around here. I fear if Satan can keep plaguing us in these areas, he'll wreck us before long. Pray against him, buddy, and let's keep our hearts in the battle sharing Christ with guys. "And they overcame him (Satan), by the blood of the Lamb, and by the Word of their testimony; and they loved not their lives unto the death." Rev. 12:11.

Let's do it!

Larry finally got to Dong Ha the next day. The first sergeant named Nick showed him around, filled him in on things, and Larry got his equipment. That evening, he went over to a small officers' club that was really a shack but a good place to have a soda and get to know some of the guys. When he got back to his quarters, he was told the colonel wanted to see him. Larry was eager to get to the field and meet his men, so the colonel's news was good. He told Larry to get set, pack his stuff, and meet him at 0600 the next morning and be ready to shove out.

When Larry got back to the CP, he got a letter off to Jim North:

I'll be picking up the 2nd Platoon, Echo Co. in Con Thien. I join them probably tomorrow or the next day. The battalion has been hitting hard and giving Mr. Charles (That's what they call the NVA up here) a run for his money. Of course, there are casualties in the front lines, but we're fightin! I just got back from the colonel's hut, and he's taking me

> *up to Con Thien with him in the morning. Tonight I have mixed emotions, but a quiet peace deep inside. (Phil. 4:6, 7) and I praise God.*

Larry's heart was filled with expectation as he went to the colonel's hut the next morning shortly before 6:00 a.m. But the colonel was not there. When they did find him at his helicopter, it was full and they took off without Larry. It was hard to be left behind, until he remembered that God was directing his steps and there was a reason for him still being in Dong Ha.

Back in the command post later that day, Larry sat down and made a tape to send to his folks.

> *Mom, Pop,*
>
> *I thought I'd send you a tape here before I head out to the field. I imagine I'll be going to the field here either tomorrow or the day after tomorrow. I was going to go out this morning with the colonel but, at the last minute, he wouldn't let me get on his helicopter, said he didn't have enough room, so I didn't get to go to the field.*
>
> *Our company is on a sweep today or, in fact, the battalion is on a sweep today. Went back into the area where they got hit pretty hard. It's been awhile back, a week ago or so. They need to check the area out again and do some search and clear. Understand they haven't met with any enemy resistance. They've had a lot of mortar fire, but not sure whether it's incoming or whether it's something that's firing from overhead from our own 81's. But they're still out on that.*
>
> *This morning I got a few things squared away. Went down and took my travel, brought it up to date.*

Took my pay record down to dispersing and got a little of this admin. done so that I'm ready to go to the field to meet my men. I'll be in charge of the 2nd platoon, which is the only platoon without an officer right now. Boy, the more I find out about the company I've been assigned to, the more I find that probably this is of God. It's an exciting deal. Echo Company is supposed to be one of the top companies around. Has a real terrific company commander, plus they've got platoon commanders for all the platoons. Been doing a real bang-up job out here. The morale is good among the men; they're ready to do the job that they're expected to do. And I understand they really have respect toward their officers, so I'm looking forward to getting out to the field and getting in there with them.

Dan is in Phu Bai. I imagine he'll be there for awhile in the Phu Bai area, I don't know. They may be moving him down to the Ka Sohn area with some of the other Marines down there. But I'm going to try to stay in touch with him.

I've had some interesting opportunities even so far, sharing Christ, you know, sharing spiritual things just a little bit; getting to talk with some of the guys. Looking forward to getting out among my men, and I guess there's going to be some good opportunity out there to spend time in the Word. It's funny, when I checked in I had a real hesitancy toward being bold. Boy, I need boldness to speak out for Christ and also just to be undeclared, man, not to be afraid to pray in front of these other officers. You know, I want to establish rapport with them, and yet, I don't want them to think that I am afraid to be proud of Jesus Christ. And the same thing goes with reading my Bible. You know, just getting some time in the Word and prayer. So boy, pray that God would give me boldness along with real wisdom to know how to do these things in these days.

Trust things are good back there at home. I left my recorder there. Tony knows how to run it. You could run me off a tape and, when I get off the field, I'll have some time to sit down and listen to that. So that will be good. Well, I don't know quite what else to share, except had a good time traveling out to the West Coast.

Things have been good so far. I'm encouraged in heart; I have a peace down inside. I'm ready to head out to the field, to get with the men and to do the job I've been trained to do. A lot of things I'm sure are going to hit me, kind of catch me unexpectedly, but I'm just going to do the best job that I can. And God willing, that, with Him on my side.

It's interesting, one of the companies in our battalion, Golf Company, has as its motto, "If God be with us, who can be against us?" Hope to get a chance to go over there and kinda find out where that little motto came from, as far as who put it up there and what the significance is to that particular company.

Well, Mom and Dad. Appreciate hearing from you. I tried to call you from Okinawa and couldn't get through. Trust to be in touch by tape and don't be worried. God's over here in a very rich and protective way and things are in His hands, so there's nothing to be worried about, except that, boy, pray that God would use the time in my life and in the lives of the men around here. Pray for my XO and some of these that I'm getting to know now, that God might give opportunity to talk to them about spiritual things and to zero in on the significance of Jesus Christ in their lives.

Well, just thought I'd take some time right now to spend a little time in prayer.

God, I appreciate what a background You've given me in spiritual things, training with men, the preparation in heart and mind and spirit, so that God, I'm ready to go. God, now I'm here and involved and in country and Father, I'm not upset, I'm not ashamed, I'm not rattled as some of the guys around here can be, but God, by Your promise, You've given real peace and a lasting security.

And now I pray that You would continue to take care, that You'd do those things that You've promised. God be with the folks there at home. Keep every one of us walking with You and loving Jesus. For I pray in His name and for His sake. Amen.

Well, I'll be looking forward to hearing from you, Mom and Dad. Hang in there. Keep encouraged and love Him.

The next day, October 11, all things were ready and Larry was flown by helicopter to the field where he met his company commander, Captain Taylor. As he listened to the 39-year-old captain explaining to him his new responsibilities as platoon commander, he was impressed with this man's grasp of the entire tactical combat situation. Larry was eager to get into the action himself. Captain Taylor told him to report to the S-3's for an operational briefing, which was soon accomplished. Then, together, they joined Echo Company, 2nd Battalion, 4th Marines, just southeast of Con Thien, and the captain introduced Larry to his 44 men.

CHAPTER 23 - HILLS OF CON THIEN

Men were everywhere! Some Americans, some Vietnamese; some running, some shooting, some falling, some being blown to pieces by the constant explosions of mortars, rockets and artillery that had been pounding Con Thien all day. Now everything was mud, blood, and the sickening stench of burning flesh and dead bodies. Larry hit the ground as another mortar round impacted 20 yards away. "Boy, I'm right in the middle of my own war story," he thought, "after less than a week in Vietnam!"

A brutal, artillery barrage had pounded the United States Marine base at Con Thien for nearly a month. Their furious shelling had caused 1,000 Marine casualties, but the Marines were determined to hold their position. If the North Vietnamese were to gain control of this strategic spot, they could bring terrific pressure to bear on Dong Ha, the Marine's main supply base. The DMZ (Demilitarized Zone) bends around Con Thien enabling the dug-in enemy mortars to fire from almost impregnable positions north and west of the camp.

Larry's battalion had spent two uneventful nights in the field on combat patrol. The men were tired and sore beneath the cold, mud-clad uniforms, drenched by the early monsoon season. Suddenly, the slushy silence was broken by enemy fire.

Larry's men were in the "point" position, ahead of the rest of the battalion. This meant that they would draw any enemy action that might be awaiting the company. As the first mortar hit "ka-whump," the men dove for the ground just in time. Their world was filled with the crackle of rockets sizzling through the air and shaking everything as they blew great holes in the already pockmarked earth.

To Larry, it seemed that all hell had broken loose. He scraped the mud from his eyes and checked on his men. So far, at least, it looked like his company was out of immediate danger. The mortars and artillery seemed to be concentrating on the nearby "G" Company. He was later to learn that the enemy had closed in on Golf Company, penetrating the command position, killing the commanding officer and one lieutenant, and wounding another. But Larry's battalion position held and the enemy was beaten.

Had he said only a week in Vietnam? The five long, noisy, crucial hours of enemy bombing that now lay behind them seemed like five years! Larry and his men set to work evacuating the seriously wounded and mopping up. The past two weeks of heavy rains made the 199-pound shells fired by the communists' biggest guns almost unmovable in the dense red mud. It was impossible to hide the fact that a battle had been fought there, for the land would long wear its scars.

Larry turned to Lieutenant Zimmerman and said that the Marines had had their Tarawa in the First World War, their Iwo Jima in the Second, and the Inchon Landing in the Korean Conflict. He was sure that Con Thien should go down with those as a major event in which the Marines had taken part and won.

It was true; the enemy had been defeated again and again. They had made hard blows, but the Marines had held and had every intention of continuing to hold.

The battle was over, but many hardships still lay ahead as they headed back to camp. Five miles on a city sidewalk is a long walk, but five miles up and down slippery, pockmarked, booby-trapped hills, sometimes knee or thigh deep in thick red mud and loaded down with the remaining supplies and ammunition, is enough to unglue even the best of men. As Larry reached the top of each hill and saw yet another ahead, Vietnam became a very real and a very large place.

Finally, a road was spotted ahead and on it the American trucks were waiting to take them back. It was all Larry could do to keep from shouting a cheer as he had done so exuberantly at ISU. The men broke out in what could almost be called a run and then, one by one, crawled into the trucks. Larry had never appreciated a big, ugly "6-By" as much as he did then!

As the trucks moved along, Larry felt like they were in a blender, soon to become a malted mud! He looked over his men, tired and worn, yet men who were willing to lay their lives on the line. They were really a team, and each one's life depended on the others.

Larry knew that the United States had to be true to her commitment to oppose atheistic communism, whatever the cost. He could see the tired lines cracked in the faces of the other lieutenants—Bill Zimmerman and Bob Postal. Bob had gone through O.C.S. and Basic with him, although they had never gotten to know one another there. They were really a sight! Larry laughed to himself as he thought about those back home who had often commented on the shine of his shoes and the crease in his slacks. Now, nothing was visible but a brownish-red mixture of mud, clay and blood.

The men were quiet except for an occasional groan or curse from a wounded Marine, as they bumped in and out of deep ruts hidden by several inches of muddy water. The busy sound of the so-welcomed choppers was heard overhead, evacuating still more of the seriously wounded and others who had now given their last ounce of devotion on the deadly hills of Con Thien.

This had been Larry's first real battle in Vietnam, and his thoughts focused on those who had died today. He asked the age-old question, *"Had they died in vain?"* The truck rattled and shook, the men muttered and cried out, the coppers buzzed and whirred. But in the silence of his own heart, down where nothing else was able to penetrate, he pleaded with God that he might be able to understand why these strong, healthy young men were required to give up life, many he knew before they had met Christ as Savior. There in that noisy truck, on that muddy bumpy road, God gave him an answer. Anything worthwhile is worth fighting for. The freedom that he, his parents, three brothers, and sister enjoyed had cost the lives of countless men and women down through the centuries. God had never said that to be in His service would be easy. Before leaving for Vietnam, Larry had said that he was willing to live or die for Jesus Christ. Now, with the smell of death all around him, he renewed his commitment to God.

Bob Postal was crammed in next to Larry in the truck and noticed his head bowed. Some weary Marine might sleep in that position, but Postal knew Larry well enough already to know that he was praying. When Larry again lifted his head, Bob was still staring at him. Larry smiled. Bob was remembering how, back at Quantico, Larry had never been afraid to reveal his love for God. He had been teased a lot and even been called Deacon Bleeker all through their days of training. But now things had changed. It was a different story here in Vietnam. What had set him apart as different and maybe a little strange back in Iowa, now made him a man and a leader that was held in great respect. Larry's testimony here had already won him a special place in the hearts of his men. Not only was he a sharp officer who knew how to lead them in the bold face of battle, but he had a strong and steady peace in the midst of crises that was something they all had come to expect and upon which they were depending. Here, with death staring them in the face, they often needed a chaplain more than a commander; they were certainly finding in Lieutenant Bleeker both of those qualities.

Larry's men marveled at his love for the Scriptures and his knowledge of them. It seemed to Bob that Larry must have the whole Bible committed to memory and, what was more, he knew how to use it and apply it. When they had talked earlier about the objectives of their men in battle, Larry quoted I Chronicles 12:33. He said that he thought their men should be as the men of Zebulun, *"such as went forth to battle, expert in war, with all instruments of war, fifty thousand, which could keep rank: they were not of double heart."* Larry said that he thought that was the kind of men they wanted to have in their unit. They wanted to get them trained and to equip them. They wanted to get them disciplined; ready to do the job they were there to do, and to see it through right to the finish with a single heart. It was Larry's single-heartedness and whole-heartedness that stood out to his men.

It was dark as the truck pulled into Dong Ha. Larry had not yet grown accustomed to how quickly day became night in Vietnam. After reporting the details of their mission, Larry walked slowly back to the hooch where he and the other lieutenants were staying. The blisters upon blisters on his feet refused to allow his normal hearty pace, and his muscles had seconded that motion. The starless sky seemed ready to dump another ton of rain upon him. But as he thought of the clouds, his mind turned to a verse he knew in Psalm 36:5, *"Thy mercy, O Lord, is in the heavens; and Thy faithfulness reacheth unto the clouds."* Well, Larry thought, with the sky heavy and the clouds low, then God's faithfulness was closer than ever. All he could do was thank God.

Inside the men, though awake, were quiet. It was good to be back with the noise of combat far in the distance. Bleek laid his utilities on the floor beside his bunk and was amused at how they resembled a suit of armor. The clay and mud had become hard and stiff and still looked like some tired, emaciated Marine might be in it.

As Larry got into bed that night, he pulled out his favorite book and began to read. One of the men took note, as he did every morning and night when Larry became absorbed in his Bible. Larry was looking forward to the day when these guys would be reading it with him. He didn't care if others questioned his interest in a book like this. It gave him the opportunity to share something out of it. God was answering his prayer, that he could have boldness to read and pray and tell others what Christ meant to him. He continued to feed his soul and seek God's guidance in the matters concerning his men. One such case was that of a missing, or perhaps stolen, wallet in which Larry was the investigating officer. Larry was praying that the guy in trouble would come to him before he risked his military career to a court martial. This was just another way in which his men saw Larry's unusual concern for each of them. They, somehow, knew they were not only valuable to him as a team but as individuals as well.

Those days in the rear were spent getting equipment squared away and the men in combat readiness. On the afternoon of October 18, Larry shot off another tape to his family, completely unaware of a letter that had arrived there earlier that morning.

The Bleekers' hearts had been excited as the postman's delivery evidenced a letter from Vietnam. It must be from Larry—but no, it was from Dan. Some of the news of Larry's recent battle had reached Dan in Phu Bai and, thinking that Larry was in "G" Company instead of "E"

Company, Dan had listened intently as news came in on their battle. When he was sure that Larry was still okay, he had written this letter to the Bleekers:

> *I am writing to you on the basis of the latest verified information available to us as of now. Larry will undoubtedly contact you with complete information at the earliest convenience, if he hasn't by the time you receive this letter.*
>
> *Larry was assigned as platoon commander of "G" Company, 2nd Battalion, 4th Marine Regiment now at Con Thien. The second night he was there, a regiment (estimated) of NVA hit their position, first with rockets and mortars and then with troops. The NVA over-ran part of the perimeter, and the action came to hand-to-hand combat. The Marines held and the NVA suffered large casualties. Many Marines were KIA (killed in action) and WIA (wounded in action), along with several officers. Contact lasted five hours. The reports coming in are still sketchy, but we know that the company CO was KIA and the other two lieutenants in the company were KIA and WIA. At last report, Larry was the remaining officer (not a casualty) and was in charge of the company. The mopping up process is still on and won't know all the details for several days.*
>
> *Since I know the lines of communication can be uncertain and/or completely cut for days, I will continue to relay all information I can possibly lay my hands on to you, until I have heard that Larry is in direct contact with you.*
>
> *My prayers are with your son.*
>
> *Dan*

That next week was filled with mixed emotion in the Bleeker household and with everyone else back home. Sadness, prayers, anxiety and waiting to know how he was and where he was occupied their every thought. Finally, on October 25, Larry's tape of the 18th arrived and an echo of joy rang through the house and hearts in Ames. Once again, they eagerly put the tape on the recorder and the notes of "You are my Sunshine" and "Kum By Yah" filled the room, as he played for them on his harmonica. Then his tired, but so welcomed voice, began to relate those things about which they had been wondering anxiously.

> *Thought I'd play a little music to let Ron and Donna know that I'm using that harmonica they gave me, and I really enjoy it. It's good to have something that you can just blow on and have a little release.*
>
> *It's the 18th of October right now. I'm making this up about 3:45 in the afternoon. I think it's Wednesday. We've been back now out of the field about four days.*
>
> *Just to bring you up to date on things. The last tape I sent was on the day before I went to the field, and I shot that off to you. They helo-lifted us out to the field where I met the company commander, Captain Taylor, a real fine man, a tremendous field mind, a man who knows his stuff and is really on top of the situation.*
>
> *I got a little scoop from the S-3 (Plans and Operations) when I got out there and then joined Captain Taylor in going back to the position we're occupying, which was just southeasterly from Con Thien. I'm not sure who it was holding the position there on the Con Thien hill.*

The battalion I'm with (2nd Battalion, 4th Marines) was out around the Con Thien area holding a phalanxing position and contributing in a significant way to several land assaults and attacks which were trying to take Con Thien.

The situation was, "Charlie" needed to take Con Thien for a psychological victory. He needed something to show that he was moving ahead and that he was winning. He's been defeated in that again and again. He's made some hard blows on units and you've probably heard about that, but we've held and will continue to hold.

When I got out there, I met some of the other lieutenants. I remember Vieses, who's been with the company, Echo Company, the longest. And we have a Lt. Zimmerman. Both of these went to the same class and, let's see, it was two days after I checked in, Lt. Postal, who went through my same class there at Basic, in fact O.C.S., checked into Echo Company. And he's with this platoon now, so we're pretty well up to strength as far as officers are concerned. We've had many replacements and, of course, there's a rotation of men who've been out here and it's changing off and on all the time. But for the most part, we're pretty much up to strength. We're trying to get them equipped right now, like in I Chronicles 12:33.

One thing I was told when I got out here was that if I take care of my men, they'll take care of me, and this is really true, Mom and Dad. The men really watch out for their unit commander. They want to make sure that his bunker's safe; they want to make sure that he's getting the right chow; they want to make sure of a lot of these things. So they watch out for me and I think it's really keen because, with God's position of provision and of taking care and these men seeing this, it really kinda encompasses a lot. I feel a peace and a security in just walking with God.

I want to express my "howdys" and my "hellos." I miss you. I'm looking forward to taking some R and R and going down to Indonesia, if that's possible, in just a few short months. My tour's up in about 12 or 13 months from now. In a few short 13 months, I'll be back in the States there and back home for a little while. I'm looking forward to that.

During the couple of nights we spent in the field, we went out on a combat patrol. My platoon was the point and it was geared to see how my men work, to see some of the areas that they need help in. We're going to be doing some training and getting these men experienced in some of this combat maneuver.

My position wasn't hit at all. Golf Company was hit pretty hard. The enemy penetrated the lines and got through to the command position. But my position held, and we actually didn't have any fighting out on our front. We came back in on the fifteenth, marched about five miles, humped it across hills, were picked up by trucks and were brought all the rest of the way back. We've been here in the rear now ever since.

It's pretty nice back here. We four lieutenants have our own hooch, and things are pretty nice.

Incidentally, any mail or packages take about five days from when you send them or five days from when I send them. From this end they go free, from your end they do cost.

There are several things, just let me list them here, that I would appreciate if you could bundle together and kinda shoot me a little package of them. One thing is a bottle of India ink. I could use that. It costs about $2.00 here for a bottle of ink if you buy it from the nationals. Another thing is nylon fishing line; a high test monofilament line is good, and we can use it here on our patrols and things. And, of course, we never get enough instant tea or instant coffee that we can take to the field. You know, a little package of condiments or Kool-Aid, too. Kool-Aid is, you know, man, it's a treat! One of the fellows showed up with instant pudding here the other day. They just put water in and it was kind of a swinging treat to have something like that out on the field, so something like that would be good, too.

Well, I see the tape is just about finished, so I'll just bid you my good-byes and look forward to hearing from you on the return tape. Thanks for everything, Mom and Dad. I love you and miss you a lot."

Then, as they listened to him play "How Great Thou Art," they brushed away proud tears. Larry was still okay.

CHAPTER 24 - FINALLY HOME!

Larry had been in the Con Thien area for two weeks when his battalion moved to a position about four miles southwest of Con Thien. Their orders were to sweep to the north, then west, so as to come to an objective area about one mile south of Con Thien. Spirits were generally high, as they were eager to get into some action again. Larry was proud of his men. During those days in the rear, God had worked into their lives some of those qualities he had asked God for from I Chronicles. They were "trained;" they were "equipped;" they were "disciplined." However, the matter of their having a single heart still concerned Larry. How many were single-hearted for God? He did not know yet. There had not been time to talk with each of them about their relationship with God. As they made their night encampment, Larry prayed that they would not go into eternity without first experiencing the joy of knowing Christ.

Wednesday morning came too soon and with it more rain. The entire day was spent sweeping the countryside for the enemy. As nightfall came, none had been found. Were they out there? Were they watching? The feeling within each man seemed to indicate that they were. And then they knew! Where a second before there had been an air of quiet edginess, suddenly the area was alive with the "whomping" sounds of the incoming rounds and the shrill complaint of flying shrapnel.

Few slept more than 15 or 20 minutes that night. As they peered into the blackness, the shadows played tricks on them and, more than once, a shot was fired at a tremulous branch or a shaking reed.

The black curtain of night was just being pulled back as they once again began their move to an intermediate objective. Here they set up a hasty defense. Larry and his men were on the portion of the perimeter facing the direction through which they had just swept. Shortly after securing this position, they again began to take a heavy pounding from enemy mortars. Feeling this was a token harassment on the part of the NVA (North Vietnamese Army), the Marine commander countered with artillery fire and the incoming rounds stopped.

All was quiet now except for an occasional curse or a canteen pouring a trickle down some dry throat. Time seemed to be almost at a standstill as the men frequently glanced at their watches, each wondering at the eternal promise of the next moment. About an hour later, Bleeker's platoon heard the report of an enemy mortar tube to the southwest. His platoon was facing the sound of the mortar, and the men were instantly alert.

Larry noticed that one young Marine, barely out of high school, who had been fighting homesickness during the last two weeks he had known him, seemed for the first time to have his mind totally on the business at hand. Larry's thoughts were then interrupted by a message from one of his squad leaders of a reported "movement" to their front. "Do you think those are 'friendlies' out there?" the squad leader asked.

Larry scanned the area in front of his men. His platoon was all present and accounted for. But, perhaps some from another platoon had not yet made it in. They may have been caught in the early exchange of fire. Not wanting any of their men still out there and trying to get back, Larry reached for his binoculars to make sure. Then he heard and felt a short "thwack" of a rifle round striking flesh and bone, and his men watched in disbelief as Larry fell unconscious into the soupy mud of Con Thien. A kind of anger ran through his men as, now, all hell seemed to have burst forth. They must fight and win for Bleeker's sake. His platoon faced the full brunt as three North Vietnamese army battalions attacked and, for awhile, Larry's whole battalion was fighting for its existence. A medic and chaplain were soon at Larry's side. The bullet had entered his forehead just below his helmet and, before they could remove him from the battle, God took him home to be with Him, face to face.

* * * * *

Two days later, a military car slowly turned the corner and came to a stop in front of 808 Hunsiker Drive, Ames, Iowa. The two men sat for a moment, dreading what lay ahead of them, and then slowly made their way up the walk and rang the doorbell.

Inside, Mom and Pop, Ron and Donna, and Hi's sister and husband were just sitting down to Saturday night dinner after having listened to Larry's tapes. When the doorbell rang, Mom asked Ron to answer it because the paper boy was due. Ron went cheerfully to the door and, as a cold October wind blew between the two officers and at him, Ron stood frozen to the spot. No words were necessary if you had a brother on the front lines in Vietnam. Ron knew why they were there, and he couldn't turn around. He couldn't look at the faces of his mom and dad.

Pop noticed his son's sudden, rigid reaction and, coming toward the door, he saw the two officers over Ron's shoulder. "Oh, no," he uttered as he reached the door and opened it for the officers to invite them in. They said they had something to tell them and Dad said, "I know you have; come on in." Then the men told them that "Larry Dean

Bleeker was killed in battle two days ago." Hi said, "I understand, please come in." So they did.

Dad pointed to two chairs and kindly asked them to sit down and listen to the tapes they had just been listening to from Larry. Following the tapes, Pop preached in all boldness that unless they had Christ in their lives like Larry had, they were doomed and had better do something about it while they could. His heart was coming up in his throat, and that was all he could do. The major said he had invited Christ into his life and he understood. The sergeant said nothing; he just stared at the floor. Then Hi prayed for them before they left his home.

Tears flowed freely then, for joy because of where they knew Larry to be at that moment, and also because of the horrible empty place that his Home-going had left in their lives. Dad steadfastly took over and called to leave word to have Tony and Marlene sent home from the hayride they were on with the church youth group. When they entered their home, God had given the rest of the family the control they needed, and a quiet peace rested upon them. Tony and Marlene were, of course, as stunned as the rest. Was it really true? Tony needed some time alone, so he left for a walk while the reality sank in. Marlene rushed to her room in tears. It was remarkable to watch Dad during those next hours and days as he notified family and friends that Larry was now with the Lord.

Dad Bleeker later shared that several months earlier, as he had sat in the church service, the thought had come, "I wonder when I'll have to bury Larry from this church. What would I do if I lost him?" And God had prepared him for this. He never told a soul, but he felt that even Larry knew. He had taken care of everything before he left—everything except the piano he wanted to get for Marlene. Well, Dad would make certain she got that.

Among the many calls that Dad Bleeker made during the next few days was one to Billings, Montana, on a Sunday afternoon. Mr. Robbie was the only one home that afternoon and as he received the news he was shocked, not so much that it had happened but that it had happened so soon. He could remember thinking, as he had shaken Larry's hand just a month before, that in some noble way Larry would give his life away unless it was God's will to prevent it, because he was forever giving his life daily to people. A sorrow, deeper than any they had known before, settled over each member of that family as they received the news. Now Barb had to be told.

Barb related that Sunday night:

> *I had gone to Fourth Presbyterian Church, Dr. Halvorson's church, out in D.C. After the service was over, I was standing and talking with friends when someone said there was a phone call for me. I couldn't imagine who could be calling me at church, but it was George and Carol Anderson, the youth pastor and his wife from Billings who now lived in the area and with whom I was living. They said they wanted to talk to me. When I asked why, George just kept saying to come right home. Finally, I got him to put Carol on the line, and she told me they had something they needed to talk to me about.*
>
> *As I hung up I thought, "Oh, something terrible has probably happened to one of the kids back home or something, and they have come to town to tell me about it. Never did it enter my mind that it could be about Larry. I never had a moment's fear for Larry. I prayed that the Lord would protect him and take care of him. The Lord had brought us together after*

> *all that time and I was just positive He was going to bring him home.*
>
> *When I walked in, I could tell by the look on their faces that they had been crying and that something was very wrong. George said that my parents had called. I thought, 'Oh no, something has happened to one of my family.' Then George continued that my Dad had gotten a call from the Bleekers and that Larry had been killed on Thursday.*
>
> *I just stood there. I couldn't believe it for a moment. Then I heard myself saying, 'Praise the Lord, he's in heaven with the Lord and he loved the Lord more than anything, more than anyone I knew could love the Lord.' Then the feelings came, and I cried.*

So the week began slowly to tick away as they all awaited the arrival of Larry's body. On Sunday, the telegram arrived saying that Larry had been killed by sniper fire while in a defensive position in Vietnam. The picture that Larry had had taken in his Marine uniform shortly before he left, for a Christmas present to his folks, now introduced the news of his death on the front page of the Ames Daily Tribune on Monday, October 30. It read in part:

> *Lt. Bleeker had made a number of tape recordings which he sent to friends and relatives. One of the most recent, sent to his parents when he left for Vietnam, said in part, "Mom, Dad, I want you to know I'm ready to go...I'm ready to live or die for the glory of Jesus Christ..."*

On Tuesday, the Ames High School sound system related to the students the death of Larry Bleeker, brother of Tony, who was then a junior at Ames High school. In memory of Larry, they all stood for a few moments of silent meditation. Later, that last picture was requested and now hangs in the high school library.

Gary and Millie came to help during that week. The doorbell and tape recorder were constantly going, as friends came by to encourage the Bleekers and went away themselves, rejoicing in what God could do. The funeral arrangements and plans for a memorial fund were taken care of during those quiet moments when they could think and plan what Larry would have wanted and what would most glorify God.

Then, on Friday, November 3, a jet landed in California from Vietnam, and the baggage crew unloaded the cargo of coffins. One white tag that fluttered in the breeze read "BLEEKER, LARRY." In just a few more hours, First Lieutenant Roger Schneider escorted Larry's body to Ames. Larry was finally home; his body now in Ames, and his soul and spirit in heaven with his wonderful Lord!

CHAPTER 25 - HE FOUND THE ANSWER

Many who read this will find themselves thinking this was a terrible tragedy to happen to such a fine family and such a promising young man. It might even be chalked up as one of God's mistakes. But those who knew Larry and those who know God cannot feel that way.

November 7, 1967. The day dawned crisp and clear. The Bleeker home was a beehive of activity as last-minute preparations were made and out-of-town guests helped to make the time pass quickly. The memorial service was to begin at 1:30 p.m. at the Campus Baptist Church in Ames.

Among those who gathered together that morning were some of Larry's buddies from the Navigators and ISU, now living in various locations not far from Ames. Still somewhat stunned at their loss, they talked together about Larry, what he had meant to them and the joy he was at that moment experiencing as he talked with the Lord and the great men from the Bible. They determined that his memorial service would be as Larry would have wanted it, if they could at all make it that way. They prayed that the lives of those who perhaps had not yet received Christ as their personal Savior would be touched. They were convinced that God would not take a young man like Larry, so sold out to God and willing to do His will here on earth, unless by his death Larry could win even more to the Lord. They would scatter and pray for opportunities to witness if God presented them.

The population of Ames climbed that day as people came from literally all over the States and Canada, to pay tribute to this young man who somewhere during his 24 years had entered their lives and left an indelible mark.

As the first notes from the organ began to penetrate the air, the feeling that it's almost over now began to settle on the crowd. The sanctuary was modestly adorned with flowers, since it had been requested that a memorial fund be established instead. The elevated casket was draped with the American flag, balanced by red and white bouquets on either side. Marines in dress uniforms banked the first rows of pews, 14 of which were to serve as honor guard and 6 to carry the flag-draped coffin. Seven of Larry's Navigator friends served as honorary pallbearers and were seated behind the Marines.

Every seat was taken now, and people were standing inside and outside of the sanctuary which holds 600. When all was ready, Dr. Paul approached the podium in the center of the platform immediately above the coffin. He began by recalling to the minds of those present how Larry's life had ended and mentioning those who would miss him dearly. Then he continued.

> *As we meet together this afternoon, we do so as those who sorrow not as others which have no hope. I would like to have you join me in prayer as we begin this service, that the Lord Jesus Christ, whom Larry loved so greatly and served so admirably, will be magnified in our meditation together today. Shall we pray.*
>
> *Our Father in heaven, we thank Thee that because of Thy grace, the Lord Jesus Christ came into this sin-sick world and willingly went to Calvary's cross to bear our sins in His body. We thank Thee that He rose from the dead, conquering the grave and sin and hell and death. We thank Thee that if any man be in Christ, he is a new creation. We praise Thee today that our memories of Larry Bleeker are memories of a young man dedicated to the Lord Jesus Christ, actively and enthusiastically telling others of Jesus, his Lord. And because he trusted the Lord Jesus Christ, we are confident this afternoon that he is with Thee. We pray that this blessed hope may comfort each of our hearts. We pray that Thou wouldst pour Thy love and grace into the hearts of Mr. and Mrs. Bleeker and the brothers and sister. May Thy grace comfort and encourage. Indeed, may we as we remember Larry's testimony, be more effective and fervent in our own witness for Jesus Christ. Speak to each of our hearts this afternoon from Thy Word. We ask it in Christ's name and for His sake. Amen.*

After the prayer, Mr. Charles Cramer sang one of Larry's favorite gospel songs. It was a song that many had heard him sing with the quartet, and it seemed to express so well Larry's feelings about this world and the next. It was titled, "This World Is Not My Home, I'm Just A Passing Through."

Then Dr. Paul continued the service.

> *Certainly Larry was a man who could say truthfully, "I have no friend like the Lord, Jesus Christ." In the eleventh chapter of the gospel of John, we have an account of a crisis which had come into the lives of three of the closest friends of Jesus, and their names were Mary, Martha and Lazarus. I'd like to read the account of this crisis and how this crisis was resolved by a Friend, Who sticks closer than a brother, even the Lord, Jesus Christ. Chapter 11 of John, verses 1-4 says: "Now a certain man was sick... When Jesus heard that, He said, 'This sickness is not unto death, but for the glory of God, that the Son of God might be glorified thereby.'" My friends, that was the desire of Larry Bleeker, that regardless of what came into his life, Jesus Christ might be glorified thereby.*
>
> *John 11:5-45. This is the hope of every believing Christian today. Jesus Christ, Who is the Resurrection and the Life, is going to speak life to this body at the resurrection day. Larry's soul is in heaven right at this moment, rejoicing in the presence of the angels of God, reunited with those who have gone before. And the good news of the gospel of Jesus Christ is that the Son of God, Who conquered the grave, Who demonstrated His authority over death while He was here and proved that authority by rising from the dead Himself, will also raise every body of every believer at that resurrection day. And so, the most comforting*

passage of Scripture in the Bible to the believing Christian brethren is in I Thessalonians 4:13-18, where Paul writes,

"But I would not have you to be ignorant, brethren, concerning them which are asleep, that ye sorrow not, even as others which have no hope. For if we believe that Jesus died and rose again, even so them also which sleep in Jesus will God bring with Him. For this we say unto you by the Word of the Lord, that we which are alive and remain unto the coming of the Lord shall not prevent them which are asleep. For the Lord Himself shall descend from heaven with a shout, with the voice of the archangel, and with the trump of God: and the dead in Christ shall rise first. Then we which are alive and remain shall be caught up together with them in the clouds, to meet the Lord in the air; and so shall we ever be with the Lord. Wherefore, comfort one another with these words."

That's why today this is a memorial service of victory, and Larry would have it no other way. Shall we bow and pray.

Our gracious, heavenly Father, we thank Thee that we serve a risen Savior, not a dead and buried religious leader. We serve One Who came to this world via the womb of a virgin, taught as no man has ever taught, with the authority of God. He demonstrated His claims by His actions, died a miraculous death on our behalf, conquered the grave and death to guarantee us everlasting life. We thank Thee that there's a Man in heaven right now, with nail-scared hands and nail-scared feet, with a scar in His side and scars on His brow where a crown of thorns was placed. A Man Who loved us and gave Himself for us, Who guaranteed that because He is the Resurrection and the Life, though we be dead, yet shall we live again. May this message of good news comfort our hearts this afternoon as we say "Good afternoon" to this body, but look forward to the day we shall say "Good morning" in Thy presence. We ask this in Jesus' name. Amen."

Then the song, "Let Me Lose My Life And Find It Lord In Thee," was sung.

Our message this afternoon is an unusual message for a funeral service. It's not usual that we refer very often to the one who has gone to be with the Lord. But I believe this afternoon there are two or three reasons why we ought to refer to Larry in this message.

First of all, this is an unusual service because of the age of the man who has gone to be with the Lord. Twenty-four years of age. I think we need to soberly reflect, once again, upon the inevitability of death. "And as it is appointed unto men once to die..." the Bible says in Hebrews. 9:27. And the Word of God says, "Boast not thyself of tomorrow; for thou knowest not what a day may bring forth" (Proverbs 27:1). No one in this audience knows at this very moment which of us will be next. It may be someone in his twenties, or thirties, or seventies, or eighties. But the urgency of your eternal relationship with God stems from the fact that you may meet God before this week is out. You ought to be ready. You ought to be prepared.

Secondly, it is unusual because of the circumstance of the death. Here's a young man who literally gave his life in the service of his country.

Thirdly, this is an unusual service because this man had an unusual testimony for the Lord, Jesus

Christ. So I'd like to build my remarks this afternoon around Larry's testimony. I think that he exemplified some things that we need to stress more urgently in the day and age in which we live.

First of all, Larry Bleeker was a man of high PRINCIPLE. In Hebrews 11:24-26, we read concerning Moses,: "By faith Moses, when he was come to years, refused to be called the son of Pharaoh's daughter; choosing rather to suffer affliction with the people of God, than to enjoy the pleasures of sin for a season; esteeming the reproach of Christ greater riches than the treasures in Egypt: for he had respect unto the recompence of the reward."

This dedication to high principle certainly demands the best of an individual. This dedication to high principle certainly demands the best of every Christian. And this testimony given here, of Moses, was the testimony of Larry. He chose to suffer, if need be, the reproach of Christ, whatever that reproach might be: the snicker of a fellow classmate; the scorn of a professor who didn't believe the Bible; the laughter of a gang that would not listen to the gospel. Whatever reproach might be, he chose to suffer that rather than enjoy the pleasures of sin, which are always "for a season." No one denies that there may be pleasure in sin, but neither can it be denied by a very thoughtful person that those pleasures are very temporary. Larry was a young man who lived for the eternal, not for the temporary; a young man who lived for that which is invisible to human eyes; a man who lived for the reality and not the shadow. Certainly, we who are here today need to dedicate ourselves to these same high principles.

Larry was a young man who had no time for the so-called "new morality." He was a man who upheld the standards of the Word of God and a man who was an encouragement and an inspiration to every young person whose life he ever touched. You who are here today, young and old, need to realize that the thing that made the United States of America great was this dedication to high principle. And, I believe it's about time all of us start speaking out against the mediocrity of our generation, the satisfaction with second best. We need to "press toward the mark for the prize of the high calling of God in Christ Jesus" (Philippians 3:14).

Larry was also a man of high PATRIOTISM. Jesus Christ was questioned at one time on this matter of patriotism. You remember the Jews of his day were under the Romans. But Jesus Christ stated a principle in Matthew 22:21 when He said, "Render therefore unto Caesar the things which are Caesar's, and unto God, the things that are God's." And in this blessed nation in which you and I live, this principle can be carried out more fully than in any other nation in the world. I can hold my head high today and say "I am an American" and, at the same time, I can freely speak of my Savior. I have freedom of worship, freedom of speech, freedom to tell others what Jesus Christ means to me. Larry was a man who was proud to be an American. He was proud of his flag, proud of his country. He loved America. He had no time for near treasonable demonstrations and unpatriotic acts of rebellion which would tend to sap the morale of our fighting men in Vietnam. He was a man who believed the United States of America ought to keep her word to her allies. He was a man who believed the United

States of America ought to be true to her commitment. He was a man who believed strongly that the United States of America ought to oppose the enslaving encroachments of atheistic communism. He was a man who was willing to lay his life on the line, that the land of the free and the home of the brave might remain that kind of a land. God grant that there might be more young men like Larry, proud to be a citizen of the greatest nation that has ever been in existence, the United States of America!

But, at the very foundation of Larry's life there was his dedication to a high PURPOSE—that which gave him incentive to high principle. That which put teeth in his dedication to patriotism of the highest type was his dedication to the highest purpose on earth. How many times have you and I, as members of Campus Baptist Church, listened to Larry on this platform, or listened to him over there in the chapel as he talked to the college students, or in a home with a group of college students? What was his passion in life?

His passion in life was the fulfillment of the great commission. He believed that the Lord, Jesus Christ meant exactly what He said in Matthew 28:18-20 when He said, "All power is given unto Me in heaven and in earth. Go ye therefore, and teach all nations, baptizing them in the name of the Father, and of the Son, and of the Holy Ghost: teaching them to observe all things whatsoever I have commanded you, and, lo, I am with you always, even unto the end of the world. Amen"

Mrs. Bleeker will remember fondly, Larry saying, "You win the little children to Christ and I'll win the men. You keep faithful in the Child

Evangelism classes, and I want God to use me to win Marines to Christ." This was his passion in life. He believed that he had the greatest message in all the universe, and he did—the message of the gospel of Christ! It is a message which could span differences in race, color and creed. A message which could go to the heart of every man he ever talked to. He could say with the Apostle Paul in Romans 1:14-16, "I am debtor both to the Greeks, and to the barbarians; both to the wise, and to the unwise. So, as much as in me is, I am ready to preach the gospel to you that are at Rome also." And I might insert the word "Vietnam." For Paul goes on to say, "I am not ashamed of the gospel of Christ; for it is the power of God unto salvation to every one that believeth..." His purpose in life was to get that message of the gospel to every man personally that he could possibly talk to.

You may say to me this afternoon, "Dr. Tassell, what is the message of the gospel anyhow?" It's simple. It's summed up in the 25 words which are given to us in John 3:16. Jesus said, "For God so loved the world, that He gave His only begotten Son, that whosoever believeth in Him should not perish, but have everlasting life." That's the greatest message you can ever hear, my friends. God so loved the world, a world of sin-stained, sin-worried individuals, carrying the load of guilt, but God loved them!

You know Larry was very adept at sitting down with a young man and saying, "Now let me share with you the greatest message in the world. The Bible says 'For all have sinned, and come short of the glory of God' (Romans 3:23). But I've got good news for you, man, God loves sinners. God loved sinners so much that He sent His Son to die on Calvary's rugged cross for their sins. God loved sinners so much that He sent His only begotten Son into the world to die for them. And Jesus Christ loved sinners so much, that He allowed them to nail His hands to the cross, His feet to the same cross. He took all of the jeering and scoffing that ungodly, wicked men could pour out upon Him. He died for your sins. But I've got good news. Death could not hold His frame. Jesus, my Savior, tore the bars away and He rose triumphantly on the third day. And the good news is that if you will receive the Lord, Jesus Christ's provision on Calvary's cross on your behalf, God will forgive your sins, give you an eternal home in heaven, and insure you, absolutely insure you, that you shall conquer the grave and hell and death.

This is the gospel he loved to tell others. Isn't that a simple message, but it's a life-transforming message. For every sinner in this building today, Christ died for you, He rose from the dead, and the only way God will forgive your sins is through His son. Any other attempt to get to heaven by any other means is an insult to God because He gave the best that He had to win you. That's the only thing that could win you. So the Bible says, "Whosoever believeth in Christ, shall not perish, but have everlasting life." You see, it doesn't say, "whosoever believeth in Campus Baptist Church." No. It doesn't say, "whosoever believeth in catechism or confirmation." No. My friends, salvation is in a Person, Jesus Christ. And the thing that made this young man's life so vibrant and radiant and exciting and exhilarating, was the fact that he had a personal relationship with the living

Son of God. That's what makes every believer's life an exciting and thrilling experience day by day. What gives these parents hope today? Faith in some dead creed? No, sir. Faith in a living Savior, Whom they talked to this morning and this afternoon in prayer. With whom they've walked many years now. Whom having not seen, they love.

We've often been asked the question in these last ten days, "Is there anything I could do for Larry?" Yes, there is. The thing that would make this young man's heart happier than anything else this afternoon, as he looks down over the battlements of heaven, the thing that would make him happiest, is if you would surrender your heart to Jesus Christ. If you, as an individual would say, 'Yes, God, I acknowledge that what You say of me is true; I am a sinner. But I believe that the Lord Jesus Christ died as my substitute, He suffered my penalty. He died so that I would not have to suffer eternal death. And I will accept Jesus Christ as my personal Savior. I'll make Him Lord of my life. I'll trust Him for forgiveness of sins and I'll depend upon Him for eternal life.'

If you would do that today, you would do exactly what Larry would try to get you to do if he were here talking to you. He lived for that high purpose.

On the tape he made before he went overseas, he quoted the verse that expressed most concisely his high purpose. Philippians 1:21: "For me to live is Christ, and to die is gain." You see, my friend, dying to the believer is but an entrance into the very presence of the Lord we love. That's why Proverbs 12:21 says, "There shall no evil happen to the just:" because the worst thing that can happen to a Christian is the best thing that can happen to him.

When that sniper's bullet snuffed out his earthly life, Larry woke up in heaven. What better thing can happen to a man?

So we encourage you today. Know this same Christ as your personal Savior. Know the satisfaction and the assurance and the joy that can only come to an individual when he knows for sure that he is rightly related to God through Jesus Christ. There's an empty tomb in Palestine this afternoon. Christ isn't there. He's in glory. If you'll reach out your hand of faith, right now, Jesus Christ will reach down and save your soul forever. That's the promise of the empty tomb.

Larry and I were pen pals. Larry always closed his letters something like this, "Hang in there. In Christ, Bleek." He seemed to like that name for himself. This afternoon, as we come to the end of this service, I'd like to salute Bleek and assure him that by God's grace, we're going to continue to tell men and women the good news of the gospel. We're going to continue to tell folks how Christ loved them and died for them and rose again, to insure them of eternal life. And when we step on that heavenly shore, Bleek will be there to greet us. He's going to have a lot to tell us, because he's gotten a head start. But when we meet him, let's be able to have the same joy and confidence he had because we've been faithful.

What says the empty tomb, to me this hallowed afternoon?
It speaks of life and victory, and glorious hope newborn.
It tells of One Who hung, in shame upon a cross of woe

That all who call upon His name, eternal life might know.
It tells me He has risen indeed, and at the Father's throne
Now daily stands to intercede, for His redeemed, His own.
It tells me that because He lives, I too shall never die
And everlasting hope it gives, of joy with Him on high.
It tells me death is overthrown, yea, tis a conquered foe,
Dispelling ever more the gloom of deaths foreboding prison
It says, Look unto Him and live, for He has power to save
Life everlasting He doth give, and victory o'er the grave."
Shall we pray?

While their heads were bowed and eyes were closed, Dr. Paul asked those who wanted to commit their lives to Jesus Christ to raise their hands. Three responded in that way, and then he prayed:

Our heavenly Father. We sorrow this afternoon, but not as others which have no hope. For we believe that Jesus died and rose again. And He's coming again to receive us unto Himself. Our hearts are rejoicing right now for these two men and this young lady, who have raised their hands indicating that right now they are receiving Christ as Savior. We pray that there will be others who, even though not raising their hand, will do this very thing, even as we bow in prayer now. We thank you

> *for Larry. Campus Baptist Church is a better church because Larry walked among us. I'm a better preacher because I knew Larry. We're better Christians because we knew him. And Thou dost take Thine own to Thyself with perfect knowledge that it is best. We commit him to Thee, and ask that Thy sustaining grace may be the portion of this dear family. In Jesus' name, Amen.*

Triumphantly, the organist began to play "This Is My Story" by Fanny Crosby, as one by one those in attendance walked through the honor guard, past the draped coffin, and out into the brisk November sunshine. The trees in their reds and golds stood like brilliant banners against the blue of the sky. Defeat and finality had no place in this day. Victory had rung throughout the service; God had been and would continue to be glorified, and each person there felt a part of the call to fill in the gap and make their lives count while there was yet time. Very few went home. They must take in as much of this event as possible. They had never experienced anything like this before and perhaps never would again.

The funeral procession left the church and began to make its way to the Ames Municipal Cemetery and the Garden of Memory. One person later commented that they had stood for 20 minutes on the corner of an Ames intersection waiting for the procession to pass. The words inscribed on the cemetery memorial just a few hundred yards from Larry's graveside had never seemed more real or more true as they were read that day by the onlookers. *John 11:25: "I am the Resurrection, and the Life: he that believeth in Me, though he were dead, yet shall he live:" Deuteronomy 33:27: "The eternal God is thy refuge, and underneath are the everlasting arms." Revelation 2:10: "...Be thou faithful unto death, and I will give thee a crown of life."* And the words of Thomas Campbell, *"To live in hearts we leave behind is not to die."*

The very reason there could be victory in such a service as this was that there could be no doubt Larry was not dead. He was more alive than any who stood there that afternoon.

As the words of I Corinthians 15:47-58 were read, they filled the hearts with new hope and victory and purpose for living. Then the full Marine honors were accorded Larry as the cannon fired a 21-gun salute and taps pierced the air like a victor's glistening sword. The flag was presented to the family, and the service closed with prayer. One by one the crowd disappeared until, at last, only the fresh-turned sod and garlands of flowers marked the spot behind the bronzed letters sparkling in the setting sun. They read:

Larry Dean Bleeker
Iowa
2nd Lt. Co. E 4 Mar 3 Mar Div
Vietnam P
June 21, 1943-October 26, 1967

His body is buried, his soul is with God, but his example lives on in the lives of men and women who had the privilege of knowing him or knowing about him. And where many had "let Larry do it," they are now moving forward themselves to get the message out to a world whose only hope for peace lies in knowing the living Person of Jesus Christ, the One for Whom Larry was ready to live or to die.

The purpose of this book was not to entertain you, but to challenge you. It was to show you that being a Christian in the truest sense of the word, is the only thing really worth giving your life to and that you can have fun and fulfillment in doing it. It was not to make you wish you could be like Larry Bleeker, but to show you "how" you, too, can be uniquely used by God to reach your world.

There is as intense a warfare going on today in our schools, businesses, city streets and quiet rooms as there was in Vietnam. For all of us, there are battles to be fought. The question is—Am I letting the enemy brainwash and seduce me, or have I taken up the *"sword of the spirit, which is the Word of God?"* II Timothy 2:4 says, *"No man that warreth entangleth himself with the affairs of this life; that he may please Him Who hath chosen him to be a soldier."* Am I willing to fight in the front lines with my Commander in Chief, that the men and women the world over might come to know Him and the *"peace of God, which passeth all understanding"?*

Larry Bleeker "Found the Answer" to living an abundant life. That life was found only in Jesus Christ. He, like us, tried other solutions only to find they fell far short of what it took to make him totally happy and fulfilled. He found in Christ a Savior always ready to forgive and a Lord always eager to lead him into bigger and better things.

When that all-important day came, Larry found Jesus Christ to be the answer to dying as well. For there in that trench in Vietnam he saw Jesus face to face and heard Him say, "Bleek. *Well done, thou good and faithful servant; thou hast been faithful over a few things, I will make thee ruler over many things: enter thou into the joy of thy Lord"* (Matthew 25:21).

Much like Enoch of old, in Genesis 5:24, Larry "*walked steadily with God. And then one day he was simply gone: for God took him."*